THE SEARCH FOR RĀVAṆA'S LAṄKĀ

THE GEOGRAPHY OF VĀLMĪKI RĀMĀYAṆA

Sukanya Agashe

Popular Prakashan
www.popularprakashan.com

Published by
Harsha Bhatkal for
POPULAR PRAKASHAN PVT. LTD.
301, Mahalaxmi Chambers
22, Bhulabhai Desai Road
Mumbai - 400 026
www.popularprakashan.com

First Published 2014

(4364)
ISBN: 978-81-7991-805-0

Design: Mahendra Ghanekar

PRINTED IN INDIA
by Rama Printer
New Delhi - 110002

"Locating the Lanka of the Valmiki Ramayana is not a new subject in scholary studies. Seeking historical validity for epic literature is immensely problematic and more so in a text where the finest poetry is enveloped in the most imaginative fantasy. Sukanya Agashe uses more recent methods of locating geographical places, and attempts to co-relate textual references with topo-sheets, Google maps and field studies that she has undertaken. The author's approach introduces new ideas into the debate and some of her suggestions are valuable in moving the debate forward and making us think afresh."

— **Romila Thapar**

TRANSLITERATION CHART FOR SANSKRIT WORDS
(IAST with Diacritic marks)

अ a	आ ā	इ i	ई ī	उ u	ऊ ū	ऋ ṛ
ऌ ḷ	ए e	ऐ ai	ओ o	औ au	अं aṃ	अः aḥ
क ka	ख kha	ग ga	घ gha	ङ ṅa		
च ca	छ cha	ज ja	झ jha	ञ ña		
ट ṭa	ठ ṭha	ड ḍa	ढ ḍha	ण ṇa		
त ta	थ tha	द da	ध dha	न na		
प pa	फ pha	ब ba	भ bha	म ma		
य ya	र ra	ल la	व va	श śa	ष ṣa	
स sa	ह ha	ळ la	क्ष kṣa	ज्ञ jña		

Note: Modern names of persons and places have been given the spellings which are currently in use, and no diacritic marks have been attached to them.

ABBREVIATIONS USED IN THIS BOOK

ASIR:	Archaeological Survey of India Report
ASR:	Archaeological Survey Report of India
ALOCP:	All India Oriental Conference Proceedings
BORI:	Bhandarkar Oriental Research Institute
CII:	Corpus Inscriptionum Indicarum
Epi. Ind.:	Epigraphia Indica
Dist. Gazet:	District Gazetteer
I. G. I.:	Imperial Gazetteer of India
Ind. Ant.:	Indian Antiquary
Ind. Anti:	Indian Antiquities
I. H. Q.:	Indian Historical Quarterly
JBBRAS:	Journal of the Bombay Branch of Royal Asiatic Society
JRAS:	Journal of the Royal Asiatic Society (Great Britain)
JASB:	Journal of the Asiatic Society of Bengal
JBORS:	Journal of the Bihar and Orissa Research Society
Jha Comm.:	Jha Commemoration Volume
JBBORS:	Journal of the Bombay Branch of Oriental Research Society
St. Ind. Ant.:	Studies in Indian Antiquities
QJMS:	Quarterly Journal of the Mythic Society
RASB:	Royal Asiatic Society of Bengal

ACKNOWLEDGEMENTS

I take this opportunity to express my gratitude to all those who helped me in this work. Prof. Dr Romila Thapar, to whom I had sent the earlier drafts of this study, was gracious enough to send her detailed critical comments and encouraging words. I express my deepest gratitude to her.

Dr M.P. Parameshvaran of Trichur shared my enthusiasm, encouraged me to publish my work, gave valuable suggestions and arranged tours to visit some of the proposed sites. I will always remain indebted to him.

I am especially grateful to late Prof. R.M. Bapat of Pune, who after reading my first draft encouraged me to go ahead with the idea of publishing the work.

This work needed the assistance of younger enthusiasts. Shri Manoj Kulkarni and his associates, from Bhopal, did the pilot touring of some of the sites and collected some interesting information and useful audio-visual material initially. My thanks go to them for their generosity of spirit and for conducting and handling these field visits. I also thank Dr Mukul Sinha for his encouragement, who personally visited the most important target sites and provided useful information. My thanks are due to Dr A.P. Jamkhedkar for his valuable suggestions.

I thank Dr Sudha Srivastav and Dr Prasad Gogate of the department of Geography, University of Mumbai, for the kind co-operation they provided whilst I was studying the topographical survey sheets, from the department library. I thank once again

Dr Prasad Gogate who also did the cartography for this book. My sincere thanks are due to Shri Dilip Ranade, curator, Chhatrapati Shivaji Museum for his full cooperation for using the museum library. I also thank all the staff members of the Asiatic Society library, Mumbai; the library of University of Mumbai, Deccan College library, Pune and Bhandarkar Oriental Research Institute library, Pune.

My sincere thanks to Shri Ramdas Bhatkal and Shri Harsha Bhatkal because of whom this work has seen the light of the day. I also thank Ms Vinitha Ramchandani, Ms Swapna Shinde, Ms Bharati Anand, Mr Mahendra Ghanekar and Ms Anjali Sawant of Popular Prakashan.

The completion of this work would not have been possible without the moral support, encouragement and actual help in editing, correcting, typing and making useful suggestions during all the stages of writing this book. This task was done by my husband Sudheer Agashe, my brother Sudheer Bedekar, and my daughter Sonia Virkar. For everything they did with great concern I prefer to remain indebted to them.

To all these persons, I express my gratitude, but I am alone responsible for any errors and shortcomings in this book.

— Sukanya Agashe

CONTENTS

LIST OF ILLUSTRATIONS
(According to present study)

Maps: Maps are complied from various sources.

Map 1: Ayodhya, Chitrakūṭ, Tāṭakāvana, Daṇḍakāraṇya, Janasthāna, Pañcavaṭī (Reva plateau), Kiṣkindhā, Ṛkṣabila, Laṅkā and other important sites from Rāmāyaṇa (in the context of some modern places).

Map 2: Routes taken by characters from Vālmīki Rāmāyaṇa.

Photograph: Ramgarh hill tunnel, Surguja district, Chhattisgarh, India, called the 'Hathipole' tunnel (image by Manoj Kulkarni).

Photograph on cover: Twenty-armed Rāvaṇa image at Mara caves, Sidhi district, M.P., India (image by Sudheer Agashe).

Illustration: Fig. 1: Illustrating the concepts of the division of the globe: Astronomical Laṅkā and Rāvaṇa's Laṅkā.

Geographical regions and site locations from Rāmāyaṇa according to present study are indicative of only the general area and locations.

PREFACE

Rāmāyaṇa has a unique place in the cultural traditions of India. Together with the great epic *Mahābhārata* it has played a major role in the formation of the Indian culture. It has permeated so deeply in the Indian psyche that for centuries and even today, in the days of T.V. serials and cinema, it has provided millions of ordinary people with entertainment, comfort, and succour. The epic form of *Rāmāyaṇa* gives it the capacity to assimilate varied cultural experiences in the shape of folk tales, bard's songs, legends, and myths. *Rāmāyaṇa* is at once a literary work in the form of an epic poem, an important religious text of the Hindūs, a very influential mythology and embedded in all this are certain historical facts.

Rāmāyaṇa has been studied by enumerable scholars, literary critics and poets, theologians and historians. The focus of the present study is the geography of *Rāmāyaṇa*. An attempt is made here to determine the location of various places mentioned in *Rāmāyaṇa* like Mt. Citrakūṭa, Pañcavaṭī, Daṇḍakāraṇya, Kiṣkindhā, and finally Laṅkā. The difficulties faced by any scientific attempt to winnow the historical facts from the heap of mythological chaff are well known. D.D.Kosambi[1] has commented on this difficulty of discriminating historical truth from myths and legends. This is also true about geographical information and place names. One would think that at least the location of such physical entities like great cities and mountains will not become wrapped in mystery and become controversial. But this is not so. Over two thousand years, the location of Laṅkā, the capital city of Rāvaṇa, has 'travelled' thousands of kilometres southwards.

If we add two more factors, the task of the researcher becomes still more complicated. Firstly, there exist innumerable versions of *Rāmāyaṇa* created by various communities or religious sects, not only in the Indian sub-continent but also in other countries. Secondly, the original Vālmīki *Rāmāyaṇa* has grown and changed over centuries by later extrapolations and modifications, to such an extent that, confusing and contradictory references to rivers, mountains and cities occur in *Rāmāyaṇa*. Last but not the least, as is well known, the researcher has to rely almost totally on literary sources and living traditions in the absence of enough archaeological data.

In view of these difficulties, what method and approach can one adopt fruitfully? The *Vedas*, the epics, *Purāṇās, Bhagavadgītā, Ṣruti, Smṛti,* the works of Pāṇinī, Patañjali, Bhāsa, Kālidāsa, Varāhamihira and Bhāskāracārya, all these and many more works form parts of our much valued ancient literature.

In the last 100-150 years *pundits* and scholars have realised that quite a sizable amount of knowledge of historical, geographical, astronomical, biological and sociological nature is embedded in our ancient literature which is of religious, legendary or mythological nature.

For carrying out geographical study of ancient India, this ancient literature, although itself of non-geographical nature, is the first source of information. References exist of kings, dynasties, descriptions of tribes and *janapadās*, names of places and of birds and animals together with plant-life of a region and descriptions of events or seasons. All such material, although incidental, if studied, analysed and interpreted properly can throw new light on ancient geography, history, or culture of a region. Besides ancient literature, inscriptions on stones, bricks or copper-plates, coins and seals, travel accounts of travellers of Indian or foreign origin, accounts of historians, geographers, pilgrims and rulers, all can give valuable information. In modern times, geological and archaeological methods like carbon-14 method for dating, mathematical and astronomical calculations are unanimously accepted scientific methods used by researchers and the results are put to scrutiny.

Such study advances the geographical knowledge derived from literary sources.

Epics like *Rāmāyaṇa* or *Mahābhārata* are works of literature created by poets like Vālmīki and Vyāsa who lived in a particular period of history in a certain social, cultural and natural environment. Whether the epics are imaginary poetry, a flight of poet's imagination or history, is not the question here. Vālmīki belonged to a certain period and environment, which will naturally be reflected in his poetry, providing it with 'historical context but not necessarily with historicity' as Romila Thapar[2] has said.

The word *Rāmāyaṇa* literally means the journey of Rāma. The real story of *Rāmāyaṇa* starts from Ayodhya. Some of the places are even today at the same geographical locations as described by Vālmīki in *Rāmāyaṇa*. The places from Ayodhya to Mt. Citrakūṭa are still identifiable, e.g. Ayodhya, Śṛṅgaverapura and some rivers and mountains.

Many other places are either wiped out in the course of history or their original names are twisted and distorted so much that they have become unrecognisable. For identifying ancient sites only their names and the tales and legends associated with them can be misleading. Other natural factors untouched by human hands like the rivers, mountains and the topography along with climatic patterns and natural flora and fauna should be applied to ancient sites for their acceptable identification. The most serious obstacle in the way of utilising the epic and purāṇic texts is the corruptions, interpolations, and intentional additions to and omissions of text from the 'original'. Even then, the numerous isolated stray references collectively will continue to provide a considerable addition to our geographical knowledge of ancient India.

Many a times material objects decay or get destroyed but things like customs and traditions of festivals, *jatrās*, religious and non-religious fares and gatherings that are traditionally practiced survive. From systematic and probing studies of such living traditions some deductions can be made and inferences can be drawn which help us reach the roots. Then to confirm such inferences other methods can be employed.

Being an epic poem *Rāmāyaṇa* and also *Mahābhārata*, present us with a complex of characters, human relationships, riddles of a psychological nature and moral puzzles. It unfolds before us a poet's world and we can appreciate and criticise the aesthetic aspects of this work of literature. However, the present study concentrates on geography and all such questions are out of the scope of this work. For example, stories like Rāma's killing of Śaṃbūka or Vālin and banishing Sītā unjustly, pose many questions of moral, social, and religious nature to the modern mind. But I have only dealt with 'where', rather than with 'how' and 'why'.

Rāmāyaṇa literally means the journey of Rāma, after being banished from Ayodhya for fourteen years of *vanavāsa*. Rāma with Lakṣmaṇa and Sītā travelled up to Śṛṅgaverapura where they crossed river Ganga and then crossed the confluence of rivers Ganga and Yamuna. They went to Mt. Citrakūṭa and visited many hermitages and spent ten years in that area. Then sage Agastya sent them to Pañcavaṭī from where Sītā was abducted by Rāvaṇa. Rāma and Lakṣmaṇa went to meet Sugrīva at Kiṣkindha and with the assistance of Hanumat and Sugrīva's *vānara* army crossed the waters to reach Laṅkā. When Rāvaṇa was killed and the war was over, triumphant Rāma returned to Ayodhya. This entire journey constitutes *Rāmāyaṇa*.

Many geographical riddles are posed by Vālmīki's account of this journey. Most scholars more or less agree that we can take as established fact that, the location of Ayodhya in *Rāmāyaṇa* is the same as present day Ayodhya. But what about other places mentioned in the course of the journey? The toughest riddle of all is the location of Rāvaṇa's Laṅkā. Along with people at large, most scholars, including F.E. Pargiter, D.R. Bhandarkar etc. believed that Laṅkā in Vālmīki *Rāmāyaṇa* was the present day Sri Laṅkā (Ceylon) and this was not questioned for a long time. However, doubts started arising. The first scholar to question this assumption and to assert that Laṅkā was situated in Madhya Pradesh, most probably on Mt. Amarkanṭak, was Sardar Madhavrao Kibe, who published a paper in Indian Historical Quarterly in 1928. Since then many scholars like T. Paramasiva Iyer, Herman Jacobi, J.C. Ghosh, H.D. Sankalia, U.P. Shah, and many others have reached similar conclusions. A short account of the works of these scholars and the nature of the controversy is given in chapter 1 of this book.

The thought of writing this book came to my mind a few years back, the reason being my going through the pages of the play *'Sītā Josyam'* and particularly the prologue to it, written by its author Narla Venkateshvar Rao in 1990. The content of the book thrilled me. The second book that I read in this connection was *'Rāmāyaṇa and Laṅkā'* written in 1940 by T. Paramasiva Iyer. These two books inspired me to study further. After going through the studies carried out on similar lines by other scholars, the scope of this subject came within view. It was also realised, that amidst the scholars there are contradicting view-points.

Gradually I came to the view that Laṅkā was not situated in Sri Laṅkā (Ceylon). It was obviously not possible to accept the sites of Australia, Egypt, Malaysia, Sumatra etc., suggested by some other 'scholars'. It was reasonable to accept the thesis that Laṅkā was in Madhya Pradesh in India. But the exact site still eluded scholars, who suggested various locations.

For the last ten years or so I have struggled with this problem. Apart from study of literature I also studied topographical maps and other geographical features of the probable areas of M.P. In addition I have studied the satellite images of the target areas of interest on 'Google Earth', which is now possible. I believe that I have discovered some 'new' evidences, made some new connections, hitherto overlooked by scholars and an attempt is made to determine the location of Rāvaṇa's Laṅkā with some degree of confidence possible under the present circumstances. I have also visited some of the proposed target sites. I humbly present the results of my studies as a tentative thesis for consideration of scholars and all those interested in the subject.

For my studies I have used the critical edition of 'Vālmīki *Rāmāyaṇa*' of Baroda, as the main source of evidences which forms the basis of my arguments presented in this book and other references that are presented are only supportive to the main logic.

A word about the organisation of the material and presentation of the argument should be added here. The strategy of research was very simple. The present author followed Rāma in his journey through the pages of *Rāmāyaṇa*. Broadly, the places are studied in the same order as that of the epic. In association with the places, the references, stories and legends, geographical data from the text or external sources, interpretations, quotations and views of other scholars that came on the way have been given at the same place. By employing this method the story line is not disturbed, the continuity of the narrative is automatically maintained and there is a minimum repetition of the matter. As mentioned earlier, Chapter 1 presents a brief review of a few chosen studies, conclusions of other scholars and my critical comments on them. Further chapters trace the journey to Laṅkā and the last few chapters deal with the argument for the exact location of Laṅkā in some details. End notes are given at the end of each chapter and appendices have been added at the end of the book to provide information about some important topics connected with the subject. Translations of all Sanskrit verses and words are given at the same place. Sanskrit verses in *Devanāgarī* are given at the end of the book. Maps, photographs, figures, tables, line-drawings etc. have been added to the text to make it more comprehensible.

I am fully aware that this study is based mainly on literary sources and the conclusions are based on the same. The next step would be to carry out multi-disciplinary research in the indicated area. For the time being, however, I hope that the work presented in this book, arouses interest of academic as well as popular nature and the problem of location of Laṅkā is studied further.

— Sukanya Agashe

1. D.D. Kosambi has said that, 'the true content of a myth is difficult to obtain, and rarely directs historical information. Indian historical figures

and events tend unfortunately to disappear into a mystery or a legend which comes more and more to resemble pure myth with the passage of time'.

2. Romila Thapar: Foreword to 'Questioning Rāmāyaṇas' Paula Richman (ed.), (2000) Oxford , p.8

Note 1: All references in this book to 'Vālmīki Rāmāyaṇa' are to the critical edition, (ed. by Bhatt G.H.) Oriental Institute Baroda (1959-75); unless otherwise mentioned and marked 'By'-for Bombay recension of 'Vālmīki Rāmāyaṇa' Translated in Marathi by S.D. Satavalekar, (1965) Swādhyāya Mandal Publication, Pardi, Balsad; Gujarat. All references to Mahābhārata are to the critical edition, ed. by Sukthankar V.S. and Belvalkar S.K., Bhandarkar Oriental Research Institute, Pune (1933-56). References to *Purāṇās*, (ed. by J.L. Shastri), are to MLBD publication, Delhi, unless mentioned otherwise.

1

INTRODUCTION AND REVIEW OF LITERATURE

Before we proceed on our investigative journey from Ayodhya to Laṅkā, it will be useful to spend some time on two considerations, firstly the socio-economic setting of the *Rāmāyaṇa* story and the probable chronology. We have to know, however broadly, as to when and in what social conditions the events could have taken place, and also when the story or stories about them were written. Secondly, a brief critical survey of the views of various scholars on the geography of *Rāmāyaṇa* will throw light on the problem and guide us as to what we should be looking for in our journey. This chapter is devoted to these two aspects.

D.D. Kosambi[1] has said that, 'The *Rāmāyaṇa* represents the conflict between agriculturists and food gatherers.' Romila Thapar[2] argues that, 'the juxtaposition between monarchical state systems and tribal 'chiefships' is reflected in the *Rāmāyaṇa*, and it presents a rather orthodox picture of political legitimacy reflecting firm faith in monarchy as the only acceptable system'. She has very effectively brought out this dimension of *Rāmāyaṇa* in detail.

In broad outline, the society in northern India, between 1500 B.C. and 200 A.D. was undergoing a tremendous transition characterised by confrontation of agriculture based, increasingly monarchical social system, with the forest dwelling tribal society. The Vedic Indo-Aryan speaking people gradually expanded their sway by moving eastward and southward, subjugating and assimilating the 'native' peoples including *rakṣasās*.

What comprises the Rāma story? Is it only mythical? Is it a legend? Or is it a story, hinting at historical context? Where did the Ikṣvākus come from? And who were the *rakṣasās* and the *vānarās*? Scholars now unanimously accept that they were actually humans, *vanacarās* or aborigines residing in the thick forests of Mt. Vindhya.

In this context it must be considered that *'Paumacariyam'* (in *prākṛt*) or *'Padmacarita'* (in Sanskrit), the earliest of all the Jain versions of Vālmīki *Rāmāyaṇa* composed by Vimalasuri in early A.D. centuries interpreted *Rāmāyaṇa* rationally and stated the humanness of the *rakṣasās* and the *vānarās*[3,4].

Romila Thapar[5] has elaborated on the purpose and function of the Jain version of Vālmīki *Rāmāyaṇa.* She points out that in addition to depicting the *rakṣasās* and *vānarās* as humans, focusing and delineating the *rakṣasās* (especially Rāvaṇa) in a better light, *Paumacariyam* states that they had a common lineage, that of the '*Vidyādharas*'.

Vidyādharavaṃśa (at Laṅkā) and *vānaravaṃśa* (at Kiṣkiṇḍi i.e. Kiṣkindhā) are said to be the two segments of a common lineage. Rāvaṇa and other main characters here are the followers of Jain ideals and *Paumacariyam* is clearly composed in conformity with Jain ideals. In addition to this *Paumacariyam* has Vindhyan region as its geographical locale and this fact therefore can be the basis of a strong argument in favour of the theory that Laṅkā be situated in the Vindhyan region is what Romila Thapar suggests.

Paumacariyam[6] gives prominence to the story of earlier Ikṣvāku king Sagara (of Sāketa) and his sixty thousand sons, echoing the *Purāṇās* and the *Mahābhārata*. What is the importance of Sagara story from *Rāmāyaṇa*? What is the connection of Sagara story with the *rakṣasās*? These questions will be dealt with in this book.

Dating the epics has been a tough problem for historians. The time periods of:

1) actual events and

2) the composition of the epic are hard to determine.

The form, the details and the description of an event may differ with the passage of time as it may also change with the local, cultural, political etc. requirements of a community.

Regarding the dating of epic *Rāmāyaṇa* various scholars have set the dating based on different norms thus resulting in chronological controversy. In the present shape the *Rāmāyaṇa* is older than the *Mahābhārata.* There is strong internal literary evidence that Rāma story was known to the poets of *Mahābhārata*.

B.B. Lal[7] suggests that Rāma or Kṛśṇa cannot be placed after Buddha, of the 6th or 5th centuries B.C. Thus, the events described in both the epics must antedate the 6th century B.C., although both the texts belong to 2nd century B.C. to 2nd century A.D. Based on his archaeological studies at Hastinapura, Kausambi and other sites B.B. Lal suggested the probable date of the *Mahābhārata* war to be sometime in the 9th century B.C. He further states that the earliest period at which the Rāmāyaṇic sites like Ayodhya, Naṅdigrāma, Śṛṅgaverapura, Citrakūṭa and Bhāradvāja hermitage could have co-existed, may go back to the 7th century B.C.

According to many scholars, it is reasonable to assume that the events depicted in *Rāmāyaṇa* could have taken place sometime around 1500 B.C. and the bardic legends and stories about the events spread to many parts of north India. As suggested by H.D. Sankalia the original *Rāmāyaṇa* written by Vālmīki was composed in epic form around 400 B.C. and the text of *Rāmāyaṇa* as we have in our hands today took shape by 200 A.D.–400 A.D. after many extrapolations, additions, probably of the *Bālakāṇḍa* and *Uttarakāṇḍa,* (making Rāma an *avatara,* an incarnation of Viṣṇu), and omissions as well. According to Sankalia the text of the critical edition is of the fifth century A.D. or later and the depiction of life is that of northern India in that period. He also suggests that the activities in *Rāmāyaṇa* relate to the destruction of Chalcolithic culture by early iron-age cultures[8].

On this background we have to begin research in ancient Indian geography. Ancient Indian geographical knowledge is scattered in many languages like Sanskrit, Pāli, etc. besides Latin, Greek, Chinese, Arabic, Persian, ancient Pahalavi, Avesta and the Indian regional languages. These are all rich sources of geographical knowledge. *Vedas*, epics, *Purāṇās*, Pāṇinī (mentioned by V.S. Agrawala)[9] etc. give geographical references, indications and guidelines. Knowing this, F. E. Pargiter[10] uncovered the geographical knowledge hidden in *Mārkaṇḍeya Purāṇa.* B.C. Law[11] and D.C. Sarkar[12] churned out *Bhuvanakośa* and Kālidāsa's works. Other ancient Indian literature, like the *Purāṇās*-were also studied by S.M. Ali[13], who through an elaborate discourse, brought to our notice the fact that the *Vedas* and the epics are the primary source of purāṇic geography. Purāṇic world map evolved out of geographical notions of the epic, making a compromise between growing scientific knowledge and traditional views. *Purāṇās* then developed the idea of the division of the world in seven *dvīpās,* S.M. Ali states. He tried to bring to light some geographical truths hidden in those apparently fanciful notions.

Bhīṣmaparvan, *Sabhāparvan* and *Vanaparvan* of *Mahābhārata* were studied as they were found to contain some important geographical indications. Pilgrimages of sage Dhaumya, Yudhiṣṭhira, king Nala, the victory march of Pāṇḍavās, *Rāmopākhyāna* were studied for clues. Mc Crindle[14] brought to light an enormous treasure of knowledge of Indian geography. Ptolemy[15], Periplus[16] and Pliny[17] have written about Indian geography. Zend Avesta points to Vedic geographical material. Dr Fleet[18] elucidated *'Bṛhatsaṃhitā'* of Varāhamihira. We were enlightened by Al-beruni[19] and Chinese visitors like Yu-an-chwang[20], Hu-en-tsang[21] etc. *Babarnama*[22] and *Ain-I–Akbari*[23] have enriched our treasure of geographical knowledge.

Regarding the geographical concepts contained in Vālmīki *Rāmāyaṇa* S.M. Ali[24] says that accounts of various countries of the four quarters of India from *Bālakāṇḍa, Ayodhyākāṇḍa* and *Kiṣkindhākaṇḍa,* and also only references of some adjacent lands, bring out more or less a complete geographical picture of India, as conceived by the composers of *Rāmāyaṇa.*

The geographical concept of the world is found in most of the *Purāṇās.*There was the concept of *'saptadvīpā vasumatī'* (earth) with seven parts (*pṛithvī*) of the *Purāṇās.* According to most *Purāṇās* the earth comprises of seven concentric island continents (*dvīpās*), separated by seven encircling seas. One of these *dvīpās,* the only one which was not in the form of a ring, was Jambūdvīpā (the whole of the then known world), occupying the entire northern hemisphere of the earth. [According to S.M. Ali a *dvīpā* literally means 'an island between two arms of water'. It may signify an island, a peninsula (division of land-big or small) or a *'doab'* i.e. land between two rivers].

Besides this, in earlier times, the earth was also conceived to be like a lotus with four petals representing only four islands, *mahādvīpās,* namely Bhadrāśva, Jambūdvīpā, Ketumāla and Uttarakurū with Mt. Meru (possibly Pamir) at the centre for its pericarp. Around Mt. Meru the central region or Illavṛtt*varṣa* was spread. Rāmāyaṇa conceived the earth with four *mahādvīpās* and four *samudrās*. In *Rāmāyaṇa,* in addition to the lotus earth theory there is also a mention of *saptadvīpā vasumatī* (the earth). Jambūdvīpā being a synonym of Bhārata for a long time in ancient geography, created confusion. According to Buddhist tradition the earth had four continents, while in Jain *Purāṇās* the seven island theory is replaced by sixteen seas separating sixteen islands.

As communication increased, the four island theory was slowly changed and the earth was divided into seven *mahādvīpās*. Jambūdvīpā was now divided into nine *varṣās,* one of them being *Bhāratavarṣa*, with nine *varṣās* (mountains). The new Jambūdvīpā was assumed to be surrounded by the sea of salt water and there are six other *dvīpās* in ring form to the south of it separated by six other seas. This, through some transitions became the world map of *Mahābhārata*, accepted and later perfected by *Purāṇās.*

Mārkaṇḍeya Purāṇa had adopted the nine-fold division of *Bhāratavarṣa* from Varāhamihira[25], who conceived the shape of Bhārata as that of a tortoise (*kūrma*) lying outspread, looking eastward and various countries and peoples distributed over its body together with corresponding lunar constellations. The nine divisions (units) or *'navakhaṇḍās'* of *Bhāratavarṣa* were separated by oceans and were mutually inaccessible. These nine *'khaṇḍās'* or *'bhedās'* are according to the geographical notions of most *Purāṇās*. They are also mentioned in the famous astronomical works *'Siddhāntaśiromaṇī'*[26], of Bhāskārācārya (II) of the twelfth century A.D. However, their identification is again a matter of controversy. These were the geographical ideas of ancient times[27, 28].

Coming specifically to the geography of *Rāmāyaṇa*, issues have been made very confusing due to uncertainty of the time period under question and complex changes in the various versions of *Rāmāyaṇa* available to us today. Where did the events of Rāmakathā take place? Initially, scholars like Pargiter[29] followed by D.R. Bhandarkar[30] intended studying the geography of *Rāmāyaṇa*. Following them, many others believed that Rāmāyaṇic Laṅkā can be identified with Ceylon - Sri Laṅkā. Some names from a long list are H. Roychaudhury[31], R.C. Majumdar[32], Vishuddhanand Pathak[33] and C.V. Vaidya[34]. However, scholars have, after great efforts, made feasible hypotheses and clarified many geographical issues as the brief survey below shows. More details of contributions of some of these researchers are included in later chapters at appropriate places. The important names of researchers whose theories proved reasonable are Sardar Madhavrao Kibe, T.P. Iyer, Hiralal, H.D. Sankalia, Romila Thapar, D.R. Mankad, V.D. Jha, T. Amrithalingam, N.V. Rao, U.P. Shah, Rai Krisnadas, G. Ramdas, J.C. Ghosh, D.P. Mishra, etc.

Some of the places and sites described in *Rāmāyaṇa* exist even today, not only in the maps but also in actual reality. Between Ayodhya and Laṅkā, there are many places with Rāmāyaṇic names and there are communities claiming themselves to be Rāvaṇa's descendents. Some even adore Rāvaṇa and Meghanāda by tradition, with their folk songs in praise of Rāvaṇa. This puzzled scholars. They thought that it was then possible that other places and sites described by Vālmīki should also be searched.

Ayodhya is still on the banks of Śarayu (Ghāghra). Rivers Ganga, Yamuna, Śṛṅgaverapura (old Singraur) and Mt. Citrakūṭa are right there at the same locations as described by Vālmīki. Scholars wanted to know if there is any historical basis for the epics. In case of *Rāmāyaṇa* the events cannot be placed after Buddha, fifth century B.C. and the text belongs to a period at least five hundred or more years later, as indicated by linguistic and internal evidences. In this scenario, some archaeological studies were also carried out by B.B. Lal, K.N. Dikshit and H.D. Sankalia. K.N. Dikshit[35] while taking an extensive review of 'The progress of Archaeology in India during the past twenty-five years', suggested that "the Gangetic valley holds many secrets in the form of unexplored sites awaiting examination'. It was thought that this could throw some light on the social life and cultural sequence of the epic period, although at the most it could provide the historical context only.

B.B. Lal carried out excavations at some of the popular Rāmāyaṇic sites like Ayodhya, including traditional spots on the right or south bank of river Śarayu (Ghagra). Excavations were also carried out at Nandigram, Śṛṅgaverapura, Bhāradvāja hermitage and Citrakūṭa. Briefly, the overall archaeological evidences collected from these sites indicated that the earliest period in which all these sites could have co-existed is that of the early stages of the Northern Black Polished Ware (NBPW) which may go back to seventh century B.C.

Certain sites are associated with certain events and up to Citrakūṭa site, these very Rāmāyaṇic names exist even today. Moreover, they match well with the description given in the epic. B.B. Lal[36] makes it clear in his introduction to the 'Archaeology of the Rāmāyaṇa sites' project that, 'There is no intention to take up any site south of Citrakūṭa'. He further writes, 'It is however hoped that someone else will continue the thread'. The reason for this fact is clear. For the remaining major Rāmāyaṇic sites like Pañcavaṭī, *Ṛkṣabila*, Kiṣkindhā, Mt. Mahendra, the south sea and Rāvaṇa's Laṅkā, logically convincing dependable literary and geographical justifications were not found, although people at large and some scholars still believe that Nashik, Bellary or Ceylon were truly the Rāmāyaṇic sites imagined by the epic poet. But then, are other sites to the south of Citrakūṭa wiped out? Or else re-established nearby or only their names have been distorted to an unrecognisable proportion? Even then, other places must have existed and should be found, may be in the form of some faint marks and indications. Researchers started studying this problem and naturally many more questions arose. Thus, there are questions regarding the location of Daṇḍakāraṇya, Pañcavaṭī, Kiṣkindhā, and above all Laṅkā. The present study is an effort to first identify the most convincing geographical positioning of these sites which can then become the ground material for thorough and multi-pronged investigations.

Ordinarily accepted common belief that Laṅkā was in Ceylon is so deep-rooted in people's minds that anything that differed from it was not to be digested by people at large. But, the scholars doubting the age-old belief asked themselves a question: When empires of great Guptas or Harṣa could not cross river Narmada and spread to the south of Vindhya and the country was so thickly forested in those times, how could Rāma traverse the distance of some 2400 km to Ceylon from Ayodhya on foot? And how could Rāvaṇa control a land as far away as Janasthāna, which was near Citrakūṭa of Vālmīki? This undoubtedly was unrealistic.

So, Rāvaṇa's Laṅkā was somewhere else, and theories opposing each other were propounded. So much so that Laṅkā was taken as far away as Assam and even out of India, e. g. Afghanistan and even up to Australia, Egypt, Java, Sumatra, Indonesia, Thailand and Maldives. One can give many other instances of misconceptions. The most reasonable and at least partly convincing thesis was put forward by M.V. Kibe[37] in 1927. His argument and explanation is derived from a study of Sanskrit edition of *Rāmāyaṇa*. He propounded a theory that Laṅkā is not Sri Laṅkā (Ceylon) but was situated in Madhya Pradesh on Mt. Amarkanṭak. J.C. Ghosh[38] (1929), after studying coins, presented evidence supporting Kibe's theory. This evidence came from a coin of a Gond king, who ruled in Madhya Pradesh in fifteenth century. The king styled himself as of *'Paulastyavaṃśa',* equivalent to *Rāvaṇavaṃśa* - and the Gonds of the region still claim their decent from Rāvaṇa. J.C. Gosh also pointed out that a certain compact area in Orissa was also called Laṅkā.

Herman Jacobi[39] had already proposed, a year before Pargiter, that Sri Laṅkā (Ceylon) cannot be Rāvaṇa's Laṅkā. Jacobi initially had said that, in his view Laṅkā was in Assam, and that it was called *'Rakṣasa-sthāna'* but later he withdrew his theory and supported Kibe's hypothesis of Amarkanṭak hill in eastern Madhya Pradesh to be Laṅkā.

Kibe[40] says that a place called Satna, 45 km to the south of Mt. Citrakūṭa, can be identified with the hermitage of sage Sutīkṣṇa. However, in his search for Laṅkā, Kibe has considered *Ṛkṣabila* to be a valley or a cave as is thought by most other scholars. It is one of the important land-marks in the geography of Vālmīki *Rāmāyaṇa*.

In our search for Laṅkā, therefore, the geographical position and the specific nature of *Ṛkṣabila* is discussed in the following pages in detail. Kibe observes that on Bengal-Nagpur railway between Bilaspur and Katni in M. P. is Pendra Road station. Ten miles from Pendra Road, on a hill, is an old fort. It is visible from Bhṛgu's hermitage (which is 3 km from where river Narmada issues out). It is known as 'Rānī Bakāvalī' fort by the locals in Amarkanṭak hill area. One has no access to it because of the marshy and swamp area around it. Kibe feels that this site could be Rāvaṇa's Laṅkā as there could have been water all around it long ago where there is marshy land today. Laṅkā of *Rāmāyaṇa* was located on Mt. Trikūṭa, surrounded by water and therefore, Kibe argues, 'In this paper it is proposed to identify it (Laṅkā) with a peak on Amarkanṭak (Āmrakūṭa) mountain. It would not be difficult to identify the other two peaks as Sālakūṭa (*Sāla*- a tree) and Madhukūṭa (*Mahuā*- a tree).'

Pargiter[41] put forward a theory that Sri Laṅkā-Ceylon is Rāvaṇa's Laṅkā and Kiṣkindha is Anegundi in Karnataka state. In his view there is another Vindhya mountain, in south India, which Saṃpātī refers to as 'south Vindhya'. The hills near Mysore are that 'south Vindhya' and the same hill ranges are the waves of the sea!

It should be considered that earlier, Emperor Alexander and Aśoka knew Ceylon as 'Siṃhala-*dvīpā*' or by the name 'Tāmraparṇī' (or 'Taṃbapannī'). By the times of Ptolemy (150 A.D.) it became 'Siṃhala'. Varāhamihira, Bhavabhūti, Murāri and Rājaśekhara, all have distinguished Siṃhala from Laṅkā (N.V. Rao)[42].

Godakumbura[43], a scholar from Ceylon, has studied the problem critically and has made abundantly clear that the chronicle of Ceylon, '*Dipavaṃśa*' (fifth century A.D.) started using the name Laṅkā for Siṃhala (Sri Laṅkā) under the influence of *Rāmāyaṇa*. A copper plate of A.D. 1080 indicates this fact and it is argued that 'This circumstance suggests the suspicion that the identification of Ceylon with Laṅkā is a much later development and had, in fact, no foundation in the classical period. The same can be said about the location of Kiṣkindhā. It is also believed that Vālin's Kiṣkindhā, the capital of *vānara* kingdom, was located at Anegundi, (near Bellari,

Karnataka state, India) where remains of ancient Vijaynagara are found. Nearby, supposed sites of Rāmāyaṇic river Paṃpā, a tributary of Tungabhadra and Mt. Mataṅga etc. are shown to the tourist.

If we look at the map of India, it becomes clear that Kiṣkindha of Vālin and Sugrīva must be in north India. This is so, since the sites that are described to be not far away from Kiṣkindhā, e.g. the northern slope of Mt. Vindhya and river Narmada to the south of Kiṣkindha according to Rāmāyaṇa itself or Mt. Citrakūṭa, stand fixed. This sounds logical. Varāhamihira[44] (sixth century) says that Kiṣkindha was in south-east direction and this should be taken to mean to the south-east of madhya-deśa, as per the prescribed orientation of *Bhāratavarṣa* as kūrma form in *Mārkaṇḍeya Purāṇa*.

'Prācina Sthalakośa[45]*'* informs us that according to *Purāṇās* and Patañjali, Kiṣkindha was situated to the north of Mt. Vindhya. It can be accepted that Kiṣkindha was on the northern slope of Vindhya, however, there was no 'sea' to the south of Kiṣkindhā. To solve this difficulty it is necessary to assume that the 'sea' of *Rāmāyaṇa* must be in reality a water reservoir of vast expanse, a notion accepted by many scholars like Sankalia[46]. In Sanskrit the word *'Sāgara'* means a water reservoir, a lake or an ocean. This has been further confirmed by studies presented in this book giving new evidences. Coming back to Laṅkā, some other scholars must be mentioned. V.D. Jha[47] gave extremely valuable information in one of his articles about the archaeology of Surguja in eastern M.P.' (modern Chhattisgarh), the region which had remained physically isolated due to its dense forests and paucity of means of communications. Jha conducted explorations and found artefacts of stone ages, rock paintings, sculptures and shrines, epigraphs, coins and ceramics and he believes that this region was closely associated with Rāma's story.

Research work done by T. P. Iyer[48] (1940) is similarly important. He has charted out Rāma's itinerary from Ayodhya to Laṅkā and believes that the entire journey could not have been of more than 373 miles or 600 km. In his opinion, on Jabalpur-Damoh railway line, near village Katangi and river Kair, is a hill called 'Indrana *parvata*'. Close to this is another hill named 'Suvela *parvata*'. River Hiran flows and encircles Indrana hill which could be Rāvaṇa's Laṅkā.

River Kair flows through a narrow pass which could be 'Mahendra *dvāra'* he believes. There is also a place called 'Singaladīpa', which T. P. Iyer takes as a supporting evidence for Laṅkā to be at this site. However, J.C. Ghosh[49] (1938) refers to a place 'Siṃhala' being close to Reva, now in M.P. If Siṃhala and Laṅkā are different, 'Singaladīpa' near Indrana hill could very well be Siṃhala but that does not identify the site with Laṅkā of *Rāmāyaṇa*. D.R. Mankad[50] (1965) shows inclination towards Iyer's view rather than towards Kibe's, whereas for scholars like U.P. Shah[51] (1975) and Rai Krisnadas[52] Amarkanṭak appears to be a more probable location of Laṅkā thus supporting Kibe's theory. This view is also shared by Hiralal[53] (1937) and G. Ramdas [54, 55, 56]. Later, H.D. Sankalia[57] personally visited Indrana hill region and found no marks of past human habitation on that hill. He therefore proposed that, Laṅkā should not be looked for near Jabalpur but should be searched for to the north of river Narmada, towards south-east regions of M.P. or near the common border of Andhra and Orissa states.

According to Rāmāyaṇa, Rāma, or for that matter any other character (with the exception of sage Agastya), never crossed river Narmada. If Ceylon were Laṅkā, by which route Rāma reached Laṅkā was the question. D.P. Mishra's[58] (1985) answer to this question was that Rāma did not go via the south sea, but along the south-eastern sea coast. Rāma could reach the south-eastern sea and then by constructing the bridge and crossing over the sea, he could reach Laṅkā. D.P. Mishra[59] proposes that Laṅkā was an island between the mouth of river Mahanadi in Orissa and the mouth of river Godavari in Andhra. The hills in that area are even today known as 'Mahendragiri'. But, this site for Rāmāyaṇic Laṅkā is an alluvial delta and has only the sea-level and is not a hill-top settlement as decribed by Vālmīki in the text.

N. V. Rao[60] opines that Laṅkā must have been situated in eastern Madhya Pradesh and in the region where the borders of Chota Nagpur, Andhra and Orissa meet. Thirty-eight percent of this region is forested even to this date and it is occupied by *adivasi* (tribal) communities like Munda, Oraon, Santhal, Ho and Asur. N.V. Rao pointed out that, although it is believed that, Rāma with his own hands had set up a place for *'Śivaliṅgam'* at Rameshvar, but in reality this place of pilgrimage (in south India) has come into existence between A.D. 1000 and A.D. 1300. *Mahābhārata* or *Purāṇās* do not mention Rameshvar or even Dhanushyakodi. Rao points out that Saivaite Cola kings established the *Śivaliṅgam* and Vaiṣṇāvas established Dhanushyakodi. He is of the opinion that Tamils from south India who had gone to Siṃhala islands, disseminated *Rāmāyaṇa* in Ceylon between A.D. 1000 and A.D. 1300.

H.D. Sankalia[61] draws our attention to the fact that, a stone inscription of tenth century, found in Bastar (Chhattisgarh) refers to a king of Gupta dynasty, Someśvara of Sonepur, who calls himself '*paścima* Laṅkādhipatī', the lord of western Laṅkā. (see B.C. Muzumdar)[62, 63]. Sankalia also notes that in south India, up to the third century, burial was a traditional practice of disposing off the dead, while to the north of Vindhya, dead bodies were cremated. *Rāmāyaṇa* informs us that Vālin and Rāvaṇa were cremated. Based on his archaeological studies, Sankalia[64] opines that Vālmīki was not properly acquainted with the rites, customs, culture and geography of south India and also for this reason the search for Laṅkā should be carried out to the north of Mt. Vindhya.

T. Amrithalingam[65] has raised two points which are extremely important in our search for Laṅkā. He says that, where there are no *Sāla* trees (Shorea robusta), Kiṣkindha or Laṅkā should not be searched for (End Note1). This suggests that north-eastern M.P. and Chhattisgarh could be the target area. Secondly he draws our attention towards the fact that while living in Pañcavaṭī, Lakṣmaṇa describes the biting and harsh winter. Amrithalingam pointed out that 'cold breezes from the west' blow only in the regions to the north of Mt. Vindhya and therefore Pañcavaṭī, Kiṣkindha and Laṅkā must be situated in the land to the north of Mt. Vindhya. This is a very important observation indeed.

It will be relevant to take a review of some recent efforts made in this direction. Studies carried out by M.R. Yardi[66] are of a different nature. He has supported the theory put forward by Kibe, Iyer and Sankalia and rejected the age old theories of Pargiter, Bhandarkar and others. R.K. Ramakrishnan[67] believes that Rāvaṇa's

Laṅkā must be situated in the southern ranges of Mt. Vindhya on Amarkanṭak. Even though one reasonably agrees that Laṅkā was in M.P. of India, the exact location was still an unanswered question. Scholars were thinking of various places as probable sites for Laṅkā. These included and ranged from Jabalpur towards eastern M.P. at Amarkanṭak and up to the borders of Andhra and Orissa to the mouth of river Godavari.

Jabalpur lies in the mid-region of Madhya Pradesh. Even if ordinary road atlas maps made for tourists are observed carefully, it becomes obvious that regions to the east of Jabalpur have maximum number of places connected with Rāma story. To the west of Jabalpur flow rivers like, Dhasan, Kali-Sindh, Chambal etc. The western Madhya Pradesh is less hilly compared to eastern regions, and as a result it is heavily populated and therefore by now has become thinly forested. The districts lying to the west of Jabalpur have less number of place names connected with *Rāmāyaṇa* than the eastern districts like Panna, Satna, Reva, Sidhi, Shahdol, Mandla, Surguja, Korea, Raipur etc., the later three are now in Chhattisgarh. These eastern districts have literally innumerable Rāmāyaṇic place names like Rampur, Ramgarh, Sitapur, Lakshmanpur, Ramanujaganj, Hanumanā etc. or as mentioned by P.V. Kane[68] like Vaiśravaṇeśvara, Rāvaṇeśvara, Māriceśvara, Sālakaṭaṅkaṭeśvara, Sugrīveśvara and many others situated to the north of Vindhya, in south Ganga plain, or in Narmadā belt (like Rāvaṇagrām in Vidisha, M.P. from where a huge *yakṣa* image has been excavated). This surely was not a coincidence, but was an indication only of an extent of influence of the epic story over the region. At this juncture, it is necessary to keep in mind that places, rivers, mountains etc. can get named after epic characters when the epic story becomes a part of local tradition. Moreover, it cannot be said that the names are of the same period as the events in the story, unless there are other evidences supporting it. Previous scholars had come to the conclusion that Laṅkā was in Madhya Pradesh and pointed at different regions in M.P. itself. It was therefore felt that more studies are required. All such studies provided the first guidelines and the direction indicated by them proved useful.

The north-eastern corner of Madhya Pradesh is the newly formed state of Chhattisgarh (A.D. 2000) comprising of sixteen districts. The entire state is hilly and forest covered even today. Till 1905 some of the districts of Chhattisgarh were included in central provinces or Chota Nagpur of Bengal. To the north of Chhattisgarh are spread Vindhyan ranges, called 'Kaimur' ranges and to the south are spread Maikal ranges. To further south of these are spread out Mt. Satpura ranges. In these mountainous regions there are very few permanent settlements. Human habitations may be found around old forts and in caves in rocky mountains. Villages are sparse and very small in size. As a result of these peculiar physical features the land from Chota Nagpur to Bastar has, from remote past, remained inaccessible for the invaders.

To the north of Chhattisgarh lies Uttar Pradesh, to the north-east is Jharkhand, to the east and south-east Orissa, to the north-west Sidhi and Shahdol districts of Madhya Pradesh, to the south-west lies Maharashtra and to the south is Andhra Pradesh. Numerous place names and the topography of the region indicate that this could be the target area where Rāvaṇa's Laṅkā must be searched for and nowhere else. Other artefacts like cave paintings and tools, found in many places in some districts of north-eastern M.P. like Reva, Panna, Satna, Sidhi and Singrauli and in Chhattisgarh state suggest that this was an area of human occupation in pre-historic times.

The strategy for this research was simple. The present author has followed Rāma through the pages of *Rāmāyaṇa,* observing minutely the twists and turns of the path he follows during his journey. In these studies it was realised that the previous researchers have not paid sufficient attention to many important points. *Ṛkṣabila* is one such instance. The fact that the description of *Ṛkṣabila* from the text if properly interpreted indicated it to be a huge tunnel and not a large cave as most scholars think. Also the fact that all the Rāmāyaṇic sites must have been closely connected cannot be ignored. The topography of various other proposed sites and the existence and abundance of crocodiles in *Dakṣiṇa sāgara,* as described in *Rāmāyaṇa* was not taken into notice.

All told, in this search for Laṅkā, *Rāmāyaṇa* should be the main guide, and it proved to be so. To conclude, this survey of the research work done by previous scholars makes it sufficiently clear that our journey should strive to confirm the thesis that Vālmīki's and Rāvaṇa's Laṅkā must have been in north-eastern M.P. and secondly locate the exact site of Laṅkā, imagined by the epic poet in that region. Further chapters are devoted to these tasks.

References: Introduction and review of literature

1. D. D. Kosambi: *'An Introduction to the study of Indian history',* Bombay (1956/75) p. 40
2. Romila Thapar: *'Exile and the kingdom: Some thoughts on the Rāmāyaṇa',* (1978), The Mythic Society Bangalore p. 18
3. V.M. Kulkarni: 'Origin and development of the Rāma story in Jain literature' (1960-62) J.O.I. Baroda, IX, no. 2, pp. 189-204
4. U.P. Shah: 'Rāmāyaṇa in Jain Tradition', (1961), International Rāmāyaṇa Seminar Proceedings, pp. 67-70
5. Romila Thapar: 'The Rāmāyaṇa: Theme and Variation', (1982), in S.N. Mukerjee (ed.) *'India: History and Thought'* Calcutta pp. 221-53. Also see 'Cultural pasts', in Collected Works (2000), pp. 660-662
6. *'Paumacariyam' Sandhi:* V, (tr. by S. Vora), pp.19,20 B.R. Publ. Corp.New Delhi/ed. and publ. by H. Jacobi
7. B.B. Lal: 'Excavations at Śṛṅgaverapura' (1993), Memoirs of ASI, vol. I, no. 88, pp.1-14
8. H.D. Sankalia: *'Rāmāyaṇa: Myth or Reality'* (1973) New Delhi, *'Rāmāyaṇa in Historical Perspective'* Macmillan India,(1973)
9. V.S. Agrawala: *'India as known to Pāṇinī'* (1953), Lucknow Univercity, pp.1-550
10. F.E. Pargiter: (ed.) *'Mārkaṇḍeya Purāṇa'* (1904/1969), pp. 160-196 The Asiatic Society of Bengal, Indological Book House, New Delhi
11. B.C. Law: *'Geographical aspects of Kālidāsa's works'* (1954), Indian Research Institute Calcutta
12. D.C. Sarkar: *'Cosmology and geography in early Indian Literature'* (1967) *'Indian Studies: Past and Present'* Calcutta, 1967
13. S.M. Ali: *'The Geography of the Purāṇās',*(1966) People's Publishing House, New Delhi

14. J.W. Mc Crindle: *'Ancient India as described in Classical Literature',* (1906) Calcutta
15. Ptolemy: *'Ancient India'* (ed. Mc Crindle (1881-1888) also [ed. by Majumdar Sastri (1927)] Calcutta
16. Periplus [tr. by W.H. Schoff of *'Periplus of the Erythraean Sea'* (1912)]
17. Pliny: *'Natural History'* (Mc crindle *'Ancient India as described in Classical Literature'*, (1901), Edinburg
18. J.F. Fleet: *'Indian Antiquity'*: (1893) *'The topographical list of 'Bṛhatsaṃhitā'*
19. Al-beruni: *'Al-beruni's India'* tr. and annotations by E.C. Sachau, London, vol. 2 (1910)
20. 'Yuan Chwang*: 'On Yuan Chwang's Travels in India':* Thomas Watters (ed.) T.W. Rhys Davids and Bushell, 2 vols. (1904)
21. Heu-en-Tsang: *'Ancient geography of India'*, vol. I, II (ed. by Watters), tr. by Beal S. London (1884)
22. *'The Baburnama'*: (English), vol. II [tr. by A. Beveridge](1922), pp. 501, 502 Lusac and co. London (Bombay)
23. Abul Fazal: *'Ain-I- Akbari',* [tr. by Jarret, Calcutta, (1949)]
24. S.M. Ali: op. cit. p. 21, 22, 26-32
25. *'Bṛhatsaṃhitā':* Varāhamihira (ed. Kern, p.32, quoted by S.M. Ali op. cit. p. 32
26. *'Siddhāntaśiromaṇī'*: III: 41, Bhāskāracārya (II) (tr.by Wilkinson, Bib.Ind Calcutta 1861)
27. S.N. Paṇḍya: *'A geographical Horizon of the Mahābhārata'* (1980) Bharat-Bharati Publication, Vārāṇasi-5, pp.1-13
28. M.R. Singh: *'A critical study of the Geographical data in the early Purāṇās'*, (1972), Punthipuṣpak Publication, Calcutta, pp.1-13
29. F.E. Pargiter: *'The geography of Rāma's exile'* (1894), JRAS.
30. D.R. Bhandarkar: 'Daṇḍakāraṇya', Jha Comm. vol. (1937), Poona pp. 47-57
31. H. Roychaudhari: *'Studies in Indian Antiquities',* (1958), Calcutta, pp. 294-297
32. R.C. Majumdar: *'Ancient India'* Book I, (1960), Motilal Banarasidas Publication, Delhi p. 197
33. Vishuddhanand Pathak: *'History of Kosālā'*, (1963), Delhi pp.182, 183
34. C.V. Vaidya: *'The Riddle of the Rāmāyaṇa'* (1971), Delhi, pp.125-135
35. K.N. Dikshit: *'The progress of Archaeology in India'*, p.263
36. B.B. Lal: op.cit. p.5
37. M.V. Kibe: *'Location of Laṅkā'* (1927/1947), pp. 1-62, Manohar Granthamala, Pune

38. J.C. Ghosh: *'Rāvaṇa's Laṅkā located in Central India'* Annals BORI, vol. XIV (1938-1939) pp.84-86; I.H.Q. vol. V. pp. 355-356
39. Herman Jacobi: *'Rāmāyaṇa',* Baroda, (1893-1960), p. 99-100, 104(quoted by M. V. Kibe in *'Rāvaṇa's Laṅkā Discovered'* as app. (a)
40. M.V. Kibe: (1947) op.cit. pp.14, 15, 18, 29
41. F.E. Pargiter: (1894) op.cit. JRAS (1894) pp.231-264
42. Varāhamihira: *'Bṛhatsaṃhitā':* 14:11; Bhavabhūti: *'Uttararāmacarita'* Murāri: Rājaśekhara:*'Bālarāmāyaṇa'* (all quoted by N. V. Rao in Introduction to his play *'Sītā Josyam'* (1990) pp. 25-127
43. C. E. Godakumbura: 'Laṅkā of the classical Indian writers', All India Oriental Conference Proceedings (1976) 27th session, pp.293-301
44. Varāhamihira: *'Bṛhatsaṃhitā': Adhyāya*: 14
45. S. Chitrav: *'Prācina Sthalakośa* (1969) Bharatiya Charitra Kosh Mandal, Pune p.494
46. H.D. Sankalia: *'The Rāmāyaṇa in Historical Perspective'* (1973), p.149
47. V. D. Jha: 'Investigations into the Archaeology of Surguja', (1973) pp.67-73
48. T. P. Iyer: *'Rāmāyaṇa and Laṅkā'* (1940) Bangalore
49. J.C. Ghosh: 'Siṃhala in Central India' New India Antiquary, vol. I, p. 463; (1938)
50. D.R. Mankad: *'Introduction to the Kiṣkindhākaṇḍa of Vālmīki Rāmāyaṇa'* c. e. Baroda (1965)
51. U. P. Shah: *'Introduction to the Uttarakāṇḍa of Vālmīki Rāmāyaṇa',* c. e. Baroda (1975)
52. Rai Krisnadas: *'Rām Vanavās ka Bhūgol',* Nagarī Pracharini Patrika, no.54:1-3
53. Hiralal 'The Situation of Rāvaṇa's Laṅkā' (1937) Jha Comm. vol. Poona, pp.151-163
54. G. Ramdas: 'Aboriginal names in the Rāmāyaṇa' (1925) JBORS, vol. XI. pp. 41-53
55. G. Ramdas: 'Rāvaṇa's Laṅkā' (1928) I.H.Q. vol. I. pp.339-346
56. G. Ramdas: 'Rāvaṇa and his Tribes' (1929): vol. V. pp. 281 ff. and vol.VI. pp. 285-289
57. H.D. Sankalia 'Times of India' Bombay, February 23,1976; (Quoted by N.V.Rao: op.cit)
58. D.P. Mishra: 'Mahakosal Historical Society Papers' vol. I Bilaspur, (1932) pp. 30ff

59. D.P. Mishra: *'The search for Laṅkā'* (1985) Agam Kala Prakashana, (Delhi), pp.1-68

60. N.V. Rao: Introduction to his play, *'Sītā Josyam'* (1990) pp. 25-127 (Marathi tr. by Nalinī Sadhle: Marathi Sahitya Parishad, Hydrabad)

61. H.D. Sankalia *'Rāmāyaṇa in Historical Perspective'*, Macmillan India, (1973)

62. B.C. Muzumdar *'Sonepur plates of Kumāra Someśvaradevā'* (19xx) Epi. Indica XII No. 29 p.239, 240

63. B.C. Muzumdar: *'Orissa in the Making'* (1925) pp.179,180, 234 University of Calcutta publ.

64. H.D. Sankalia: *'Rāmāyaṇa: Myth or Reality'* (1973), New Delhi; p.17

65. T. Amrithalingam: *'Rāmāyaṇa Vimarśa',* (19...)' Madras p. 466 [Quoted by N.V. Rao, op. cit.]

66. M.R. Yardi: *'The Rāmāyaṇa: its origin and Growth'* (1994) 'A Statistical study, BORI, Poona.

67. R.K. Ramakrishnan: *'Rāvaṇa and Laṅkā',* (2003) Global Vision Publication, New Delhi

68. P.V. Kane: '*Dharmaśastraka Itihas* (Hindi): IV, *Tirthasuci'* p. 1471, 1476, 1490, 1499 (tr. Chaube Arjun Kashyap (publ. Hindi Samiti Suchana Vibhag, Lucknow) also referred P.V. Kane: *'History of Dharmashastra',* IV, List of Tīrthās (publ. Govt. Oriental series, Class B/4, BORI Poona, (1953)

End Notes:

(1) SĀLA TREE: (Shorea robusta) The importance given to *Sāla* tree in *Vālmīki Rāmāyaṇa* indicates the locations where the events described might have taken place. *Sāla* trees grow in a region with an annual rainfall of 1250 to1800 mm (40-50 inches) and at altitudes between 300 metres to 450 metres. *Vālmīki Rāmāyaṇa* mentions Sāla trees at a number of places. Different geographical areas have been described in *Rāmāyaṇa* with poetic imagination. Various forests, trees and seasons have also been described. The importance given to *Sāla* tree speaks indirectly about the location of the event.

Late T. Amrithalingam was the first scholar, to recognise and point out this fact in his book *'Rāmāyaṇa Vimarśa'* (19....). His original book was not available to the present author. As a result, some of its part that is referred to by N. V. Rao is given here in brief.) T. Amrithalingam pointed out that, in *Ayodhyākāṇḍa* (1:5:12) city Ayodhya is described as *'sālamekhalām'*, meaning, ornamented with a girdle of *Sāla* trees. Rāma's brother Bharata crossed a *Sāla* forest on his way from *rājagṛha* to Ayodhya (2: 65:11, 12). There were *Sāla* trees on Mt. Citrakūṭa **'sa gireścitrakūṭasya sālamāsādya puṣpitam'** (2:92:13). In a tussle which took place in Janasthāna between Rāma and *rakṣasās* Khara and Dūṣaṇa, the *rakṣasās* had used *Sāla* trees as weapons **'sālatālaśilayudhāḥ'** (3:24:27). When Rāma forms an alliance with Sugrīva, Hanumat breaks a branch of *Sāla* tree, keeps it down and requests Rāma to sit on it. *Sāla* seems to be a sacred tree for the *vānarās* living in Kiṣkindhā. Rāma in order to prove his prowess to Sugrīva shot through seven *Sāla* trees with a single arrow (4:12:1-5), and when an encounter had taken place between Vālin and Sugrīva, both had used *Sāla* trees as weapons. Amongst the variety of trees seen in Pañcavaṭī or even in Laṅkā *Sāla* trees were predominant. When Hanumat sets Laṅkā afire, and when *Nalasetū* was being constructed, *Sāla* trees were used.

Sāla trees grow in Himalayan lower ranges, Ganga plain and valleys, Madhya Pradesh, Santhal, Reva, Chota Nagpur, western Bihar, Orissa, Bastar and Chhattisgarh. The tree also grows in some parts of Uttar Pradesh. However, it does not grow to the south of Palakonda mountain range in south India. It does not grow to the south of Mt. Vindhya (*'The Wealth of India'* 1972 vol. IV and *'A Dictionary of Indian Raw Materials and Industrial Products',* Publication and Information Directorate, CSIR, New Delhi) Buddhā's 'Lumbini *vana*' was a *Sāla* forest. The tree is known by many names in different languages.

Most importantly *Sāla* tree does not grow at all in Ceylon. It is not mentioned in the flora and fauna of Ceylon (Ceylon Gazetteer ed. by Chitty Mudliar - 1834). In spite of this, *pundits* refuse to abandon the age old and deep-rooted belief that Ceylon was Rāvaṇa's Laṅkā. The tree grows straight and reaches a height of 18 metres or more, up to 60 metres. It is a deciduous tree. North India, north-eastern part of M. P. north-east India (some parts) and the central and eastern M.P. have *Sāla* forests and thick *Sāla* forests occupy large areas of M.P. even today. A point to note here is that northern and eastern districts of M.P., Chota Nagpur, Chhattisgarh and Jharkhand have *Sāla* forests in much larger proportion than central and western districts of M.P. like Jabalpur and districts to the west of Jabalpur. To the south, towards Bastar, *Sāla* forests are in great proportions.

We may recall here that the ancestor of Rāvaṇa's lineage was Alaṃbuṣa *rakṣasa,* whose name is 'Sālakaṭaṅkaṭa'. Kaṭaṅkaṭas were a tribe as has been suggested by researchers. Kaṭaṅkaṭa or *'Kaṭaṅkaṭaḥ'* (Sanskrit) means god 'Śiva' (*Gīrvāṇalaghukośa* p.137). However, U. P. Shah suggests [*'Introduction to Uttarakāṇḍa of Vālmīki Rāmāyaṇa',* c.e. (1975) p. 44, 45] that the word *'Kaṭaṅkaṭa'* seems to be of a non-Aryan origin and that they were a tribe of the Gondavana. Thus, Sālakaṭaṅkaṭa and Narmada *gandharvī* being Rāvaṇa'*s* ancestors, (see Appendix D) the theory that Rāvaṇa's Laṅkā was situated in M. P. State of India is hard to disapprove.

The thesis of T. Amrithalingam, that all the places like Pañcavaṭī in Daṇḍakāraṇya, Kiṣkindhā, *Ṛkṣabila* and Laṅkā were in *Sāla* forest areas is convincing.

§§§

2

DAṆḌAKĀRAṆYA, JANASTHĀNA AND PAÑCAVAṬĪ

Daśaratha was the Ikṣvāku king of Ayodhya. He had promised his queen Kaikeyī that his eldest son Rāma will be sent away into *vanavāsa* (exile into forest) for fourteen years and Kaikeyī's son Bharata will be enthroned as the crown prince of Ayodhya in Rāma's place. The old king agreed to fulfil Kaikeyī's demand with a heavy heart.

It should be noted here that before the birth of his sons, Daśaratha's *Putrakāmeṣṭī yajña* had taken place on the left bank or north bank of river Śarayu, as is repeatedly mentioned in *Bālakāṇḍa*. The verses are-

sarayvāścottare tīre yajñabhūmirvidhīyatām ||[1]
ath saṃvatsare pūrne tasmin prāpte turangame |
sarayvāścottare tīre rajño yajñobhyavartata ||[2]

Grand scale preparations were made for this yajña including the constructions of housing complexes for invitees, large kitchens, shelters for animals and vehicles etc. The detailed description[3] in *Bālakāṇḍa* suggests that Ikṣvāku capital, Ayodhya was also spread on the northern bank of river Śarayu.

Rāma with his wife Sītā and brother Lakṣmaṇa left Ayodhya [26°48′ N, 82°12′ E]. After leaving Ayodhya, the trio took a night-halt on the banks of river Tamasā (Upper Tamasā of U.P., and not river Tons) and then the next day, they crossed rivers Vedaśṛutī, (Bisui)

Gomatī and Syandikā (Sai), thereby left behind Kosālā, ultimately to reach Śṛṅgaverapura (topo-sheet no. 63 G/10)[25°34′N,81°39′E] on the north bank of river Ganga (see End Note 1 and map 2). Rāma, Lakṣmaṇa, and Sītā were welcomed by Guhā, the king of *niṣādās* (a tribe of fishermen). Guhā was a friend and admirer-devotee of king Daśaratha. Guhā helped Rāma cross the mighty river Ganga, with the assistance of his boatmen. Sumantra, Daśaratha's minister speaks of Guhā, thus-

eṣa jñātisahasreṇa sthapatiḥ parivāritaḥ |
kuśalo daṇḍakāraṇye vṛddho bhrātuśca te sakhā ||[4]

Meaning: 'This old king of the fishermen tribe, a friend of Daśaratha, who rules in Daṇḍakāraṇya, is approaching with his thousand clan-men'. After crossing Ganga, Rāma enters Vatsa-*deśa* a land of plenty and populated with happy people. The three of them walk the whole day eastwards, towards the confluence and then come near the *sangama* (confluence) of rivers Ganga and Yamuna. They take a night halt in the hermitage of sage Bhāradvāja (map 2). The sage advises them that the three should then go to stay at Mt. Citrakūṭa, two and a half *yojanās* away, (see End Note 2) i.e. 10 *krośās*, or 20 miles (32 km) from his hermitage. Next morning they start from the *sangama* and take a route by the northern bank of Yamuna in the western direction to reach a spot most suitable for crossing river Yamuna by using a raft. After crossing the river they follow the sage's instructions and walk through the forest towards south-west to reach Mt. Citrakūṭa[5] (see map 2).

The whole description here indicates that Guhā, who was ruling over that part of Daṇḍakāraṇya, had helped Rāma (accompanied by Daśaratha's men) to cross river Ganga and come to Bhāradvāja's hermitage near the Ganga-Yamuna confluence. This indicates that the northern boundary of Daṇḍakāraṇya forest had started even before Rāma had reached the north bank of Ganga, where Guhā lived. The army of Ayodhya had come along with their much loved hero, right up to the hermitage of Bhāradvāja. He very clearly mentions that Mt. Citrakūṭa is located in a desolate area where river Mandākinī flows. They cross Yamuna by a raft and walk towards Mt. Citrakūṭa. Sage Vālmīki had his hermitage in Citrakūṭa forest. Mt. Citrakūṭa, as the name itself suggests, is described as uniquely colourful amidst the sandstone hills of the region due to its red, yellow and black rock formation and also with *aśokavana* on it[6]. (*Rāmāyaṇa* mentions and describes two other *aśokavanikās,* the second one in Laṅkā and the third one in Ayodhya[7, 8]. Thus *'aśokavanikā'* seems generally to mean a pleasure garden of kings.) This hill alone stands out and is of granite as explained by Sankalia[9]. Lakṣmaṇa constructs a temporary hut in the area and later, Rāma performs *vāstuśāntī* (the due rites) by offering deer meat on the banks of river Mandākinī and the trio starts living there.

Rivers Mandākinī and a larger river Paiśunī flow near Mt. Citrakūṭa. Mandākinī flows over the northern slope of Mt. Citrakūṭa, (To the north of Mandākinī flow rivers Kalind and Baghain (topo-sheet no. 63 C/11+15) (**'uttaram pārśvamāsādya'**)[10] as can be seen in some of the maps of India even today (see maps 1 and 2). It is not shown in topo-sheet # 63C/16 of 1925 which shows the spot of *gupta* Godavari, about nine km to the south-west of Citrakūṭa. Pippalaśroṇī (*Vāyu Purāṇa*) and Pippalaśyenī (*Matsya Purāṇa*) were also the rivers flowing in the same area. Topo-sheet 63C/16 shows a river Piprawal to the north east of Mt. Citrakūṭa. Mandākinī, [synonymous with Paiśunī/ Payasvinī] was a tributary of Paiśunī according to Jain literature. *Rāmāyaṇa* mentions a river Mālyavatī (which cannot be identified) on Mt. Citrakūṭa. Thus-

suramyamāsādya tu citrakūṭam |
nadim ca tām mālyavatim sutīrthām ||[11]

Back in Ayodhya the news of Rāma having reached Mt. Citrakūṭa reaches Sumantra (on the third day). Rāma's mother, queen Kauśalyā grieves-

'nivartaya ratham śīghram daṇḍakānnaya māmapi' | [12]

Meaning: 'Let the chariot turn back and let it take me to the forest Daṇḍakāraṇya' (O, Sumantra!). Anguished Bharata then marches with his army towards Mt. Citrakūṭa, to bring back Rāma. He halts at Śṛṅgaverapura on the northern bank of river Ganga and asks Guhā, the route to Bhāradvāja's hermitage. Here again Guhā is described as a ruler of the forest Daṇḍakāraṇya[13].

Where was Daṇḍakāraṇya?

Daṇḍakāraṇya was the locale of Rāma's exile. A large part of it was under Kosālā domain. After Rāma's eventless stay at Citrakūṭa the *Araṇyakāṇḍa* begins with Rāma's entry in the thicker part of Daṇḍakāraṇya, where confrontation with *rakṣasās* was expected. U.P. Shah[14], after considering various views says that Daṇḍakāraṇya can also be explained as a hilly region with marshy land abounding in water-logged areas.

Mahābhārata mentions Daṇḍakāraṇya at various places. Balarama's pilgrimage has been described in *Mahābhārata*[15] wherein Balarama is said to have visited forest Daṇḍakāraṇya. *Mahābhārata* also mentions the presence of goddess 'Daṇḍā' in that forest.

Pargiter[16] opines that in *Rāmopākhyāna* of *Mahābhārata* the word *'Daṇḍakāraṇya'* is used many a times as a common noun and the extent of Daṇḍakāraṇya is from Śarabhaṅga's hermitage near Mt. Citrakūṭa, to river Godavari of south India; in other words, from Bundelkhand to river Godavari of the south. D.R. Bhandarkar[17], who shares Pargiter's view, feels that Daṇḍakāraṇya must be in Maharashtra and was spread also to the south of it.

D.P. Mishra[18] suggested that Daṇḍakāraṇya must have been in the present Bastar district ('Vastara *deśe*') of Chhattisgarh state, as per the testimony of Śaṃbūka. However, scholars like Hiralal[19], M.V. Kibe[20] and Sankalia[21] argued that Rāmāyaṇic Daṇḍakāraṇya lay to the south of Mt. Citrakūṭa in the present state of Madhya Pradesh. Navinchandra Dās[22] says that immediately after leaving Mt. Citrakūṭa, Rāma enters a thick and vast forest and that is Daṇḍakāraṇya. T.P. Iyer[23] places Sutīkṣṇa's hermitage at a place called Mohadra in Panna district and Pañcavaṭī at Hindoria in Damoh district pointing at Daṇḍakāraṇya. Iyer identifies Daṇḍakāraṇya with the tract to the north of Panna hill range in M.P. Rai Krisnadas[24] has suggested that Damoh-Maihar tract of the Panna range could be Mt. Śaivala, the southernmost boundary of Daṇḍakāraṇya.

In the times of *Rāmāyaṇa*, the entire Indian subcontinent was a heavily forested land, a fact not to be overlooked while studying the geography of *Rāmāyaṇa*. This necessarily implies that right from the foothills of Mt. Himalaya and river Ganga, the land was forest covered. Not that there was no forest land between Ayodhya and river Ganga but human habitation had already started in the region to the north of Ganga. Different regions and their city capitals had flourished and with it heavy axing down of forests had started too. Even then the country was full of forests, only some forests were thicker and uninhabitable than others. In fact, Rāma's brother Bharata, when he wanted to go to Mt. Citrakūṭa with his followers, had to get the roads widened by cutting down the forest[25].

Bharata returned to Ayodhya with Rāma's instructions that he should be the king of Ayodhya in Rāma's absence. Rāma with Sītā and Lakṣmaṇa then went to visit sage Atrī and his wife Anasūyā. Their hermitage was in the vicinity of Mt. Citrakūṭa. Anasūyā hill (height 660 feet) exists even today (topo-sheet no. 63 C/16) [25° 10′ N, 80° 53′ E] in Citrakūṭa area (see map 2). After leaving that place, Rāma entered the thicker part of Daṇḍakāraṇya (*mahāvana*). He visited many hermitages in the area where a number of *ṛṣīs* welcomed him and expressed their grievances concerning the *rakṣasās*. They reminded Rāma that since they lived in the land which was under Ikṣvāku control, it was Rāma's duty to protect them under any circumstances. The *rakṣasās* were living in that same forest where water, fruits, roots and animal meat were in abundance and easily available. The *rakṣasās* were the aboriginal tribes and are called *'rakṣasās'* throughout the epic, as is now widely accepted by scholars.

The next day, Rāma, after leaving sage Atrī's hermitage, entered a forest infested with predators and here itself, near Mt. Citrakūṭa, he killed Virādha *rakṣasa.* T.P. Iyer[26] mentions that Virādha *kuṇḍa* is shown even today at a distance of about eight and a half km from the confluence of river Śarabhañja with river Paiśunī (see topo-sheet # 63C/16). At about one and a half *yojanās* away from this place, was the hermitage of sage Śarabhaṅga. It should be noted here that in fact there was a river named Śarabhaṅga (or Śarabhañja) flowing in the vicinity of Mt. Citrakūṭa[27]. The epic description indicates that sage Śarabhaṅga had his hermitage on the banks of river *gupta* Godavari, a tributary of river Mandākinī, which in turn was a tributary of a still larger river Paiśunī (Payasvinī). Thus rivers Paiśunī, Mandākinī, Gupta Godavari and Śarabhañja all seem to be flowing towards north over the northern slope of Mt. Citrakūṭa, and adjacent hills.

Rāma requested sage Śarabhaṅga, to suggest a suitable dwelling place for the three of them. The old sage suggested that if Rāma takes the route in the opposite direction of the flow of river Mandākinī, carrying loveliest flowers along the current, then he would reach the hermitage of sage Sutīkṣṇa, who was the disciple of sage Agastya (this stanza is omited from the c.e. of Vālmīki Rāmāyaṇa of Baroda). Mandākinī flowed over the northern slope of Mt. Citrakūṭa towards river Yamuna. This points out to the fact that, if Rāma takes the south route as suggested by Śarabhaṅga, he would reach the hermitage of Sutīkṣṇa. Śarabhaṅga's disciples inform Rāma that the area affected by evil deeds of *rakṣasās* covered Mt. Citrakūṭa, and rivers Mandākinī and Paṃpā. The verse is:

pampānadī nivasānāmanumandākinīmapi |
citrakūṭālayānām ca kriyate kadanam mahat ||[28]

Curiously, the topo-sheet #63C/16 shows a spot named Paṃpeśvar close to Mt. Citrakūṭa. After walking a long distance (Vālmīki only says 'dūramadhvānan') and crossing many rivers they finally reach Sutīkṣṇa's hermitage. When Sutīkṣṇa suggests that the three could stay with him, Rāma promptly explains that the *ṛṣīs* do not want him to waste any more time but visit the troubled area immediately. Rāma thus politely declines Sutīkṣṇa's offer and leaves. Sutīkṣṇa then suggests that after their mission is completed, Rāma should return to his hermitage.

After this Rāma wandered through many forests and crossed many rivers and mountains, ultimately to reach a large lake which belonged to sage Maṇḍakarṇī. The lake was named 'Pañcāpsarās' and was a permanent and secret dwelling place of five *apsarās* (celestial damsels). This must be a place with a perennial water source, a very large lake, with a cascade, a waterfall and a place with extraordinary natural beauty. Rai Krisnadas[29] identifies Pañcāpsarā lake with a large water reservoir in Sagar district of M.P. According to M.V. Kibe[30] near Satna, 45 km from Mt. Citrakūṭa, was Sutīkṣṇa's hermitage. D.R. Mankad[31] made certain enquiries, through personal communication which suggested that, Atrī hermitage may be located in Citrakūṭa district and sages Sutīkṣṇa and Agastya had their hermitages in district Panna. As suggested by U.P. Shah[32], since Sutīkṣṇa often used to visit Mt. Citrakūṭa it could not have been very far from his hermitage and that Sutīkṣṇa's hermitage must have been to the immediate south of Mt. Citrakūṭa. District Satna as a probable location for Sutīkṣṇa's hermitage is a notion also shared by the present author. The most probable site for Sutīkṣṇa's hermitage can be imagined to be near Jaitwara railway station on Manikpur-Satna route as per the local tradition mentioned by D.R. Mankad, a notion shared by the present author. Until Rāma reached Sutīkṣṇa's hermitage, Vālmīki's geography can be traced without any difficulty (see map 2).

After this, Rāma visited many hermitages and hermitages of many group of ṛṣīs (sages) and spent as many as ten years in that area. He then returned to Sutīkṣṇa's hermitage. After a stay of four days Rāma left Sutīkṣṇa's hermitage and went to the hermitage of Agastya's brother, at a distance of 4 *yojanās* to the south. His hermitage was situated in a thick grove of *Pippalī* trees and they could recognise the place by the pungent smell of *Pippalī* fruits. *Mahābhārata* mentions a river Pippalī having her origin in Mt Ṛkṣa. It is possible that a river flowing through *Pippalīvana* might have been named Pippalāvatī, Pippalaśyenī, Pippalaśroṇī or simply Pippalī. Was this sage, Agastya's brother, 'Vasiṣṭḥa Maitrāvaruṇī'or 'Vasiṣṭḥa Āpava', Vālmīki does not clarify (see End Note 4). After a night's halt, they walked a distance of one *yojana* (7 km) to reach the hermitage of sage Agastya. Many sites on the southern banks of river Ganga are also identified as Agastya's hermitage by various scholars, the reasons for this are discussed in end note 4. However, it would be logical to imagine that the hermitage of Agastya who directed Rāma towards pañcavaṭī plateau might have been near (as per the local tradition mentioned by D.R. Mankad) village Sarang at the southern tip of Satna district between rivers Son and Tamasā-Tons. This is so since it is somewhere near Gidhailā and Gṛdhrāj mountains - presumed Jaṭāyu abode by the present studies.

Rāmāyaṇa gives the story of how Agastya had annihilated two *rakṣasās* namely Vātāpī and Ilvala in that area and also that Agastya's presence in that 'southern territory' had deterred the *rakṣasās* from approaching (see End Note 4).

Agastya promptly offers Rāma many valued weapons[33] and then explains that if Rāma and Lakṣmaṇa stay with Agastya, Rāma's mission may not be completed as there was no chance of the *rakṣasās* coming in that area. Rāma and Lakṣmaṇa should therefore go a little further, a distance of two *yojanās* (14.5 km), and stay at a place called Pañcavaṭī which was not very far from river Godavari and where there was an abundance of fruits, meat and clear water. Sītā could happily spend her time there, he says. Agastya advised them thus:

'ito dviyojane tāta bahumūlaphalodakaḥ |
deśo bahumṛgaḥ śrīmānpañcavaṭyabhiviśṛtaḥ ||[34]
sa deśaḥ ślāghanīyaśca nātidūre ca rāghava |
godāvaryāḥ samīpe ca maithilī tatra raṃsyate' ||[35]

Agastya also instructs Rāma that Pañcavaṭī has predominantly Banyan trees in the forest and many other trees as well and the route to Pañcavaṭī goes from the north side of Mohavana, i.e. forest having *Mahuā* trees predominantly (Madhukā - *Bassia latifolia*). Agastya tells Rāma that Pañcavaṭī *deśa* is at a slightly elevated plain land (a vast plateau) near the mountain and one has to climb to reach there and this clue is very important for identification of Pañcavaṭī area. The verse is-

tataḥ sthalamupāruhya parvatasya vidūrataḥ |
khyātaḥ pañcavaṭītyeva nityapuṣpitakānanaḥ ||[36]

From this it can also be inferred that Agastya's own hermitage must have been at the base of the table-land or plateau of Pañcavaṭī, situated in the vicinity but at a lower level. On their way to Pañcavaṭī, they meet Jaṭāyu (map 2), a *grdhṛa* (a vulture) who pronounces that he was a close friend of Rāma's father. Jaṭāyu happily accompanies the trio and then he too starts living at Pañcavaṭī. (A village named Gṛdhrakūṭa (Giddhaur or Giddheshvar in Bihar (to south of Jamui) according to a local legend is identified as a place, where Jaṭāyu gave a fatal fight to Rāvaṇa, but it is also connected with Buddha legends[37]). Interestingly enough is the fact, that there are places or mountain peaks with names like Gidhodā (dist. Panna), Badgiddha (dist. Surguja), Mt. Gidhailā peak (dist. Satna), or Gṛddhraraj *parvata* (dist. Reva) near Bansagar, at 24^0 17′ 56″ N, 81^0 14′ 55″ E all these spots being in the adjoining region attract attention (see map 2). Was this close to Pañcavaṭī *deśa* area? And was this the initial abode of or a natural habitat of Gṛddhraraj, Jaṭāyu and Saṃpātī - the vultures? It indeed is a believable notion.

Rāma, after leaving Sutīkṣṇa's hermitage, spent ten years, inspecting various hermitages of many unnamed *ṛṣīs*. During this period of ten years, Rāma does not come across either Agastya's hermitage or Pañcavaṭī. This indicates that his journey from Citrakūṭa to Pañcavaṭī via Sutīkṣṇa's hermitage might not have been in a straight line in one direction (Map 1).

In previous pages we have seen different views of scholars regarding the boundaries of Daṇḍakāraṇya, which we must now examine to get a comprehensible picture, so that we can identify Janasthāna and Pañcavaṭī both situated within it.

It is important to note that our entire country being heavily forested in Rāmāyaṇic times, regions and their boundaries could not be defined with any precision or certainty. Land that one could bring under one's control and maintain was taken as one's territory or domain. Therefore it becomes difficult today, to locate a place in question and decide whether it is a large area or a small place or a mere site. There are a few places with proper names unchanged till today. Using other criteria such places can be identified. But then, where was Daṇḍakāraṇya and where was Pañcavaṭī? To find an answer, the first step would be to dig into ancient literature. We will now come back to the problem of identifying the boundaries of Daṇḍakāraṇya and begin with the name itself which may be indicative.

Rāmāyaṇa gives the story of Daṇḍakāraṇya as follows. (***Daṇḍakāraṇyanāmotpattikathana***[38]) Daṇḍā, the son of Ikṣvāku, king of Ayodhya, being rude, foolish and unpopular, the king had given him a separate piece of land, away from Ayodhya to rule. He was enthroned as king of the land between two hills named Mt. Vindhya and Mt. Śaivala (***vindhyaśaivalayormadhye***[39]). Between these two arms of Mt. Vindhya, Daṇḍā set his capital, a city named Madhumatta or Madhumanta. He ruled over his country for a long time righteously. Then, one day as he went hunting in the forest, he saw a beautiful dame Arajā, daughter of sage Uśanas or Śukrācārya. (Who was also a *purohita* of Ikṣvākus?) King Daṇḍā raped the girl. When the sage returned he cursed the king for his evil deed, as a result of which Daṇḍā was annihilated and his vast land (which was 100 × 400 *yojanās* in extent) was ruined by a dust storm and was turned into an arid, deserted and desolate region. Since it was originally king Daṇḍā's domain it was called 'Daṇḍakāraṇya'. Later, when it was again partly populated by sages and *ṛṣīs* etc. that part of the land was called 'Janasthāna'. Pañcavaṭī with its thick forest was a small part of the same Janasthāna. (Daṇḍā, Kaliṅga and Mataṅga were the territories that became arid by the curse of a sage, according to Buddhist literature[40]). Thus goes the story of Ikṣvāku king Daṇḍā and Daṇḍakāraṇya. The story itself indicates that Daṇḍakāraṇya area must have been away from Ayodhya but still under Ikṣvāku rule. However, *Rāmāyaṇa* informs us that Daṇḍakāraṇya, with Janasthāna within it was inhabited by the *rakṣasās* as well.

U.P. Shah[41] quotes G. Ramdas[42] who remarks, 'The word *'daṇḍaka'* does not mean 'of king Daṇḍā' but signifies 'full of water' in Savara language'. U.P. Shah feels that the story of king Daṇḍā, cursed by Uśanas Bhārgava, from *Uttarakāṇḍa* could be an interpolation and a Bhārgava attempt at redacting *Rāmāyaṇa*, in order to prove their supremacy over the Ikṣvākus. This derivation of the word will not alter the geographical perception of Daṇḍakāraṇya area, as discussed below.

Mount Vindhya is spread east-west in central India, with its south-eastern limit being Mt. Amarkanṭak in the Maikal range. Towards the north, arms of Mt. Vindhya, called Kaimur range, touch the Mirzapur area (the southern district of Uttar Pradesh). *Rāmāyaṇa* thus suggests that Daṇḍakāraṇya lay between ranges of Mt. Kaimur and Mt. Śaivala, both necessarily being the arms of Mt. Vindhya. Can we locate Mt. Śaivala? Quite unexpectedly the answer to this question is found in the story of Śaṃbūka which appears in *Uttarakāṇḍa*.

After the battle of Laṅkā was over, Rāma returned to Ayodhya and was enthroned as king. He wandered in Puṣpak *vimāna* in the country to find out if any evil deeds were taking place in his kingdom. He found nothing wrong in the eastern, western and northern regions. Finally when he searched in the south direction, he came across a vast expanse of water or a lake which was situated to the north of Mt. Śaivala. Thus:

dakṣiṇām diśāmākrāmattato rājarṣinandanaḥ |
śaivalasyottare pārśve dadarśa sumahatsaraḥ ||[43]

He noticed on the southern shore of that lake, a man called Śaṃbūka practicing penance. He was a *śūdra* (of low caste). He had hung himself head down. Rāma came forward and cut his head as Śaṃbūka was a wrong doer according to Rāma.

The above narrative makes it clear that this Mt. Śaivala, to the south of a vast expanse of water, was the southern boundary of Rāma's empire or Ikṣvāku territory. That arm of Mt. Vindhya was also the southern boundary of king Daṇḍā's domain and so also that of Daṇḍakāraṇya. Between Mt. Vindhya and Mt. Śaivala was the city of Madhumanta, Daṇḍā's capital city. As we have argued, this whole land was basically under Ikṣvāku control and the land to the south of Mt. Śaivala and Mt. Vindhya was never under Ikṣvāku control. Nandalal Dey has argued that the hill named Ramagiri at Ramtek, twenty-four miles (37 km) to the north of Nagpur (Maharashtra), must have been the place where Śaṃbūka was practicing penance. He is of the opinion that from the point, where the northernmost arm of Mt. Vindhya touches river Ganga the boundary of Daṇḍakāraṇya begins[44]. This point is a place named Chunar (*charaṇādri*), in Mirzapur district of U.P. and southernmost boundary of Daṇḍakāraṇya could be at the most Ramgiri hill near Nagpur. Evidence is provided here, that Guhā *niṣād* was the ruler of a part of Daṇḍakāraṇya on the north bank of river Ganga. This must have been the northern boundary of Daṇḍakāraṇya.

It is interesting to note that before sage Agastya narrates the story of Ikṣvāku King Daṇḍā, Vālmīki *Rāmāyaṇa* gives an account of king Śveta of Vidarbha[45]. According to this narrative king Śveta of Vidarbha practiced penance on the shore of a lake. This lake was located in a dry and deserted forest devoid of any birds or animals. In fact that forest was totally uninhabited is specifically mentioned. This forest is called the forest of Daṇḍakāraṇya in king Śveta's story also and why it became so deserted is then further explained to Rāma by sage Agastya, by narrating king Daṇḍā's story[46]. The story of Vidarbha king Śveta suggests that he must have naturally chosen Daṇḍakāraṇya to practise penance since it was in the vicinity of his Vidarbha-*deśa*. *Purāṇās* also refer to Vidarbha and the Daṇḍaka together as 'Vindhyamūliyās' (***vidarbhah daṇḍakaih saha***) (Sarkar D. C)[47]. It can therefore be inferred that the extent of Daṇḍakāraṇya in the southern direction could at the most be up to northern Vidarbha according to Uttarakāṇḍa.

In this connection V.V. Mirashi, after exploring and critically examining the Ramtek area says that, king Daṇḍā or Dāṇḍakya is called king Bhoja elsewhere. He further says that, Bhojās were the rulers in ancient Vidarbha, is well known. He suggests that Śaṃbūka-*sthāna* was Ramagiri at Ramtek in Vidarbha, furnishing this theory with evidence, where the hill is also named 'Mahaśaivala' in one of the psalms of '*Bṛhatsindūrāgirimāhātmya*' (indeed a later work of thirteenth century). 'Sindūragirī' and 'Tapogirī' are other special names of Ramagiri hill. V. V. Mirashi also points out that there is a large lake now called 'Ambale', at the foothill of Ramagiri. He therefore infers that Mt. Śalvala can be identified with Ramagiri hill at Ramtek in Vidarbha[48]. This evidence, even if proved to be a later addition, the description of the site and its location in Vidarbha is consistent with *Purāṇās* and with the description in *Rāmāyaṇa* of Śaṃbūka-*sthāna.* U.P. Shah also has stated that, according to *Purāṇās*, both the Vidarbha and the Daṇḍaka were referred as 'Vindhyamūliya'[49]. T.P. Iyer's identification of Mt. Śaivala with Panna range[50] is therefore, not acceptable.

All these evidences thus point to the general area of Daṇḍakāraṇya, with its southern boundary to be northern Vidarbha. The western boundary of Daṇḍakāraṇya could be Mt. Citrakūṭa. Its eastern boundary must have been formed naturally by the eastern ranges of Kaimur or the north-easterly flow of river Son and river Karmanāśā (see map 1).

Where was Janasthāna?

Rāvaṇa was aware that if Aryans and the *vānarās* of Kiṣkindha form an alliance, their united force would threaten the existence of his rule in that area. Janasthāna was his outpost, where Rāvaṇa had employed Khara and Dūṣaṇa, his generals with their 14,000 men strong army. When Rāvaṇa heard the news of total annihilation of that army along with Khara and Dūṣaṇa by Rāma, he, without any delay, re-employed a few chosen men in or near *Janasthāna*.

There are some indications regarding the location of Janasthāna in the epic and elsewhere. *Prācina Caritrakośa* by S. Chitrav gives the list of *śaktipīṭhās* with place names and the names of corresponding goddesses. For instance, Mt. Kiṣkindha has goddess Tārā, (the name of Vālin's wife), or Mt. Citrakūṭa has goddess Sītā. Similarly Janasthāna *śaktipīṭha*[51] and Triśrota *śaktipīṭha,* (This may be a place where Ganga flows in three currents or it could be a meeting place of any three streams or rivers.) both are associated with goddess Bhrāmarī. The wife of Rudra was also delineated with honeybees and resembled goddess Bhrāmarī, it is said. This indicates a derivation from word *'bhramara'* [52, 53].

P.K. Bhattacharya[54] has made a mention of Mt. Bhramara situated between the rivers Banas and Son flowing through Reva state of M.P. (actually it would be situated at the north-western corner in present Sidhi dist. of M.P.) Bhrāmarī is also another name of goddess Viṅdhyavāsini [55].

Kalhana also mentions goddess Bhramaravāsini[56]. *Brahmā Purāṇa* states that, 'on the south bank of river Ganga was an area 4 *yojanās* in extent known as Janasthāna'[57]. By connecting these loose threads from the bulk of information a coherent and convincing picture emerges, which we can take as evidence to identify the Janasthāna area, which must be located east-west between the rivers Son and Banas of M.P. and Mirzapur to Son in north-south directions. It can be stated that Janasthāna included Citrakūṭa, river Mandākinī embeding river Paṃpā region between Citrakūṭa and Mirzapur within it. (**Paṃpā Nadī Nivasa..........Kadanam mahat**[28]). Like Paṃpeśhwara near Citrakūṭa there is a place called Paṃpāpur about 20 km to the north-east of Mirzapur though river Paṃpā cannot be identified. The Imperial Gazetteer of India of

Sidhi District provides a very interesting piece of information[58]. It mentions Bhanvarsen, (24⁰ 19'N, 81⁰ E) a deserted locality, situated in Shikarganj area of Gopad-Banas *tahsil*, lying to the north of river Son. It is near Chandrehi or Chandresh (24⁰ 18' N,81⁰ 29' E), a small village near the right bank of river Son, close to the confluence of Son and Banas rivers in Sidhi district. The place is of great antiquity and has yielded a few early stone-age tools (see map 1).

The Chandresh inscription of Prabodha Śiva of the Kalacuri (A.D. 724-A.D. 973) refers to this place as 'Bhramaraśaila' (Bhramara hill)[59] and further indicates that Bhanvarsen was then an important seat of the Śaivaite. Bhramaragiri is modern 'Shrishaila hill. Ganjam copper-plate of Tivaradeva (eighth century) mentions an area called 'Bhramaravadra', (modern 'Barm') in south Kosālā, *Dakṣiṇa* Kosālā *mandala* area[60]. Thus, it is not out of place to imagine that this Bhramaragiri seems to be the landmark hill for identifying Janasthāna area around it, within the boundaries of Daṇḍakāraṇya of Rāma story.

Brahma Purāṇa describes *Bhāratavarṣa,* which in turn describes the *tīrtha* (a place of holy water) of Janasthāna. *Brahmā Purāṇa* states - God Varuṇa advised king Janaka (of Vaivasvata Manu line, who might not be the king Janaka of Mithilā, Sītā's father, Janaka being a family name) to perform his *Aśvamedha yajña* on a piece of land called 'Daṇḍaka' *kṣetra*, where 'Gautamī Ganga' (Godavari) *tīrtha* also existed. Therefore that sacrificial ground of Janaka became 'Janasthāna'[61]. (It should really be- '*janaka-sthāna*'!) This story from *Brahmā Purāṇa* seems mixed up, but the fact that the story shows some connection between Daṇḍaka *kṣetra* and Janasthāna, is important.

According to *Rāmāyaṇa*, Śūrpaṇakha, after being defaced by Lakṣmaṇa, goes to Laṅkā, (like Akaṃpana *rakṣasa*) weeping and shrieking to report to Rāvaṇa, saying- 'Rāma has made Daṇḍaka area safe, and invaded Janasthāna'... etc[62].

In another instance Rāvaṇa tells Mārīca that he had never imagined that Janasthāna would ever be invaded, as he had kept his security guards at that outpost ... etc.

All this suggests that Janasthāna area might have come partly under Rāvaṇa's control. Daṇḍakāraṇya was an area of huge extent and therefore, sage Agastya had instructed Rāma to establish a settlement in Pañcavaṭī, which was within Janasthāna, where *rakṣasās* were moving.

Now we know the boundaries of Daṇḍakāraṇya, as the north bank of river Ganga and Mt. Śaivala to the south. (This according to Uttarakāṇḍa - a later addition - was the southern boundary of Ikṣvāku rule of Ayodhya.) River Son and Chota Nagpur hill ranges are the eastern boundary. (This makes a natural wall like barrier north-south.) Mt. Citrakūṭa and river *gupta* Godavari flowing in the vicinity are the western boundaries. The statement that can be made, based on the above discussion, is that Daṇḍakāraṇya had not spread to the south of Mt. Vindhya and towards southern India.

More about Daṇḍakāraṇya

According to *Mahābhārata*[63] the following places were parts of Daṇḍakāraṇya: Śarabhaṅga hermitage, Śukaśrama, Śūrpāraka, Bhṛgutuṅga, Tuṅgakāraṇya, Kālanjar, Devahṛada, Citrakūṭa and river Mandākinī. Although number of places from this list cannot be identified, on the whole this list is indicative of the area. Mārīca *rakṣasa* advises Rāvaṇa, that he should not antagonise Rāma, whose valour is unsurpassable. Mārīca narrates his past experience. Sage Viśvāmitra had performed a *yajña* and his hermitage was in Ganga-Son *doab*, which was towards the eastern boundary of Daṇḍakāraṇya. Rāma, even at that young age, had killed Tāṭakā in Tāṭakāvana and protected the sage's *yajña*. Rāma at the same time had driven Mārīca out of that area, 100 *yojanās* away, until Mārīca had fallen into the 'sea'[64]. After gaining consciousness, Mārīca had gone to Laṅkā[65]. Mārīca also says that earlier he had entered Daṇḍakāraṇya with an intention of eating human flesh[66]. This narrative indicates that Mārīca was thrown out of Ganga-Son *doab* and his second home must have been near Daṇḍakāraṇya. Mārīca had then become dependent of Rāvaṇa. It will now be interesting to locate the second dwelling place of Mārīca, where Rāvaṇa visits him. It was also called 'Mārīcaśrama'.

Kālakeya Mārīca's second abode: When Rāvaṇa thought of enlisting the help of Mārīca he went to meet Mārīca. After the scheme was planned, both of them travelled a long distance by Rāvaṇa's ass-drawn cart and entered Daṇḍakāraṇya and Pañcavaṭī, where Rāma, Sītā and Lakṣmaṇa (also with Jaṭāyu around) had their *parṇakuṭī* (a hut)[67]. Rāvaṇa makes two trips to Mārīcaśrama in his ass-drawn chariot. During his second trip Rāvaṇa threatens Mārīca and after the scheme of abducting Sītā is planned, the trip is extended up to Pañcavaṭī. In his first visit to Mārīca, he is said to have gone 'beyond the sea'[68] but later *ślokās*[69] do not state that he crossed the sea waters. In fact the natural beauty of abundance, exclusively of the sea-shore and the land track that comes in his view while travelling, is described in great details. Rāvaṇa is said to have crossed the marshy land mass, with rocks emerging in between (**saśaila sāgarānūpam**)[70].

Rāvaṇa's route to Mārīca's place, as given in *Mahābhārata*[71], starts from Trikūṭa *parvata*, Kāla *parvata*, then Śiva's favourite place Gokarṇa and after crossing the sea Rāvaṇa reaches Mārīca's *sthāna*.

Elsewhere the sea is mentioned and the land-mark Banyan tree standing on its shore is also viewed by Rāvaṇa, but he does not have to 'cross the sea'[72]. D.R. Mankad[73] states that, this was the sea, which Hanumat crossed and over which Rāma built a bridge, as it was shallow but a vast expanse of water. This argument is not tenable as *Rāmāyaṇa* clearly states that Rāvaṇa saw trees, lakes with boats, large hermitages and even cities at the sea-shore. Rāvaṇa also saw the great Banyan tree. D.R. Mankad says that this character of the sea does not fit in with that of an ocean. This sounds logical, but since there would be many such *Sāgarās* in the region it need not be *Dakṣiṇa Sāgara,* or **'sāgaro makarālayaḥ'**, because if it were *Dakṣiṇa Sāgara,* it would not be passable by a chariot drawn by asses for the fear of crocodiles. It is more likely that Rāvaṇa passed via this sea by its shore. It can only be inferred from the description that this 'sea' was close to 'Subhadra-*vaṭa',* Mārīca's abode and Pañcavaṭī, Laṅkā being slightly away and therefore this could not be *Dakṣiṇa Sāgara* which Hanumat crossed.

Mārīca *rakṣasa* (Kālakā's husband) was originally a 'Kāleya' or a 'Kālakeya'[74] and *Mahābhārata* tells us that Kālakeyās had their original home at Hiraṇyapura or Maṇimatī *nagarī* situated on the banks of river Ganga[75]. Yudhiṣṭhira's pilgrimage account also states that sage Agastya had his hermitage right there near Prayāga and Gayaśira *parvata*. This was a place where Vātāpī was killed by Agastya, it is clearly stated.

ilvalo nāma daiteya āsītkauravanandanaḥ |
maṇimatyām puri purā vātāpistasyacānujaḥ ||[76]

Meaning: (Arjuna is informed that) a *daitya* named Ilvala lived in Maṇimatī *nagarī* with his younger brother Vātāpī. A definite conclusion that we can draw from this information is this -the hermitage of Agastya and also Vātāpī-*sthāna* was an area that was in south Ganga plain to the south of Kaśi (Vārāṇasi). Ilvalapura, Ilvaleśvara, Vātāpiśvara *tīrtha* and the city of Durjayā/Maṇimatī, all these place names point to a single and specific area. In essence, the original home of Kālakeyās was definitely in south Ganga plain. It is interesting to see what Rāma says before killing Mārīca. Rāma pronounces that at this very place Mārīca had killed many sages and hermits before. 'At this same place, Vātāpī used to kill many hermits by tearing their stomachs from within'-.

purastādiha vātāpiḥ paribhūya tapasvinaḥ |
udarastho dvijānhanti svagarbhośvatarīmiva ||[77]

He further says-This is the same place where sage Agastya had earlier killed *rakṣasa* brothers Vātāpī and Ilvala. We can infer from all this that, the event of killing of Vātāpī by Agastya had taken place at or very close to Pañcavaṭī and that Mārīca had his home not very far from Pañcavaṭī. Hiraṇyapura, the original home of Kālakeyās, can be identified only when we locate Durjayā or Maṇimatī *nagarī.* In this connection it is tempting to give a small but very interesting piece of information here. The very first travel account *'Tīrthayātrāprabandh*[78]*'* in Marathi, written by Ganesh Shastri Lele Tryambakkar, was published in AD 1885 although the tours were conducted in 1770, not by the writer himself but by a statesman of Vinchur state (in Nashik area, Maharashtra). The account is based on notes written by Sardar Abasaheb Vinchurkar and his friends and aides. He was on an all India pilgrimage with his huge paraphernalia. He has referred to two holy places (*tīrthās*) namely, Vātāpiśvara and Ilvaleśvara in Kurukṣetra, to the east of Delhi and on the banks of Bhāgīrathī Ganga. These places do not exist anymore, however we may still be able to infer from the discussion above that these places were situated in south Ganga plain, near Pañcavaṭī.

'Gaṇeśa kośa'[79] gives an additional interesting clue. A poet named Dikshit says in one of his prayer songs, that he (the poet) worships lord Gaṇapatī who dwells in Vārāṇasi in the domain of Vātāpī. From the above evidences it can be argued that Pañcavaṭī must have been somewhere near Vārāṇasi and most probably to the south of it.

In and around Pañcavaṭī, - Malada and Karuṣa deśa.

Bālakāṇḍa[80] gives some indications about the probable site of Pañcavaṭī. We are told that sage Viśvāmitra guided young Rāma and Lakṣmaṇa and crossed the confluence of rivers Ganga and Śarayu (or Ghāghra from Sanskrit *gharghharā*) by boat and entered an extremely thick forest. Rāma asks Viśvāmitra a question as to whom that forest belongs to. In reply Viśvāmitra explains how that particular forest had come into existence. He says that, when Indra fought a fierce battle with mighty Vṛtrāsura and killed him, gods washed away the *'mala'* (filth) accumulated on Indra's body. They also washed out hunger from Indra's body (*'Karuṣa'* meaning hunger). The place where this was done was therefore called Malada and Karuṣa *deśa* and Indra showered prosperity over this land[81]. Later on, a *yakṣī* named Tāṭakā, who was extraordinarily powerful in spite of being a woman and that too of a frail *yakṣa* stock, took this area-Tāṭakāvana (see map 1) under her control. She was the wife of Sunda and the mother of Mārīca and Subāhu. As Tāṭakā was an obstacle for Agastya, Rāma then slew her on Viśvāmitra's instructions. Then Rāma, Lakṣmaṇa and sage Viśvāmitra took a night halt in Tāṭakāvana. Next morning they moved to the site of Viśvāmitra's sacrificial platform where the young princes provided full protection for the *yajña* and that place, called Siddhāśrama, became so in the real sense of the word[82]. Rāma however, at the same time, banished Mārīca 100 *yojanās* away into the 'sea'. Mārīca, thus dispirited then became Rāvaṇa's dependant.

We are told that after achieving this, the three men camped for the night on the bank of river Son or Sumāgadhī, from where they could get a glimpse of Vasumatī *nagarī* or Girivrajā[83]. The next day they walked towards river Ganga, crossed the river, then visited Viśāla *nagarī* and finally reached Mithilā where they were welcomed by king Janaka of Mithilā, Sītā's father.

Malada and Karuṣa *deśa* are thought to lie between the Kaimur ranges (the north-eastern ranges of Mt. Vindhya) and the Cedi-Māgadha country, or between Bundelkhand and Baghelkhand or between Ayodhya and Mithilā. *Prācina Sthalakośa*[84] gives a detailed description of this land and also of *janapadās* Malada and Karuṣa. *Mahābhārata* mentions in *Udyogaparvan* that Śri Kṛśṇa had killed Dantavaktra, the king of Karuṣas and that Karuṣa country lay to the east of Daśārṇa and Niṣād countries. S.M. Ali[85] suggests that in the purāṇic tradition Karuṣa *deśa* is coinsided with Ganga-Son *doab*, also including the lands of the *janapadās* Matsyās, Kaśīs, Cedīs and Pāncālās and extending upto the lands in Son-Ken *doab*. All the above indications lead to an inference that the main area of Karuṣa's activity was Baghelkhand, south Mirzapur and districts of western Bihar amidst north-eastern slopes of Kaimur ranges.

The above evidences indicate that, the region where Rāma killed Tāṭakā, was Ganga-Son *doab* and land adjoining Daṇḍakāraṇya and to the east of it. Thus, it can now be imagined that Kālakā and Mārīca might be having their domain near Tāṭakāvana and also Daṇḍakāraṇya. In later times all these *rakṣasās* from Tāṭakāvana and Kālakāvana must have got reorganised under the leadership of Vidyujjiva, the '*Kālakeyādhipatī*'. This point will be further discussed in chapter 5. It is interesting to note that in eastern Madhya Pradesh, near modern Daltonganj, is a place called Kalakapur even today. Patañjali mentions '*Kālakāvana*' around Baxar in central *paragaṇa*, (province of Bihar)[86] supporting inferences drawn above.

The 'Vaṭa' tree of Pañcavaṭī - an important landmark

Rāmāyaṇa informs us that Rāvaṇa went to see Mārīca in his ass-drawn cart. As Rāvaṇa was moving towards Mārīcaśrama, he passed by many forests, rivers and he also passed one vast expanse of water (or 'sea', but not *Dakṣiṇa Sāgara* as we have argued). On the shore of this sea was a plain land of huge extent and with abundance of natural beauty. It was a flat land-mass, a plateau (as specifically mentioned in *Rāmāyaṇa*). It is clear that Rāvaṇa on his way to Pañcavaṭī had picked up Mārīca. Rāvaṇa also viewed on the shore of that vast water reservoir a very large Banyan tree, its name being *'Subhadra-vaṭa'*. Sages and hermits like Vālakhilya, Marīci and others had taken shelter in the shade of that huge tree, it is mentioned. Thus *Araṇyakāṇḍa* informs us –

anūpam sindhurājasya dadarśa tridivopamam |
tatrāpaśyatsa meghābham nyagrodhamṛṣibhivṛtam ||
nāmnā subhadram nyagrodham dadarśa dhanadānujaḥ |
tam tu gatvā param pāram samudrasya nadīpateḥ ||[87]

The story of this Subhadra-*vaṭa* further informs us that very large branches of this tree, as much as 100 *yojanās* in length, were sweeping in all directions. One magnificent eagle bird with very large wing span came and sat on one of the branches and the branch broke under the weight of the bird. As the branch was falling on the ground, the bird swiftly lifted it in its talons, in the air so that the *ṛṣīs* resting under the tree would not get hurt. As the broken branch was falling down it ruined and devastated the land below called 'Niṣād-*deśa*' (**niṣādaviṣayam hatvā śākhayā patagottamaḥ |**)[88] and the Subhadra-*vaṭa* was left with a big scar at the spot from where the branch had broken off. The bird had lifted the branch along with its prey, which were an elephant and a tortoise (two *ṛṣīs* transformed into animals) both also of huge dimensions like the bird (and the tree). The eagle then flew away in the direction of Mt. Himalaya to fetch *amṛta* (nectar).

Mahābhārata also gives a detailed story of this Banyan tree[89] with a little difference. It does not mention Rāvaṇa. The huge eagle picks up its prey from the sea or lake, it is said. Niṣādās were a fisherman tribe and lived at the 'back side of the sea'. Niṣād country is said to have been devastated by the falling branch and then Garuḍa, (an eagle), we are told, flies away first towards Mt. Gandhamādan and then towards Mt. Himalaya. However, *Mahābhārata* does not mention the name of the Banyan tree.

Most importantly both the epics inform us, that there was one magnificent Banyan tree, which stood on the shore of a very large reservoir of water and a branch of the tree held in the eagle's talons fell on the way and caused destruction of Niṣād-*deśa* . The clues from *Bālakāṇḍa* of *Rāmāyaṇa* point to the fact that Mārīca's abode must have been at a distance of 100 *yojanās* from Viśvāmitra's

Siddhāśrama, which was in Ganga-Son *doab* or Tāṭakāvana, land between rivers Son and Ganga, as we have earlier inferred from literal evidences.

From the story of 'Subhadra-*vaṭa*' given above and from the description of Rāvaṇa's journey it appears that there was a plain land with incomparable natural beauty between Mārīcaśrama and Niṣāda *deśa. Niṣādādhipatī* Guhā was a headman of a tribe of fishermen and the settlements of Niṣāda people were spread over large areas around Ganga banks.

All these clues, if put together and analysed, lead us to infer that the land mass, with the magnificent landmark tree Subhadra-*vaṭa* spread over it, was in the vicinity of Pañcavaṭī of *Rāmāyaṇa*. Banyan trees, especially those on the banks of river Ganga, were of huge dimensions as the epic tells us and for this reason also Pañcavaṭī table-land, we can safely say, was located in the southern plain of Ganga.

The people of Niṣāda *janapada* were known to be out of the framework of four '*varṇās*' (being the progeny of a brāhmin man and a '*śūdra*' woman). They were hunters and fishermen and these practices were considered to be sinful. A village 'Niṣādagrāma' exists near Vārāṇasi till this date[90].

Pañcavaṭī was an area of huge extent not far away (*nātidūre)* from Agastya's hermitage, or also from Godavari. It was a plain, but elevated land ('**tataḥsthalamupāruhya**'), a plateau, of huge extent (a '*deśa*') and not a hilly region. It had a variety of trees including *Sāla*, Banyan and many others. However, the most important thing to note is that the Banyan tree named 'Subhadra-*vaṭa*', with the peculiar legend about it, was in the vicinity of Pañcavaṭī only and nowhere else. The tree was like an identification mark of Pañcavaṭī land. In his return journey from Laṅkā to Ayodhya by Puṣpak *Vimāna,* Rāma points out (to Sītā) this huge Banyan tree near Pañcavaṭī:

dṛṣyatesau janasthāne sīte śrīmān vanaspatiḥ |[91]

Meaning: 'O Sītā! See that (Banyan) tree in Janasthāna'. Thus there are numerous indications and evidences from the epic itself which help us locate Pañcavaṭī with Subhadra-*vaṭa'* as an exclusive landmark between Mārīcaśrama and Niṣāda *deśa,* all in south Ganga plain.

Banavari in his book *'Pañcavaṭī'* has explained that Pañcavaṭī means a beautiful *vana* (forest), or a grove having not only five trees of special importance (names also differ with locality) i.e. Banyan, Pippal, Aśoka, Dhātri, Mango etc. but a *vana* with many other trees as well. He says that the 'concept' of Pañcavaṭī and such groves existed in India from very ancient times, even before the times of *Rāmāyaṇa*[92].

More about Pañcavaṭī

Sage Agastya's advice to Rāma was-

ito dviyojane tāta bahumūlaphalodakaḥ |
deśo bahumṛgaḥ śrīmānpañcavaṭyabhiviśrutaḥ ||[93]

Meaning: 'at a distance of only two *yojanās* from here, is a region Pañcavaṭī *deśa* famous for its abundance of natural resources like fruits, roots, water and deer'. Agastya further says:

etadālakṣyate vīra madhūkānām mahadvanam |
uttareṇāsya gantavyam nyagrodhamabhigacchatā ||
tataḥ sthalamupāruhya parvatasya vidūrataḥ |
khyātaḥ pañcavaṭītyeva nityapuṣpitakānanaḥ ||[94]

Meaning: 'O brave man, if one wants to go to that grove of Banyan trees then one should go from the north side of this forest of Madhukā trees and then 'ascend' to an open and plain table-land close to the hillock to reach Pañcavaṭī, a place always blooming with flowers'. Agastya further says that *rakṣasās* move about in that area and the place is not far from Godavari. This suggests that Agastya's hermitage must have been in the lower plain, at the base of that table-land. *Rāmāyaṇa,* on the other hand suggests that it was somewhere near the south bank of river Ganga, where Vātāpī and Ilvala *rakṣasās* also had their abode. Thus it can be imagined to be somewhere to the north of Pañcavaṭī plateau in district Allahabad. On the contrary, Rāma's return journey from Laṅkā to Ayodhya gives Agastya hermitage's site between Godavari and Śarabhaṅga's hermitage. This suggests that another Agastya's hermitage must have been set up to the south of Citrakūṭa and might have been established after Agastya or his descendents crossed over Mt.Vindhya and made that south territory free from *rakṣasa* terror. Both these Agastya *sthānas* must have been close to Pañcavaṭī plateau (see End Note 4).

Rāma on his way to Pañcavaṭī saw beautiful river Godavari with a variety of birds and deer herds at its waters. A variety of trees were in blossom. The three of them settled in a *parṇakuṭī* (a hut). They were also accompanied by Jaṭāyu. Days passed and it was the beginning of winter. Winter at Pañcavaṭī in the testimony of Lakṣmaṇa was like this: He says, 'Mt. Himalaya with its snow capped peaks is now all the more covered with snow, as the sun's rays are not reaching Himalaya any more. Thus its name truly explains it. It is now Himalaya (Home of snow) in the real sense of the word'. Lakṣmaṇa also describes how piercingly harsh the winter is. He says that 'the naturally cool morning breeze has now become doubly harsh and chilly'[95]. No doubt Mt. Himalaya is mentioned here which was hundreds of kilometers away from Ganga plain, but the rest of the description is of unbearable conditions due to very harsh winter. One experiences such conditions only in north India, to the north of Mt. Vindhya, where many a times the temperature drops to near zero degree.

It was T. Amritalingam who first drew the attention of scholars to Lakṣmaṇa's words: 'Chilly winds coming from the west'. He expounded and interpreted the geographical significance of this description of winter at Pañcavaṭī. He explained that to the south of Vindhya the western winds are hot or warm but not cool ....etc[96]. (The original book of T. Amrithalingam- *'Rāmāyaṇa Vimarśa'* of 19XX was not available to this author). Though the point noted by T. Amrithalingam is very important, scholars have neglected and ignored it.

The present author has produced many other evidences which suggest that Pañcavaṭī was located in north India, more precisely in the south Ganga plain. It should also be noted that the epic description indicates that Pañcavaṭī was not a land-mass in Himalayan ranges, since there were deciduous trees as well as a variety of other trees, fields rich with barley crop and especially the roaming herds of wild elephants, suggesting that it was not a hilly country with extremely cold climate.

Most scholars who believe that Rāvaṇa's Laṅkā must have been to the north of Vindhya also believe that Pañcavaṭī must have been an area to the north of Vindhya. Rai Krisnadas[97] identifies Pañcavaṭī near the region where river Ken rises (Śuktimatī rising in the middle and western ranges of Vindhya) in district Jabalpur of M.P. and flows by the western boundaries of Panna (M.P.) and Banda (U.P.) districts to join Yamuna.

T.P. Iyer identifies Pañcavaṭī at Hindoria in Damoh district[98]. However it is not a plateau of vast extent and river Godavari is not in the vicinity. Also as Hindoria is situated far to the south-west and slightly away from the south Ganga plain, it does not satisfy the description of Rāmāyaṇic Pañcavaṭī. M.V. Kibe[99] opines that Pañcavaṭī was near river Godavari and also near Mt. Citrakūṭa. He believes that 'Pañcavaṭī was certainly not so far away as is the current belief.' However, he does not specify or identify Pañcavaṭī with any specific region.

The most characteristic geographical feature of Rāmāyaṇic Pañcavaṭī was that it was a vast table land at a higher level than the plain, a plateau described as a *'deśa'*. Rāmāyaṇic Pañcavaṭī plateau should therefore be looked for at a site near Mt. Citrakūṭa and *gupta* Godavari, in south Ganga plain. Sights identified by the above scholars do not meet these requirements, and hence cannot be identified with Rāmāyaṇic Pañcavaṭī.

D.P. Mishra believes that what Vālmīki meant was that, the larger river Godavari flowed by Pañcavaṭī and hence Rāmāyaṇic Pañcavaṭī should be looked for near Bastar[100]. However, Bastar is not an upland plateau or a vast table-land, and moreover Mishra's identification takes Pañcavaṭī far away from Citrakūṭa and this is not acceptable.

Pañcavaṭī and Godavari-

The belief that Rāmāyaṇic Laṅkā was in Ceylon is so deep rooted that it stretched the extent of Daṇḍakāraṇya as far south as river Godavari of the south. Bastar area, through which larger Godavari flows, thus became Pañcavaṭī for some and Nashik for some others. There are numerous evidences[101] suggesting the existence of another river, named Godavari, connected with *Rāmāyaṇa*, which was in north India flowing in north direction near Mt. Citrakūṭa. (This notion proposed by Cunningham, is supported by Hiralal and others including the present author). Cunningham has stated that there is another Godavari flowing from a cave in a hill as a weak current at a distance of 9-11 miles south-south west of Mt. Citrakūṭa, and the river is called *gupta* Godavari[102]. Topo-sheet 63/C/16 shows Anasūyā hill and Virādh Kuṇḍ on the banks of river Paiśunī (Mandākinī) and also the cave site of *gupta* Godavari to the south west of Mt. Citrakūṭa (Gupt Godā cave is at 25° 6′ N,80° 46′ E; Alt. 200 m).

Hiralal[103] supports the theory that *Rāmāyaṇa* talks about this north Godavari (Citrakūṭa Godavari). He says that *'godā' or 'godārī'* is a non-Aryan word (perhaps Dravidian) meaning simply 'river'. *Mahābhārata*[104] gives a list of place-names of *tīrthās* visited by sage Pulastya during his pilgrimage. They seem to be generally in the order of their geographical locations e.g. after the mention of Godavari, river Payoṣṇī (or Paiśunī) is mentioned. Further on, Daṇḍakāraṇya, Śarabhaṅga's hermitage etc. are mentioned. Most of the place names point to an area in a very specific region from where river Godavari of north India was flowing near Mt. Citrakūṭa. Excepting the mention of Śūrpāraka *kṣetra* all other names are of places from north India.

Perusal of a legend from *Skanda Purāṇa*[105] tells us that Koṭi *tīrtha* on the banks of Goutami (Godavari) was a place where both sage Ṛcika and sage Jamadagnī used to practice penance. Fearing the power of sage Ṛcika, river Godavari was divided into two parts. One part was in the vicinity of river Mandākinī and Mt. Citrakūṭa. This explanatory tale suggests that Mt. Citrakūṭa and river Godavari were in the same area as can be inferred since Koṭi *tīrtha* was on the banks of river Godavari (north) flowing near Mt. Citrakūṭa only. Topo-sheet 63 C/16 shows a hillock 280 metres (909 feet) high at the base of which lies Koṭi *tīrtha* surrounded by many rivulets, which join river Paiśunī (25° 10′ N; 80° 55′ E). Rai Krisnadas says that even now in Bundelkhandi dialect, *'godā'* is a place where a river divides into two streams forming an island in between[106]. Thus, the legend given above seems to have a basis in this geographical characteristic feature of the river. *Skanda Purāṇa* tells us that a Tryaṃbaka *sthāna* (a Śiva *sthāna*) was on the banks of river Godavari, where Guhā (Skanda) had acquired special powers that helped him annihilate

Tārakāsura. Another piece of information is given by *Mahābhārata*. In *Vanaparvan*[107], Śiva's sojurn, along with his subjects towards Bhadra *vaṭa* is delineated. This Bhadra *vaṭa* could most probably be the Subhadra *vaṭa* near Pañcavaṭī and *Rāmāyaṇa* says that Pañcavaṭī was not far from Godavari. It is also obvious that Skanda was not given special powers by Śiva on the banks of south Godavari. The particular abode of Śiva given in *Skanda Purāṇa* i.e. Tryaṃbaka *sthāna* could be the very ancient place of Śiva on Kālanjar (Kālanjar is also the name of Śiva). The list of place names of Pulastya's pilgrimage mentions Kālanjar, a natural hill fort in Bundelkhand, 50 km to the south-west of Mt. Citrakūṭa and river Mandākinī. The information about Kālanjar (or Kālājina) is given in *Prācina Sthalakośa*[108].

Certainly noteworthy are some references from ancient literature which indicate river Godavari of the north. Following examples must be considered in this regard, e.g. 'Aśva *tīrtha*' is a place near Kanyākubja, (modern Kanauj) on the banks of Godavari and Aśvini Kumārās were born here according to *Brahmā Purāṇa*[109]. Similarly, Atreya *tīrtha* and Atrī-Anasūyā hermitage were situated on the north bank of Godavari. This Atrī hermitage was situated in the vicinity of Mt. Citrakūṭa[110]. Topo sheet 63 C/16 shows Anasūyā hill near river Paiśunī.

We get some geographical knowledge from Rāma's testimony itself. He says that, if I am to find Sītā, I will search for her in this area i.e. in and around river Mandākinī, Janasthāna and this Mt. Prasravaṇa[111]. All these descriptions from *Rāmāyaṇa* suggest that Janasthāna, Godavari near Pañcavaṭī, river Mandākinī and Mt. Prasravaṇa are all referred collectively here by Rāma.

Araṇyakāṇḍa states that after Jaṭāyu's death at Janasthāna Rāma entered a much thicker forest (*mahāraṇya*), walked a distance of three *krośās* and came out of Krauñcavana (see End Note 3 and map 2). Then to the east, three *krośās* away, they saw a dark, deep and mysterious valley with terrifying depth. There came a *rākṣasī* named Ayomukhī (meaning dark or iron faced) who tried to seduce Lakṣmaṇa, but ran away when Lakṣmaṇa defaced her. Heu-en-Tsang in his travel accounts, has written that Ayomukhā (Ayomukhī) was a country to the east of Ayodhya. He calls it 'A-YE-MU-KA' and opines that it was in the district of Raybareli[112] (which is in fact to the south-west of Ayodhya.) Kielhorn says that it could be the name of a demon or a mountain[113]. Also a king, descendant of Sahasrārjuna Kārtavīrya's Haihaya dynasty, had conquered Kālanjar *deśa* and Ayomukhā *deśa*[114]. All this information suggests that, this Ayomukhā *deśa* must be somewhere near Citrakūṭa and Kālanjar, the hills which can be identified even today. However, the identification of Ayomukhā country is not possible at present.

Bhavabhūti[115] has described the dwelling place of Jaṭāyu to be on Mt. Prasravaṇa. If we recall that Rāma had first met Jaṭāyu on his way to Pañcavaṭī, we can say with certainty that the original dwelling place of Jaṭāyu must have been near Pañcavaṭī. Curiously, there are places like Gidhodā (dist. Panna), Gidhailā *pahārā* (ht. 2354 feet) [topo-sheet no. 63 H/3+7], to the south-east of Amarpatan of dist. Satna, or Gṛdhrāj *parvata* (south-west of Reva). All these sites are in the vicinity of Shikarganj (Shikargarh) area where we have placed Janasthāna (see map 2). Gṛdhrāj Parvat has many caves and is a habitat of thousands of vultures.

Rāmāyaṇa describes Rāma's return journey from Laṅkā to Ayodhya in northern direction and gives place names in the order of their occurrence. After Mt. Ṛṣyamūka → Paṃpā → Śabarī hermitage → Janasthāna → Death spot of Jaṭāyu → Pañcavaṭī → Godavari (or Mandākinī Paiśunī?) → Agastya hermitage → Śarabhaṅga hermitage → Death spot of Virādha → Mt. Citrakūṭa → river Yamuna → river Ganga → Śṛṅgaverapura → Ayodhya[116]. It can easily be pointed out that all these place names are in order and that order unambiguously identifies the geographical locations of these sites. For example: in this order of place names, no river, mountain or a site from south India is mentioned and we can conclude that Rāmāyaṇic Godavari was the river flowing near Mt. Citrakūṭa. It cannot be the Godavari of south India.

Prācina Sthalakośa mentions that Mt. Kālanjar is an important Śiva *sthāna* on the banks of river Godavari, where it is called, 'Yayāta *tīrtha*' or a place of king Yayāti[117]. Kālanjar hill is a part of Vindhyan range, situated to the south-west of Mt. Citrakūṭa at a distance of a 50 kilometres. The hill is situated at a strategic place from military point of view. There is an old fort and numerous remains which make it an extremely interesting site for Indologists and archaeologists. Kālanjar is considered to be a holy place and has been referred to in ancient literature. It is also mentioned in *Ain-I-Akbari*. Detailed information about this hill and the fort is given by K.D. Bajpai[118] and also in District Gazetteer of Banda, the southernmost district of U.P.[119]

Mt. Citrakūṭa lies to the north-east of Kālanjar. Citrakūṭa '*parikṛamā*' is performed by devotees. On or near the hill are sites like Koṭi *tīrtha*, Devāngaṅa, Hanumanā-dhārā, Faṭak-Shilā, Satī Anasūyā hill, *gupta* Godavari and Bharata-*kūpa* etc, most of them having some connection with the story of *Rāmāyaṇa*. Citrakūṭa is also known as 'Kāmtānāth' and 'Kāmadāgirī'.

Emperor Yayātī had a land of huge extent under his control and had distributed all the provinces to the north of Mt.Vindhya, amongst his five sons. *Prācina Caritrakośa*[120] gives the extent of each one's territory. Emperor Yayātī ruled the land between Kanyākubja (Kanauj) to the west of Ayodhya and Madhya *deśa* up to Ganga Yamuna *doab*. His rule never spread to the south of Mt. Vindhya. Yayātī's capital city Pratiṣṭhāna was at Ganga Yamuna confluence. It was also said to be situated on the banks of Godavari of north India (*gupta* Godavari), the river, which at one time had joined river Ganga according to purāṇic literature. Paiṭhan (also called Pratiṣṭhān) city of Maharashtra is entirely different from Pratiṣṭhāna the city of Yayātī.

Gupta Godavari was not very far from Mt. Citrakūṭa (17.6 km away). The river is said to have entered the earth and is shown today to exist in one cave only, in the form of a thin and weak flow of water. *Skanda Purāṇa*[121] gives an interesting piece of information about *gupta* Godavari of the north. It informs us that along with all other rivers coming to join the mighty river Ganga, also comes river Godavari (and joins Ganga at Prayāga). We are told that the rivers meet at a holy and 'secret' place. The length of Godavari of Daṇḍakāraṇya was only about five *yojanās* (about 35 km) according to *Brahmā Purāṇa,*[122] whereas, that of south Godavari is 1444 km.

The most interesting fact is that if we look at the maps and topo-sheets of the indicated areas in districts Allahabad, Banda and Citrakūṭa of U.P. and those of districts Panna, Satna, Reva and Sidhi of M.P., the following things attract our attention. As per the description in the epic, Pañcavaṭī was an elevated land or a plateau, close to Mt. Citrakūṭa and not far from river gupta Godavari. Reva district seems to be the indicated area. It consists of four natural parts; Kymore pahārā, Binjha pahārā, Reva plateau and lower northern plain. Reva is basically a plateau, its average altitude being between 1000 to 1200 feet and from south to north its height decreases (see map 1). Reva table land from river Panna of west to Hanumanā as its eastern end stretches to about 200 km and its north-south width near Satna is 80 kms. Thus this huge plateau was rightly described as Pañcavaṭī *deśa*.

(1) To south-east of Mt. Citrakūṭa, (25° 10′ 12″ N.; 80 ° 50′ 51″ E.-altitude 310 m) to the north of Chachai falls and to the south of river Kakarahi is a minor hill range named 'Godā *pahārā*' as given in topo-sheet No. 63 G 44, or topo-sheet No. 63 H/5. It lies between Simaria and Sirmaur (25 N. 81° 9′ E.), both these places being in central Reva district. Godā *pahārā* lies to the north of river Tamasā (Tons), which flows from south-west to north-east through district Reva to join river Yamuna. Godā *pahārā* reserved forest located to the eastern side of Godā *pahārā* hills is also shown in the map (topo-sheet Reva # 63H/5-1:50.000;# 63H/2+6 and 63 H/10+14). Apart from *gupta* Godavari spot shown to the west of Citrakūṭa, topo-sheet 63C/16 or 63G/L 1:250,000, also shows another river named 'Gadwā' or 'Gadaiyā', a small feeder of river Paiśunī, joining it from the east.

(2) It is therefore logical to believe that river *gupta* Godā and/ or another river named Gadwā [topo-sheet no. 63 C/15] were flowing near Mt. Citrakūṭa. Both were flowing in the vicinity of Godā *pahārā*, to the north of river Tons. (Less than 50 km to the south-east of Mt. Citrakūṭa). Cunningham thinks that Rāmāyaṇic Godavari to be to the south-west of Mt. Citrakūṭa. However it could also be Gadva flowing by the eastern side of Citrakūṭa. It can therefore be hypothesised that this river *gupta* Godā was the Rāmāyaṇic Godavari.

(3) Another interesting thing is that there exists an extremely vast table-land in Reva district to the north of river Son, (on the northern border of district Sidhi of M.P.) which forms its southern boundary. It is to the south of Meja (25^0 N, 82^0 7′ E) of district Allahabad. Godā *pahārā* is to the north-west of this tableland. At the eastern end of this tableland, 100 km from Citrakūṭa, is a village Hanumanā (topo-sheet # 63L/G44W 1:250,000 (map 1)) which is on national highway no. 7, as its eastern boundary. The present studies suggest that this vast high-land (east-west from river Panna to Hanumanā - 200 km and north-south width near Satna - 80 kms), but plain region of Reva, could be the Pañcavaṭī *deśa* of *Rāmāyaṇa*. There is a place, probably a very large water body called 'Devtālāb' (topo-sheet # 63 H/10+14) on this high-land (map 1). Curiously, in districts Sidhi and Reva are villages with names like 'Parṇakhuri' (Padkhudi), 'Pāchokhar', 'Pankhaura', 'Pārkhuri', which remind us of Rāma's *parṇakuṭī* (topo-sheet # 63H/11+15).

Rāma and Lakṣmaṇa entered 'Krauñcavana' at three *krośās* or nine km to south of Pañcavaṭī (see End Note 3 and map 2) and after coming out of Krauñcavana met Kabandha *rakṣasa*. He showed them the way to Mataṅgavana, where they met an old *Śabara* woman, 'Śabarī' (see End Note 5). Vālmīki refers to her as '*Pampāsaranivāsinī*'.

Pañcavaṭī, Godavari and Nashik

Pañcavaṭī, according to the epic was a part of Janasthāna in Daṇḍakāraṇya. The city of Nashik is situated on the banks of a large river Godavari in northern Maharashtra. Common belief is that Nashik with its surrounding area is the Pañcavaṭī of Vālmīki *Rāmāyaṇa*. A deeply rooted belief is that it is the holiest place of all *tīrthās* where one should perform the rites for the deceased in the waters of river Godavari (because Rāma performed such rites for his father Daśaratha right there?). However this is not true. *Rāmāyaṇa* states that Bharata had approached Rāma on Mt. Citrakūṭa and announced the news of their father's death. Grieving Rāma then got into the waters of river Mandākinī and ceremoniously performed the rites for his deceased father. Offerings were prepared from the pulp of Ingudi fruit mixed with Ber fruit (***aingudam badarimiśram***)[123].

Nashik is a place, where Śūrpaṇakha's nose was cut by Rāma and Lakṣmaṇa, is a wrong belief (and that is why the place name-Nashik, for 'Nasa' meaning nose, came into being). It is believed that Mārīca was killed by Rāma here, Jaṭāyu by Rāvaṇa and it is from here that abduction of Sītā took place. Now, this wrong belief is prevalent also amongst scholars. In fact the name 'Nasikya' does not appear in Vālmīki *Rāmāyaṇa* at all. *Mahābhārata* also does not mention Nashik. Neither *Rāmāyaṇa* nor *Purāṇās* give literary justification for Pañcavaṭī to be at Nashik in Maharashtra.

Tryambakesvara was a small village, about 32 km from Nashik, very thinly populated five centuries ago. Its importance was heightened during the 'Peshva' (Maratha rulers) period. Tryaṃbaka or Triyambaka is the name for Rudra. Kuśāvarta *tīrtha* was then built. However, there exist at least three Kuśāvarta *tīrtha*, one near Haridwar at the foot hills of Himalayas, another according to Jain literature on the banks of river Yamuna, and the third Kuśāvarta is located in Gujarat state[124].

In and around Nashik are sites like Nilambika temple on a hill-top called 'Neel *parvata'*. Trirashi (or Trirashmi) are three small hills with Buddhist caves narrowing towards the apex. Añjaneri (or Añjanagiri) are wrongly called 'Pāṇḍava-*leṇi*' (or caves) which are actually caves of fifth century and could be Jain caves. In the vicinity of Nashik are sites like Ramshej, Govardhan, Saptashrungi hillock, Brahmagiri hill with Tapovan (penance grove) and the rise of Godavari. Nashik is known as *'paścima* Kāśi', whereas Paiṭhan (near Aurangabad, also in Maharashtra) is known as *'Dakṣiṇa* Kāśi'. Nashik is one of the five *'mahātīrthās'* according to *'Kṣetramahatmyā'*[125], although *Purāṇās* have omitted Nashik from their seven holy cities of *Bhāratvarśa,* namely Dvāraka, Avantī (Ujjayini), Mayapuri (Haridwar), Kañcī, Ayodhya, Kaśi (Vārāṇasi) and Prayāga. References to Nashik can be found in ancient literature like Patañjali (second century B.C.), Ptolemy (150 A.D.), *Vāyu Purāṇa,* Jain and Buddhist literature etc. Jain literature mentions Godavari and explains that Nashik is a *'tapovana'* where Brahmā practised penance in *'padmāsana'* (Lotus pose) and therefore it is also called

'Padmapurā'. In *tretāyuga,* it is here that Rāma annihilated three *rakṣasās*, namely Khara, Dūṣaṇa and Triśirā and so Nashik is also called *'trikaṇṭaka'*. In *dvāparayuga*, it was king Janaka's sacrificial ground and hence called Janasthāna. However, we have seen in earlier pages, the story given by Vālmīki himself, about how Janasthāna came into existence in Daṇḍakāraṇya. Janasthāna, therefore, cannot be identified with Nashik, in any case.

The local legend[126] about Pañcavaṭī *kṣetra* of Nashik tells us that five young sages metamorphosed into five Banyan trees and were later on blessed here by Rāma. They then acquired their original forms. However, Vālmīki *Rāmāyaṇa* describes Pañcavaṭī in a different way.

The birth place of Hanumat according to Jain literature is believed to be on Añjanagiri (Añjaneri) hill near Nashik. Some believe this abode to be at Hampi in south India (and also in Afghanistan on Mt. Suleman, ancient Mt. Trikakud!) However, *Rāmāyaṇa* tells us that Hanumat was a *vānara*, an aide of the lord of Kiṣkindhā, Sugrīva, and in fact Hanumat had no connection with Pañcavaṭī.

In reality, the place name Nashik might have a derivation from the name of a *janapada* named 'Nasikyāv'[127] which was a place in north-west frontier. Through the pages of this chapter we have seen that Nashik, which cannot be identified with Pañcavaṭī and therefore was not a place where Śūrpaṇakha's nose was cut as is wrongly believed. According to this author, Nashik or Nasikyāv, the place-name or a *janapada* with the same name, should be connected with the birth story of Aśvinikumārās who had taken birth from the nostrils of a mare[128], their birth-place being Uttara Kuru[129], in the northwest frontier of India of ancient times. The river name Godavari or Gautamī Ganga similarly appears to have a direct connection with the 'Go' of Dīrghatamas/Gotama rescued by Nasikya Aśvinaus, from legend in the Ṛgveda. S.M. Ali[130] has discussed Uttara Kuru at great length. He identified it with Taiga belt of Saiberian region. He says that Uttara Kuru is not mentioned in Ṛgveda, but *Purāṇās* mention it as the northernmost region of Jambūdvīpā, stretching out to the arctic ocean.

References: Daṇḍakāraṇya, Janasthāna and Pañcavaṭī

1. 1:11:15
2. 1; 13:1
3. 1:12:1-12
4. 2:78:11
5. 2:50:22
6. 2:88:1-6
7. 3:56:32-By
8. 7:41:1
9. H.D. Sankalia: *'Rāmāyaṇa in Historical Perspective'*, (1973) p.146, New Delhi,
10. 2:86:11
11. 2:50:22
12. 2:54:3
13. 2:44:9,10
14. U.P. Shah: 'Introduction to c.e. Uttarakāṇḍa' (1975), p.40
15. *'Mbh'. Sabhāparvan, Vana.* 2:27:15
16. F.E. Pargiter: *'The Geography of Rāma's exile'* (1894)
17. D.R. Bhandarkar: 'Daṇḍakāraṇya' Jha Comm. vol. Poona (1937) pp. 46-57
18. D.P. Mishra: *'The search for Laṅkā'* Agam Kala prakashan Delhi, (1985) p.39
19. Hiralal: 'The situation of Rāvaṇa's Laṅkā' Jha Comm. vol. Poona (1937) p.161
20. M.V. Kibe: *'Location of Laṅkā'* (1947), Manohar Granthamala Pune
21. H.D. Sankalia: *'Rāmāyaṇa in historical perspective',*(1982),Mac Millan, Bombay, p.57
22. Navinchandra Dās: (1871/1896), p. 43
23. T.P. Iyer: *'Rāmāyaṇa and Laṅkā',* (1940), pp.106-109
24. Rai Krisnadas: 'Rām vanavās ka bhūgol' Nagarī Pracharini Patrika 54:1, p.25
25. 2:74:1-10
26. T.P. Iyer: (1940) op.cit.p.102
27. *'Imperial Gazetteer of India',* North-Western Provinces, Bundelkhand, vol.1 (1875)
28. 3:5:16
29. Rai Krisnadas: op.cit.p.21
30. M.V. Kibe: op.cit. p.29
31. D.R. Mankad: *'Introduction to Kiṣkindhākaṇḍa',* c. e. (1965) p. 54-55
32. U.P. Shah: *'Introduction to Uttarkaṇḍa,* c. e. (1975) p. 40,
33. 3:11:29-34
34. 3:12:13

35. 3:12:18
36. 3:12:22
37. *'Bhāratiya Sanskṛti Kośa'* vol.III Bharatiya Sanskriti Kosh Mandal, (1965-87) Pune, p.100
38. 7:70:79, 80, 81 *'Daṇḍakāraṇyanāmotpattikathana'* (By)/ 7: sargās 70-72
39. 7:70:16, 17
40. Majjhima Nikaya: 1:378 (quoted by S. Chitrav *'Prācina Sthalakośa',* p.395)
41. U. P. Shah: op.cit. p. 40
42. G. Ramdas: 'Aboriginal Names in the Rāmāyaṇa', JBBORS, vol. XI (1925) pp. 41-53; 'Aboriginal Tribes in the Rāmāyaṇa', I.H.Q. vol. IV (1928),pp. 339-346, *'Man in India'* vol.V. pp. 281-299; 'Rāvaṇa and His Tribes', vol. VI. pp. 285-289;
43. 7:66:12
44. Nundalal Dey: *'Geographical dictionary of ancient and medieval India'* New Delhi (1927/1971), Oriental Reprint and IInd ed. (1979) Cosmo publ. New Delhi
45. 7: 69, 70
46. 7:71
47. D.C. Sarkar: *'Studies in the geography of ancient and medieval India'* MLBD Publ. New Delhi (1960), p. 43
48. V. V. Mirashi: *'Kautilīya Arthaśastra',* (1958) 1:3 (quoted by V. V. Mirashi) *'Ramagiri of Meghadūta is Ramtek'* (Marathi), (1958), Vidarbha Samshodhan Mandal.
49. U.P. Shah: op.cit.p.39
50. T.P. Iyer: op.cit.p.103, 104
51. S. Chitrav: *'Prācina Caritrakośa'* (1964), p. 302 (See Entry: *'Devipiṭha'*) Bharatiya Charitra Kosh Mandal, Poona
52. *'Mārkaṇḍeya Purāṇa*, canto. XCI, 47, 48 [tr. and notes by Pargiter F.E. (1904/1969]
53. *'Devī Bhāgavata Purāṇa' Skandha* 10:6-13
54. P.K. Bhattacharya: *'Historical geography of M.P. from early records'* MLBD Vārāṇasi (1977) p.81
55. *'Śabdeśvarī',* (1999), p.169
56. Kalhana: *'Rājataraṅginī',* 3*:* verse 394
57. P.V. Kane:*'History of Dharmaśastra',* vol.4: List of Tīrthās, BORI Poona (1953), p.759
58. *'Imperial Gazetteer of India',* Sidhi District, (1994)
59. V. V. Mirashi: *'Corp. Inscr.'* vol. IV. Part 1, p.198, 199
60. S. Chitrav: *'Prācina Sthalakośa',* p.626
61. *Brahmā Purāṇa':* 42
62. 3:31:1
63. *Mbh'. Vanaparvan.* 84:85
64. 1:29:15, 16

65. 3:36:17
66. 3:37:1-6
67. 3:40:9
68. 3:33:7
69. 3:33:8-27
70. 3:33:11
71. *'Mbh'.Vanaparvan. 'Rāmopākhyāna'* 3:261:53, 54
72. 3:42:8-11
73. D.R. Mankad: op.cit.p.62
74. S. Chitrav: *'Prācina Caritrakośa',* p.138
75. *'Mbh'. Vanaparvan. Tirth.* 102:98:170
76. *'Mbh'. Āraṇyakaparvan.* 3:94:4
77. 3:41:39
78. Ganeshshastri Lele: *'Tīrthayātrāprabandh'* (1885/1964) (Based on Sardar Abasaheb Vinchurkar's all India pilgrimage in 1770), Deshmukh and co. Pune
79. *'Gaṇeśa kośa'* p.577 ed. Amarendra Gadgil, 2nd ed. (1981), Shri Ganesh Kosh Mandal, Pune
80. 1:24
81: 1: 23: 23
82. 1:28:15, 16, 18
83. 1:31:5-7
84. S. Chitrav: op. cit. p.377, 592
85. S.M.Ali: *'The geography of the Purāṇās'*,(1966), pp. 159, 160, PPH, New Delhi
86. Patañjali {quoted by N. Dey p. 84 *'Prācina Sthalakośa'* (1979) (entry: *'Kālakāvana'*)}
87. 3:33:27, 35, 36
88. 3:33:32
89. *'Mbh'. Ādiparvan. Astik.* 5:25
90. *'Mora Jatak'* 2:36(quoted by *'Bhāratiya Sanskṛti Kośa',* p.138 ed. by Mahadeoshastri Joshi, (1968) Bharatiya Sanskriti Kosh Mandal, Pune
91. 6:123:42
92. Banavari: *'Pañcavaṭī'* : Indian approach to Environment [tr. Hindi by Asha Vora(1992)]
93. 3:12:13
94. 3:12:21, 22
95. 3:16:14-24
96. T. Amrithalingam: (19....) (Quoted: N. V. Rao (1990), p.69
97. Rai Krisnadas: op.cit. 54:1, p.24
98. T.P. Iyer: op.cit. p.108
99. M.V. Kibe: op.cit. p.10
100. D.P. Mishra: op.cit.p.37
101.*'Bhāratiya Sanskṛti Kośa',* 5:83 (1968). According to *Kṣetramahatmyā,*

river Godavari flowing in south direction is difficult to find, although, it is holy and gives salvation. However, the larger river Godavari in Maharashtra does flow towards south. Why then does *Kṣetramahatmyā* make a statement that the flow of Godavari in south direction is difficult to find? (Or is non-existent?) Or is there any north bound Godavari flowing in northerly direction that is referred by *Kṣetramahatmyā?* An answer to this question is in the affirmative.

102. A. Cunningham: (1894) ASIR, vol.XXI, pp.11-13
103. Hiralal: 'The situation of Rāvaṇa's Laṅkā' Jha comm. vol. (1937) Pune, pp.151-161
104. *'Mbh'.Vanaparvan.* 3:83:55
105. *'Skanda Purāṇa'* (*Sahyadri Khaṇḍā* 8-*Reṇuka Mahatmyā, Adhyāya* 8:4,5)
106. Rai Krisnadas: 'Rām Vanavās ka Bhūgol' Nagarī Pracharini Patrika, 54:1 p.25
107. *Mbh. Vana. Ara. Adhyāya* 221
108. *'Mbh.Vana. Ara.* Fasicule 11, *Adhyāya* 80:22-133 c.e. BORI Poona
109. *'Brahmā Purāṇa'* p.147/1, 123/117-120
110. *'Mbh'. Vanaparvan. Āraṇyakaparvan Tirth. Adhyāya*: 85
111. 3:60:14
112. Heu-en-Tsang: (quoted by *'Prācina Sthalakośa'*: pp.128-129)
113. Kielhorn: *'Epi.Indica'* 7:86
114. *Corp. Inscr.* I:4:2:385 (quoted by *'Prācina Sthalakośa'*, pp.128-129)
115. Bhavabhūti: *'Uttararāmacarita'* Act I, text with commentary of Ghanashyama, notes, Intro. and English tr. by P.V. Kane and C.N. Joshi, MLBD Delhi, 5th ed. (1971) pp.74-76
116. 6:111:19
117. *'Brahmā Purāṇa'*: 146:1-43
118. K.D. Bajpeyi: *'Geographical Encyclopaedia of Ancient and Medieval India,'* (1967) vol.1, pp.448-449 Indic Academy, Vārāṇasi
119. *'Imperial Gazetteer of India'*: dist. Banda, U.P.
120. S. Chitrav: *'Prācina Caritrakośa'*, p.682
121. *'Skanda Purāṇa', Avantī Khaṇḍā, Gaṅgeśvara mahatmyā*
122. *'Brahmā Purāṇa'*: 123:117-120
123. 2:95:20-30
124. S, Chitrav: *'Prācina Sthalakośa'* p.553
125. *'Kṣetramahatmyā'* (quoted in *'Bhāratiya Sanskṛti Kośa'*:5: ed. 1968 p.83 Mahadevshastri Joshi, Bharatiya Sanskriti Kosh' Mandal, Pune
126. Ibid: 5:82-86
127. *'Śrī Mārkaṇḍeya Purāṇa'* 54:50-51
128. S. Agashe: *'Nashikche Nāmarahasya'* (Marathi) (Lokasatta daily, 10th Dec.2006)

129. A.J. Karandikar: '*Mahābhāratachi Parśvabhūmī-Paśchim Asia*' (1980), (Marathi) Shubhada Sarasvat Publication Pune, p.169 (Quotes Mark. 89, 90)

130.S.M. Ali: op.cit. pp. 72, 73 84 101

End Notes:

(1) ŚṚṄGAVERAPURA: Singraur is identified with Śṛṅgaverapura as shown by convincing topo-sheet evidences furnished by T.P. Iyer: ['*Rāmāyaṇa and Laṅkā*' (1940) p.100] Near Prayāga, (Allahabad 25° 27′ N, 81° 51′ E) was a village Singraur, which existed at 25° 35′N, 81° 30′E on river Ganga till 1935 and latter was probably swallowed up by the river. It is not seen in the degree-sheet 63B of Government of India standard maps, revised in 1936. It is also argued that Bhāradvāja's hermitage might have been on the banks of Yamuna because from here Mt. Citrakūṭa is at a distance of about 25-30 km (see map 2).

T.P. Iyer has further stated that there was no Prayāga in *Rāmāyaṇa* days, although Vālmīki mentions Prayāga (2:48:5) and that Bhāradvāja hermitage was near the confluence of rivers Ganga and Yamuna. Iyer suggests that rivers Ganga and Jumna (Yamuna) together formed a vast lake with an extent of 400 square miles, which the rivers entered by distinct mouths. This *Sāgara* lies between the bevelled stumpy ridge of the Bindhachal between Meja, east of the south Tons, and Partabpur on the south bank of river Yamuna and shown as 'stoney waste' in degree-sheets 63K and 63G (or # 63 G/11+15) as conclusive proof that it was an old *Sāgara* now dried up (T.P. Iyer 1940, p.28-29).

Rai Krisnadas opines ('*Rām Vanavās ka Bhūgol*', Nagarī Pracharini Patrika 54: 4: p.15, 16) that, in those days Ganga -Yamuna confluence itself might have been at Rajapur [topo-sheet # 63 G/16] on the southern or right bank of Yamuna, from where Citrakūṭa is 10 *crosas* (32-35 kms) away. He interprets Vālmīki as follows - Ganga and/or Yamuna had turned towards west and the rivers did not unite at Prayāga, but at Rajapur. Thus,

gaṅgāyamunayoḥ sandhimādāya manujarṣabha |
kālindimanugacchanti nadīm paścānmukhāśritām || (2:55:4-By)
yatra bhāgīrathī gaṅgā yamunāmabhivartate | (2:48:2)

This notion is not tenable since Vālmīki mentions both Prayāga and Bhāradvāja hermitage being close to the confluence. Instead, a believable solution to this problem of a distance of 32 km between Bhāradvāja's hermitage and Mt. Citrakūṭa can be like this: Rajapur is more than 50 km away from Prayāga. The sage says that he visits

Citrakūṭa very often. At a certain point river Yamuna (and not Ganga) seems to flow in a reverse direction, i.e. from east to west, perhaps on a natural downward slope towards west. A glance at any map shows that such a place is to the north of Rajapur where for just a few miles Yamuna appears to be flowing from east to west. This also must be a spot most suitable (as the sage suggests) for crossing the river by raft. It can then be imagined that Rajapur must be a resting point and Bhāradvāja must be naturally having another hermitage somewhere there. It then follows that Vālmīki's statement that Citrakūṭa was at 10 *krośās* (32 km) from this second Bhāradvāja hermitage on the north bank or at Rajapur is justified. The distance from Rajapur to Mt. Citrakūṭa is 36 km. One more possibility is that a small branch of river Ganga might be flowing southwards to meet Yamuna near Rajapur. This problem of course needs further investigation.

Śṛṅgaverapura is believed to have derived its name from sage Ṛśyaśṛṅga, whose hermitage was thought to be at this place on the north banks of Ganga. At present there is a small modern temple of Ṛśyaśṛṅga at this site. However this notion is not acceptable for the following reason. Meanings of the word *'śṛṅga'* as given in *Gīrvāṇalaghukośa* (p.480) are horn/apex/greatness/crescent moon. The meaning of the word *'ver'* is given as 'body' (p.456). From this place name 'Śṛṅgaverapura' the word 'Ṛśya' (meaning deer) is absent, although a female deer was connected with the birth story of sage Ṛśyaśṛṅga according to the epic.

It should be noted that Ṛśyaśṛṅga's hermitage was on the banks of river Kauśikī (Kosi) in a forest, in the viscinity of ancient Añga *deśa,* (capital Campā, North Bihar) ruled by king Romapāda, a friend of Kosālā king Daśaratha. *Bālakāṇḍa* also says that the prostitutes visited the sage often to lure him and finally succeeded in bringing him to Champa. According to the epic, Daśaratha's *Aśvamedha yajña* had then taken place near Ayodhya and that too on the north bank of river Śarayu. These events obviously must have taken place far away from Śṛṅgaverapura, which is about 35 km to the north-west of Allahabad-Prayāga. At the site of Śṛṅgaverapura B.B.Lal observed, (in his 'Excavations at Śṛṅgaverapura'; Memoirs of ASI 1993 no.88, p.13) that here river Ganga takes a horse-shoe curve. Regarding the derivation of the name Śṛṅgaverapura, it can therefore be argued that here river Ganga takes a horn-like (or crescent moon like) curve and hence this site must have been named Śṛṅgaverapura, thus Ṛśyaśṛṅga story cannot be associated with this place.

(2) WHAT IS A 'YOJANA'?: T.P. Iyer [(1940) p 3, 37, 38] explains, 'The *yojana* is used in two senses in Vālmīki *Rāmāyaṇa*. In the ordinary sense of four krośās of 1000 *dhanuṣ* each. A *dhanuṣ* is four *hastas* or two yards and that gives 8000 yards or four and a half miles to a yojana (*'Kautilīya Arthaśastra'-Encyclopaedia Asiatica).* [Vālmīki also uses it in the sports sense of a 'stadium' where one stadium or one yojana is 200 yards or 660 feet, Thus, Mt. Mahendra to Laṅkā could be eleven and a half miles (17 km). 100 yojanās is equal to 100 stadia'.] The present author has followed the same standard. T.P. Iyer [*'Rāmāyaṇa and Laṅkā,'* (1940)] has studied the geography of Rāma's journey in search of Sītā and Rāma's itinerary as given in *Rāmāyaṇa*. He has estimated the distances from one place to another. Thus, according to Iyer's study, the total distance which Rāma covered from Ayodhya to Laṅkā (identified with Indrana hill near Jabalpur) can at the most be around 373 miles or 600 km.

(3) KRAUÑCAVANA AND PAÑCAVAṬĪ: *Araṇyakāṇḍa* says that after Jaṭāyu's death at Janasthāna, Rāma and Lakṣmaṇa entered *mahāraṇya,* (a much thicker forest) and walked a distance of 3 *krośās* and came out of Krauñcavana (3:65:5). Interestingly, in the districts of north-eastern M.P. there are forests with names like Mohadra, Jiavan, Majhgavan, Managavan, etc. The Map of Sidhi district shows Kehanjua [topo-sheet # 63 H/11and #63 L/2+6] reserved forest as well as a river named Kehanjua, which joins river Adva near Son-Banas confluence.

M.V. Kibe imagined a forest in Kenjua, an offshoot of Vindhyas, to be Krauñcavana, where Rāma goes from Janasthāna in search of Sītā. Krauñcavana was at a distance of 3 *krośās* (9.6 km) to the south of Pañcavaṭī. Thus –

tataḥ param janasthānāttrikrośam gamya rāghavau |
krauñcāraṇyam viviśaturgahanam tau mahaujasau || (3:65:5)

In fact the *'Imperial Gazetteer of Reva state'*, vol. IV, (1907) informs us that, the area lying between Kaimur and Maikal mountain ranges, up to Panna range is called 'Vinjh *pahārā'* (Mt. Vindhya) in local language, while its eastern branch is called 'Kehanjua' (or 'Kenjua' *pahārā*.) This name reminds one of Krauñcavana as is rightly thought by a few researchers. Rāmāyaṇic Krauñcavana therefore, is more likely to be in Reva range, towards the northern border of dist. Sidhi rather than near Mt. Amarkanṭak. The present studies suggest Pañcavaṭī to be on a vast table land in Reva district to the south of Meja, a few kilometres to the south-west of Mirzapur. An area to the south of Reva plateau can be identified with Krauñcavana of Vālmīki. Two rivers, namely a branch of Adva and Kehanjua, join together in this area (topo-sheet # 63L/5).

(4) SAGE AGASTYA: *Rāmāyaṇa* (3:10:77-83; entry 185, 186) describes Agastya as the master or preceptor of all mountains. *Vanaparvan* of *Mahābhārata* (*Adhyāya* 85) describes the pilgrimage of Yudhiṣṭhira. He comes across Akṣaya-*vaṭa* of Prayāga and then the sacrificial ground of Gayāsura (Gayapura of U. P.) and then the place where sage Agastya, whose hermitage was said to be near Prayāga, had killed *rakṣasa* Vātāpī (at Durjayā also known as Maṇimatī *nagarī*) near river Bahudā (*'Mbh'. Vanaparvan.* 85:21/86:10, 14). Could this be a river in Ikṣvāku domain? Perhaps a feeder of river Raptī near Oudh? (there is a legend about river Bahudā involving a Ikṣvāku king).

There are numerous places in India believed to be Agastya's places. *Vanaparvan* also describes the pilgrimage of sage Dhaumya (*'Mbh'. Vana. Tirthayatraparvan* 85). The places to the east are given in the order of their occurrence. They are: Naimiśāraṇya → river Gomatī → Gaya mountain → Brahmasara → (or Ganga?) Mahanadi (as adjective of river Ganga?) → Gayaśira → Akṣaya-*vaṭa* → Falgu Mahanadi (the smaller Mahanadi?) → Kauśikī → Kālanjar-Hiraṇyabindu → Mt. Agastya → Ganga → Kanyākubja (modern Kanauj) → Agastya's hermitage at Prayāga → Mt. Mahendra of Paraśurāma (This was Mahendragiri of eastern-*ghats* in Orissa!) *'yajña-vedī'* of Brahmā (where Bhāgīrathī-Ganga sinks in Maṇikarṇika lake-which was in Vārāṇasi) → Mataṅgakedāra hermitage (this was near Paṃpā, Mt. Ṛṣyamūka, etc.) → Kuṇḍoda *parvata* → Devavana → rivers Bahudā and Nandā.

This list gives food for thought indeed. In this chaotic order of sites and also in accordance with information from *Prācina Caritrakośa,* Agastya had a hermitage on Mt. Mahendra and *Gaṅgāvatarana* site was also near Mt. Mahendra. Obviously in the above narration there seems to be a mix-up between these two facts. Vālmīki's (and Agastya's) Mahendra is definitely not the one in eastern *ghats* in Orissa (see Appendix G). Therefore Mt. Mahendra of *Rāmāyaṇa* must be located on the north slope of Mt. Vindhya, in watery region.

Ilvala and Vātāpī had their abode in Durjayā, also named Maṇimatī, as we have seen (*Mbh. Sabhāparvan. Ara.'*.97, 98). It seems to be closely connected to Ganga, Yamuna and Prayāga or South Ganga plain. Thus Maṇimatī of Vātāpī cannot be identified with Badami of south India. *Prācina Caritrakośa* mentions that Agastya was initially a resident of Kaśi (Vārāṇasi) but later left Kaśi, mastered Mt. Vindhya and crossed over its ranges. Thus according to the description in *Araṇyakāṇḍa* he settled 'to the south', and his second hermitage must have been slightly to the south of Mt. Citrakūṭa but still very close to Mt. Citrakūṭa and Pañcavaṭī. In addition to this it can also be said that Agastya Maitrāvaruṇī, Son of Urvaśi, (like sage Vasiṣṭha, both born of a pitcher) (*Ṛgveda* 7:33:13), Agastya, who consumed the 'sea', Agastya of Vārāṇasi who exterminated Vātāpī and Ilvala and Agastya who advised Rāma to settle down at Pañcavaṭī could not all be the same person, and seem to have appeared in different times. Agastya of *Rāmāyaṇa* and his 'brother' (*Agastyabhrātā*) living to the south of Citrakūṭa could be the descendents of the great sage Agastya of pre-Rāma days, and it can be argued that Rāma might have approached Pañcavaṭī highland from south of Citrakūṭa from Agastya hermitage situated to the south of Citrakūṭa. P.V. Kane makes a note of river Pippala or river Pippalī rising from Mt. Rsyavanta of *Purāṇās*. This name of the river reminds us of a Pippalī grove near the hermitage of Agastyabhrātā. ('*History of Dharmaśastra* vol. IV, list of *tīrthās* p. 791) Interestingly, according to Purāṇās river Pippalāvatī (or Pippalaśroṇī or Pippalaśyenī) was the same as river Paiśunī rising in Mt. Ṛkṣa and flowing near Mt. Citrakūṭa in Bundelkhand. (P.V. Kane p. 791, *Prācina Sthalakośa* I, p. 287)

While Rāvaṇa was wandering 'all over the world' he went to Bhogāvatī city of Nāgās and from there to Maṇimayī *nagarī* of Nivātakavacās. (Kālakeyās and Paulomās together were called Nivātakavacās) Can Maṇimayī be Maṇimatī of Vātāpī and Ilvala? These two *rakṣasās* were the grandsons of Hiraṇyakaśipū and were also known as 'Saiṃhikeyās' (being two out of thirteen of them). This indicates that their original place could be the same as that of Hiraṇyakaśipū. Perhaps Hiraṇyaparvata, valley of river Hiraṇyavāhā (Sonabhadra or Son) and Hiraṇyapura was originally the domain of Hiraṇyakaśipū and/or Bali *daitya*. *Prācina Caritrakośa* (page 1111) informs that Saiṃhikeyās, Bali vairocana, Virādha, Kālakeya Mārīca, Nivātakavacās and Jarāsandha all were of Hiraṇyakaśipū lineage. Cunningham in his '*Ancient Geography of India*' (ed. by S.N. Mujumdarshastri 1924 p.545) writes that Hiraṇyaparvata could be a hill near Monghyr (Bihar) on the banks of river Ganga. Moreover the mythical Mt. Maināka, (submerged in *Dakṣiṇa Sāgara*) which acted as a barrier for daityās is also called Hiraṇyanābha by *Rāmāyaṇakaras* (6:111:12). This matter needs further investigation. At this point we can only reach a conjecture that Durjayā-Maṇimatī and the hermitage of Agastya, who killed Vātāpī and Ilvala *rakṣasās* must be located somewhere between Prayāga and Kaśi (Vārāṇasi), to the south of river Ganga.

(5) **THE ŚABARĪ EPISODE:** After Sītā was abducted by Rāvaṇa, Rāma and Lakṣmaṇa, wandering and searching for her in the forest, met Kabandha *rakṣasa*. He showed them the way to Mataṅgavana. There they met an old ascetic tribal woman, 'Paṃpāsarnivasinī' Śabarī living in the hermitage of sage Mataṅga, who was also a '*śūdra*' (a low caste in Hindū hierarchy).

In the medieval period purāṇic literature helped glorify '*bhākti*' (devotion) by popularising this story. This popular story tells us that

Rāma ate the *'bers'* defiled by Śabarī and that proved the greatness of Rāma as well as that of Śabarī. However, according to the epic, with special care and devotion, Śabarī had collected many fruits from the banks of river Paṃpā and not just a few *'bers'* (3:70:9-13). Śabarī of the epic poet certainly did not offer defiled *bers* to Rāma.

These 'Śabara' tribes were the dwellers of southern part of north India (*Prācina Caritrakośa* p.944,). They are referred to along with Ābhirs, Aṭavyas, Pulindās, Vaidarbhās and Daṇḍakās (*Mārkaṇḍeya Purāṇa*: 54:47) (*'Vāyu Purāṇa'* 45.126). It must be remembered that in those times, the southern boundary of *'Āryāvarta'* was Mt. Vindhya or river Narmada. However, these Śabaras were also living in Pennar river surroundings in south India. They were to be found in Rajasthan and at the foothills of Himalayas as well. To the south of Bilaspur in Madhya Pradesh is a village named 'Śabarīnarain'. A river named Śabarī flows in the southern part of M.P. The hills of Orissa, Bihar and forest clad areas of eastern M.P. had Śabara settlements. Pliny calls them 'Suari' and Ptolemy calls them 'Sabarae'. These Śabarās did not have a permanent settlement at one place but had spread over vast areas. Śabarās from Orissa used to practice witchcraft known as *'Śabarīvidyā'.* The rights and control of the temple of Jagannatha at Puri in Orissa have always been with Śabara community, till this date.

§§§

3

KIṢKINDHĀKAṆḌA OF RĀMĀYAṆA

For scholars studying *Rāmāyaṇa* from a geographical point of view *Kiṣkindhākaṇḍa* poses the most difficult challenge. Yet, it provides the most interesting and exciting material to investigate and explore through. It is still a disputable source of geographical knowledge. Politics of *Rāmāyaṇa* starts getting clearer here. There are new associations and alliances; new friendships, new plans and strategies crystallise, take shape and advance in Kiṣkindhā. Rāma and Lakṣmaṇa are wandering about in the deep forest of Daṇḍakāraṇya in search of Sītā. They follow Kabandhā's instructions after which Rāma's search for Sītā and for Rāvaṇa's Laṅkā for the first time gets proper direction. It is in Kiṣkindha that Rāma sees a ray of hope.

Kabandha had advised Rāma to make friendship with *vānara* king Sugrīva. This advice was for three reasons. Firstly, since the *vānarās* residing in the immediate viscinity of Pañcavaṭī, must have been a tribe of robust, sturdy people, well adapted to life in hills and valleys of Mt. Vindhya ranges and hence *vānarās* alone could guide and assist Rāma in jungle-warfare. Therefore, as a fighting force *vānarās* alone would be of some use, and not the army of settlers of plain and cities like Ayodhya. Secondly, Sugrīva, the king of *vānarās* or *vanacarās* had good knowledge of the geography of various regions 'of the earth', and for this reason Kabandhā's advice was very important. The third reason was that Sugrīva had been dethroned by his brother Vālin and Sugrīva's wife Ruma was now under the control of Vālin, a situation similar to that of Rāma.

The name of the capital city of *vānara* kingdom 'Kiṣkindhā' is a very peculiar proper noun, and invites an enquiry regarding the derivation of the word. Kiṣkindha was the dwelling place of Vālin and Sugrīva whose birth story is curious. Ṛkṣarajas, their father once had acquired the form of a beautiful woman. Indra and Sun god both were excited when their eyes fell on this dame and from the drops of semen of Indra which fell on the hair of Ṛkṣarajas was born Indraputra Vālin. Also from the semen of Sūrya (Sun god) falling on the neck of Ṛkṣarajas Sūryaputra Sugrīva was born[1].

'Kikhih' in Sanskrit means *vānara* (a monkey). The word *'kandhara'* means - (1) neck or throat, (2) shoulder (3) name of a particular plant[2]. Similarly, word *'kandhī'* means (1) ocean, (2) nape of neck. The word *ṛkṣa'* means bear, monkey or deer, and word *'vāla'* means tail, hair, wool or a particular plant. If we consider the birth story of Vālin and Sugrīva and examine collectively all the above mentioned words with their meanings, we may arrive at a derivation: *'kikhi' + 'kandha'* = Kiṣkindha (If grammar can allow this!). It is tempting to imagine that this could be so, because of the phonetic similarity between the words. However, this conjecture could be only a peripheral argument.

As per Kabandhā'*s* direction Rāma meets Śabarī near Mataṅgavana to the east of which was river Paṃpā. Mt. Ṛṣyamūka was located right opposite river Paṃpā, very close to river Paṃpā, also referred to as Paṃpā-*saras* (*sarovara*) or *puṣkariṇī*. Vālmīki tells us that Ṛṣyamūka was a high hill difficult of ascend. This hill and Paṃpā were adjoining each other and were important landmarks on Pacavati-Kiṣkindha route as well as Pañcavaṭī-Laṅkā route as can be easily inferred from the descriptions. *Rāmāyaṇa* informs us[3] that Paṃpā was a tributary of river Mandākinī or Anumandakinī. This suggests that Paṃpā could not be very far from Mt. Citrakūṭa and Kiṣkindha (there is a site called Paṃpeśvara (topo-sheet # 63 C/16) near Mt. Citrakūṭa!).

Kiṣkindha is described by Vālmīki as a *guhā* or *giri-guhā* e.g. **'guhām praviṣte sugrīve'**[4], **'kiṣkindhā girigavhare'**[5]. Mataṅga *parvata*, hermitage of Mataṅga, Mataṅga-*kedāra* and Mataṅga *saras,* all were parts of Mt. Ṛṣyamūka, and Kişkindha was near Mt. Ṛṣyamūka and river Paṃpā. All these places were situated in thick *Sāla* forest and picturesque surroundings as Vālmīki describes in *Kişkindhākaṇḍa*. Rāma and Lakṣmaṇa saw river Paṃpā, bathed in Mataṅga-*saras* and they then started to ascend the Ṛṣyamūka hill. Seeing the two armed strangers, Sugrīva ran to the neighbouring peak-'Malaya'. Now appears Hanumat, Sugrīva's minister, for the first time in *Rāmāyaṇa* story, who meets Rāma on the banks of river Paṃpā. They all then gathered on Ṛṣyamūka hill, which was a safe place for Sugrīva, as his brother Vālin was deterred (by sage Mataṅga's curse) from approaching Mataṅgāśrama on Ṛṣyamūka. On Mt. Ṛṣyamūka, sitting on the branch of *sāla* tree laid on the ground, *'Sūryavaṃśī'* Rāma and *'Sūryaputra'* Sugrīva entered into a friendship treaty according to which Rāma should then espouse the cause of the then exiled prince Sugrīva by killing Vālin and Sugrīva in turn should help Rāma in locating Rāvaṇa's abode Laṅkā and finding Sītā. Sugrīva offered Rāma, his army of *vānarās* for this cause. After the strategy was planned, Sugrīva led Rāma to Kişkindhā-*dvāra,* which was an arena of combatants Vālin and Sugrīva, where Rāma killed Vālin. Sugrīva, now friend of Rāma, enthroned as king of *vānarās,* then entered Kişkindhā. Thus-

abhiṣikte tu sugrīve praviṣṭe vānare guhām |
ājagāma saha bhrātrā rāmaḥ prasravaṇam girim ||[6]

Meaning: Rāma's new friend Sugrīva then entered Kişkindha cave and was crowned as the king. After this, (during the four months of rainy season), Rāma and Lakṣmaṇa stayed in a cave on Mt. Mālyavān (or Malaya?) or Prasravaṇa hill, (which was quite close to Kişkindhā).

The rainy season was over. Earlier, Sugrīva had told Rāma, that he had seen Rāvaṇa along with Sītā crossing Paṃpā and going in southward direction. He had also shown Rāma some of the ornaments, which Sītā, while being dragged by Rāvaṇa, had dropped down towards *vānarās*, sitting and watching from the hillock below. Sugrīva now tells Rāma that he still doesn't know the exact place where Rāvaṇa lives or about his prowess and resources or about his parentage. In spite of this admission of ignorance on his part, Sugrīva sends four groups of his army of *vānarās* in four different directions. It is obvious that since he had seen Rāvaṇa carrying Sītā southwards, he employs more efficient and intelligent *vānarās* like Añgada (Vālin's son), Tāra and Hanumat to search for Sītā in the south direction.

Sugrīva explains that earlier when he was threatened by Vālin, who was chasing him, Sugrīva had to run from place to place to save himself from Vālin and that is how he had acquired the geographical knowledge of 'the whole Earth'. Quite naturally and rightly, Sugrīva's geographical conception has been questioned by scholars.

D.R. Mankad[7], who critically edited the *Kiṣkindhākaṇḍa* of Vālmīki *Rāmāyaṇa,* is of the opinion that the four *sargās* (39, 40, 41, 42), where Sugrīva's knowledge of geography is detailed out are a later addition. Also in *sarga* 40 only a few *ślokās* (1-8, 9-11and 21-26) must have been by Vālmīki. All the other *ślokās* must be a later addition. Scholars question as to why Sugrīva sends his four divisions of *vānarās* in all four directions, if he had already seen Rāvaṇa going in south direction? I feel that probably this could be an attempt of these composers to list out even the imagined regions of the earth and of the then known world as well as the conception of the division of the globe and delineate the world geography based on the lotus earth theory of that period. We will consider here only the places the south bound search party would come across in somewhat detail and the rest will only be referred to. *Uttarakāṇḍa*[8], while delineating Vālin's prowess, tells us that Vālin everyday visited all four *samudrās* including *'Dakṣiṇa samudra'* (and not *'Dakṣiṇa Sāgara'*?). This again appears to be a delineation based on the fanciful geographical conception of the earth of the rāmāyaṇic period, comprising of four *dvīpās* and four *samudrās*. (In addition, words like *saptadvīpeśvaro, saptadvīpādhipa* and earth as *saptadvīpāsamudrānta* also appear in *Uttarakāṇḍa*) *Kiṣkindhākaṇḍa*[9] however mentions that to the immediate south of Kiṣkindha Hanumat's search party comes across an arid zone, where sage Kaṇḍu lived and it is specifically mentioned that the whole region had become useless for any kind of life to susatain as a result of sage Kaṇḍu's curse. Then, it is only after a long search further to the south but still in Vindhya itself that the *vānarās* come across *Ṛkṣabila*, in the south-west direction. This suggests that there was no *'Dakṣiṇa samudra'* (or *Dakṣiṇa Sāgara*) to the immediate south of Kiṣkindhā.

Kiṣkindha and the geographical knowledge of Sugrīva

To the group going towards south, Sugrīva gives following instructions, saying, "As you turn towards the south, (of Kiṣkindhā) you will see the great Mt. Vindhya with thousand peaks. You will then come across rivers Narmada, Godavari, Mahanadi, Kṛṣṇavenī, Mekala and Utkala *deśas*, Daśārṇa *deśa*, Ābhrayantī, the city of Avantī (Ujjayini), Vidarbha, Ṛṣṭika, beautiful Mahīṣaka, Matsya, Kaliṅga, Kauśika, Daṇḍakāraṇya, Godavari, Andhra, Puṇḍra, Cola, Paṇḍya, Kerala, Mt. Ayomukhā, river Kaveri, Mt. Malaya, river Tāmraparṇī, Mt. Mahendra with its own arm planted into the 'south sea', and then, you will see on the other shore of that sea, an island quite inaccessible and that is the place (Laṅkā) where Rāvaṇa lives. In that 'south sea', which surrounds Laṅkā lives a *rākṣasī* (a demoness) named Aṅgārakā who guards Laṅkā. The expanse of the 'south sea' is 100 *yojanās* and beyond which you shall see mountains like Puṣpavān, Sūryakāntā, Vaidyuta and Kuñjara. After that is the home of sage Agastya, the city named Bhogāvatī of *sarpās* (Nāgās?), Mt. Ṛṣabha, [with abundance of *'candana'* (sandalwood) trees], guarded by Rohita *gandharvās*. After that comes the end of the Earth".

If we look at the place names in all the four directions (*sargās* 4:39-42) it can easily be noticed that the places in the south direction are admixed to a great extent. The listed places are not in the order of their natural locations. Also they do not present a coherent picture of any region from a geographical point of view. The order of place names towards the west is not so incorrect, and then comes the order of the place names in the east. Places and sites listed as situated to the north of Kiṣkindha seem to be (mostly) located towards the north thus presenting a geographically more or less correct picture[10,11,12]. *Rāmāyaṇa* does not specify the exact locations of many sites of the Rāma-story, Kiṣkindha being no exception. No landmarks can easily be pinpointed. Moreover, because of such chaotic and mixed up geography inherent in the *kāvyā*, Ceylon was conveniently accepted as Laṅkā and Anegundi of Karnataka state in south India was believed to be Vālmīki's Kiṣkindha by laymen and researchers alike. There would be reasons for such incorrect assumptions and geography. Nevertheless, in spite of this chaos we do get some clues from Sugrīva's imperfect knowledge.

Kiṣkindha was inaccessible and was like a hiding place situated deep in the hills. It was from here that Sugrīva sent out four groups of *vānarās* in all four directions and based on his own knowledge instructed them as to how to go about their search (s*argās* 4:39-42). But where was this central point Kiṣkindhā?

Sugrīva says that *vānara* group going towards east (39th *sarga*) will come across rivers Bhāgīrathī, Ganga, Śarayu, Kosi, Son and Videha (North Bihar), Malava, Kaśi-Kosālā, Māgadha-*deśa*, (South Bihar) Puṇḍra, Añga, Mandara-*parvata* (near Girivrajā), Gṛdhrakūṭa *parvata* (in Bihar) etc. (A few doubtful places are listed here, but the above mentioned places mostly outnumber such doubtful place names) and even today their geographical locations can be identified, e.g. river Son can be located even today. According to Sugrīva, *vānarā*s would come across river Son towards the east (of Kiṣkindhā) can only mean that Kiṣkindha should be located to the west of river Son. Similar argument can be extended for many places in the other three directions as well. If Kiṣkindha were near Anegundi in south India it would come to the south of river Son, and not to its west, as per Sugrīva's instructions. Similarly, Kiṣkindhā, according to his geographical knowledge should be to the west of Videha, Māgadha i.e. Bihar, and other correctly listed places.

Sugrīva's statement that *vānarās* venturing in the south direction (40th *sarga*) would see Mt.Vindhya, river Narmada, Daṇḍakāraṇya and rivers Godavari and Mahanadi which join the eastern sea, is a clear proof of the fact that Kiṣkindha lay to the north of Vindhya and could not be in south India. There is also a smaller river Mahanadi flowing in M.P. which is a tributary of river Son. Sugrīva might be referring to this Mahanadi, or else the larger

Mahanadi of Orissa and countries Mekala, Utkala, Daśārṇa, Avantī, Vidarbha and Kaliṅga *deśas*. This clearly indicates that Kiṣkindha of *Rāmāyaṇa* must be located towards the north of all the places listed above. In this list however, are also places like Andhra, Puṇḍra, Cola, Paṇḍya, Kerala and river Kaveri !

If Anegundi of Karnataka state in south India were Kiṣkindha of Sugrīva, places like Mt.Vindhya, river Narmada, Daṇḍakāraṇya, Godavari (both), Mahanadi (both), Mekala, Utkala, Daśārṇa, Avantī (Ujjayini), Vidarbha, Matsya and Kaliṅga would be to the north of Kiṣkindhā! Which is not what Sugrīva says.

It is not possible that *vānarās* going to the west of Kiṣkindha would first come across Balhikā and Saurashtra omitting all the places in between. (*sarga:* 41) If Anegundi is Rāmāyaṇic Kiṣkindhā, all the places that Sugrīva listed (e.g. Balhikā, Saurashtra, Avantī, Mt. Meru etc. as westward places would not be to the west of Anegundi-Kiṣkindhā. All those places would be to the north of Anegundi-Kiṣkindhā.

If we examine the list of places *vānarās* venturing in the north direction would come across, (*sarga* 42) it can easily be seen that all those sites are located not only to north of Mt. Vindhya, but to the extreme north in the map of India. If Anegundi were the Rāmāyaṇic Kiṣkindhā, then in this list, according to geographical order, rivers Tungabhadra and Kaveri would come first and then the *vānarās* should be able to see Mt. Sahyadri in Maharashtra and so on. But here again the same question can be posed, was Sugrīva's geographical knowledge so poor? And if it were not so where was Sugrīva's Kiṣkindhā?

D.R. Mankad has examined this question and found the position to be as follows[13] - Out of the eastern places mentioned in the text, the westernmost point is river Son and Yamuna. Out of the southern places, the northernmost point is Mt. Vindhya. Out of the western places the easternmost point is Avantī (Ujjayini) and out of the northern places, the southernmost point is the Śūrasena country. Thus, the central point of this geography seems to be bounded by river Son and Yamuna, Ujjayini, Śūrasena and Vindhya, and naturally, Kiṣkindha should be situated in between these four points, from where Sugrīva had described various other places.

It is now imperative to explore our ancient literature to see what information it provides about Kiṣkindhā, Kiṣkindhāka, Kiskindhya, Kikarava and Kikarva. (a country, *janapada* or city)In this connection, we need to answer questions like, who were the Kiṣkindhakās? Who were the *vānarās* of Vālmīki *Rāmāyaṇa*? And where were their original and later settlements? A common Vidyādhara lineage for both *vānarās* and *rakṣasās*[14] has been suggested. *Bālakāṇḍa* says that the *vānarās* were robust forest dwellers, well aquainted with mountain warfare and were born to Apsarā and Vidyādhara (and also Nāgā and Gandharva) mothers. Thus the verse is

apsarāsu ca mukhyāsu gandharvānām tanūṣu ca |
yakṣapannagakanyāsu ṛkṣavidyādharīsu ca ||[15]

Curiously, *Mārkaṇḍeya Purāṇa* mentions Ketumāla *varṣa* to the west of Mt. Meru (modern Pamir plateau to the north-west of India) and one of the sub-divisions of this is mentioned as Kiṣkiṇḍi-Paṇḍubhūmika, which in medieval period was known to be the Kaśk-Dariyā river delta and people living by Mt. Paṇḍura were called Vidyādharas![16] What connection can this have with *vānarās* of rāmāyaṇic Kiṣkindha ?

As of today, village Anegundi is believed to be the Kiṣkindha of *Rāmāyaṇa.* Anegundi is situated near the city of ancient Vijaynagar, on the banks of river Tungabhadra in Karnataka state. The place name is supposedly a derivation from two words, an (a) + *mandi* meaning Hanumat. At a distance of one kilometre from here the place of Vālin, the site where Rāma shot through seven *sāla* trees, the cave where Rāma rested, are all shown.

On the opposite bank of Tungabhadra a place is shown as a spot where Vālin was killed. A white stone from which white powder issues is taken to be remnants of the bones of Vālin. In addition, three hillocks, with names like Sugrīva *'śikhara'* (peak), Tāra and Añgada peaks are shown as evidences for presuming that in rāmāyaṇic times Kiṣkindha was located here.[17, 18, 19] But, in fact *Rāmāyaṇa* does not refer to Tungabhadra at all[20]. *Rāmāyaṇa* suggests that Sugrīva's Kiṣkindha was not very far from Janasthāna in Daṇḍakāraṇya, which extended only slightly to south of Mt. Vindhya. Was Vālmīki's Kiṣkindha in Karnataka state of south India or in the eastern region of Mt.Vindhya? It must be remembered that the possible locations of rāmāyaṇic sites should be looked for in relation to each other, as much as possible and not in isolation.

D.R. Mankad has stated after an exhaustive study that the purāṇic tradition knew Kişkindha to have been situated in the Vindhyan region, to the north of river Narmada[21]. *Bṛhatsaṃhitā* tells us that Kişkindha was a *deśa* (country) to *'āgneya'* (south-east) of Bhāratvarśa/Āryāvarta. It was a *pīṭha* of the goddess named Tārā' (Tārā was *vānara* king Vālin's wife). The *āgneya* (south-east) direction as given in Purāṇās must be according to *Mārkaṇḍeya Purāṇa*, which places *Kişkindhyā* in its *pūrva–Dakşiṇa pada* of the *kūrma*, meaning *āgneya* (south-east) [22,23,24]. *Mārkaṇḍeya Purāṇa* says that Kişkindhāka was a name of a janapada living in Vindhyas to the north of Narmada[25]. Monier Williams[26] suggested that Kişkindha must be situated in Odra *deśa. Mahābhārata* explains, that Sahadeva in his expedition of the south had conquered Kişkindha associated with Odra *deśa.* Odra people have been referred to along with Utkala, Mekala, Kaliṅga and Andhra people[27].

Prācina Sthalakośa mentions that Kişkindhāka was a *janapada* of Mt. Vindhya and had its place in the watershed area to the north of river Narmada (*Brahmā, Matsya, Vāyu* and *Mārkaṇḍeya Purāṇa*). All the *janapadās* with which Kişkindhāka has been collectively referred to were on the northern slope of Mt.Vindhya[28]. This information also clearly suggests that the rāmāyaṇic Kişkindha must be situated on the northern slope of Mt. Vindhya.

According to *Purāṇās,* 'Kikarva' was another name of Kişkindhāka *janapada* of 'southern India'[29] and it must be noted that this 'southern India' was to the north of Mt. Vindhya. *Mahābhārata* also tells us that Ikşvāku king Sagara had conquered many a communities, Kişkindhakās being one such community[30]. Here it should be remembered that the empire of Ikşvāku king Sagara had never spread to the south of Mt. Vindhya. Later, in the times of *Mahābhārata* Kişkindha was under the rule of Mainda and Dvivida (brothers of Tārā-Vālin's wife) and Sahadeva had conquered this area during his 'southern' expedition[31]. *Vāmana Purāṇa* informs us that the country called 'Kikarava' was situated in Vindhyan ranges[32], the corroboration of which comes from *Varāha*

Purāṇa[33] which lists Kikarava with the *janapadās* of Vindhyamūla mountain, indicating that Kiṣkindha must be located within the Vindhyan ranges.

Varāhamihira (sixth century) says that Kiṣkindha is to the north-east of Ujjayini[34]. *'Vālmīki Rāmakośa'* similarly mentions that Kiṣkindha was to the north of Abhravanti or Avantī (Ujjayini) or to the east of Avantī[35]. Does it not then mean that Kiṣkindha was to the north-east of Ujjayini? Rājaśekhara says that Kiṣkindha was to *āgneya* (south-east) of Pāñcāla *deśa* pointing out to the same conclusion that it was situated on the northern slope of Mt. Vindhya[36]. However, these references from ancient literature have not been considered by some scholars while suggesting a site for Sugrīva's Kiṣkindhā. A few examples are like these: D.R. Bhandarkar[37] suggests that the village named 'Mandor' near Jodhpur in Rajasthan was believed to be a place where Mandodarī's father Mayāsura dwelled. Twenty-four km from this village is another village named 'Kekind'. Two stone inscriptions (of A.D. 1176 and A.D. 1230) found in the nearby area inform us that an old name of 'Kekind' was 'Kiṣkindhā', and also that the name Kekind may be a corrupted form of Kiṣkindhā. However, Bhandarkar suggests that Anegundi, a place on the banks of river Tungabhadra in Karnataka state, should be identified with rāmāyaṇic Kiṣkindhā. One river, a tributary of Tungabhadra, is called Paṃpā and a hill nearby is named Ṛṣyamūka. Two inscriptions of A. D. 873 and another of thirteenth century support this assumption, Bhandarkar opines[38].

B.C. Law in his geographical essays writes about Kiṣkindhakās, 'It is doubtful that they are identified with the people of Kiṣkindha mentioned in *Rāmāyaṇa*, for Kiṣkindha of *Rāmāyaṇa* was situated far below in south India'[39].

P.V. Kane[40] opines that Kiṣkindhā-*guphā* (cave) referred to by Patañjali[41] and by Vyāsa in *Mahābhārata*[42] should be the same as Kiṣkindhā-*nagara* (city) and should be identified with the city of modern Anegundi.

S.M. Ali[43] says that Kiṣkindha was an important place from political as well as military point of view. However, according to him it was situated on the main road crossing the Khāndva plain between rivers Narmada and Tapi. All such sites for Kiṣkindha are unacceptable for various obvious reasons. N.V. Rao has rightly pointed out that there was an abundance of *sāla* trees which have gained maximum importance in the *Kiṣkindhākaṇḍa*. Kiṣkindha therefore cannot be at Anegundi in south India.

It was M.V. Kibe[44] who first pointed out that if we go according to Sugrīva's order of listed place names, Rāmāyaṇic Kiṣkindha is situated to the north of river Narmada. He cites *Matsya* and *Vāyu Purāṇās* supporting his opinion, saying that Kiṣkindha is associated with Maikal range and should be searched for near Bilaspur in Madhya Pradesh. His theory actually overthrows the belief, popular among laymen and a few scholars alike, that Anegundi was Sugrīva's Kiṣkindhā. The present author, however, beyond a point cannot agree with Kibe's Bilaspur theory for Kiṣkindhā, as will be discussed later. M.V. Kibe says that a village named 'Kandho' situated on the northern slope of Mt. Vindhya at a distance of 94 miles (140 km) from Citrakūṭa or Sutīkṣṇa's hermitage is Kiṣkindha of *Rāmāyaṇa*.

Pāṇinī and Patañjali[45] say that Kiṣkindha was a *janapada* near Gandikā *deśa* that was outside the boundaries of Āryāvarta. However, V.S. Agrawala[46] has suggested that Patañjali might have referred to some other *janapada* from Uttar Pradesh as 'Kiṣkindhā'. Agrawala conclusively says that Kiṣkindha can be identified with a place named 'Khukhundo' near Gaddi (meaning ancient Gabdika) of Champa in Gorakhpur district (u.p.). U.P. Shah suggests that Gandikā (Gabdika) should be identified with the people speaking the Gadaba dialect[47] and that these people must be living in a region close to the region inhabited by Kiṣkindhakās.All the above evidences point to north Vindhyan region.

In this connection the most convincing reference has been cited by N.V. Rao[48] who has drawn our attention to an old play of ancient times. The name of this play is *'Kaumudī mahotsava'*. The writer of this play is unknown/i.e. not mentioned, but is thought to be a woman named Vijjika. The style of writing suggestes that it must have been written in the fifth or sixth century according to most *pundits*. The plot or story of the play is clearly based on historical events of earlier times (i.e. the times of Emperor Candragupta Maurya (B.C. 322-B.C. 185) and Canakya[49].

The story of the drama unfolds in Pāṭaliputra or Kusumapura (modern Patna), the capital of Māgadha (modern Bihar), in the area around Ganga-Son confluence. The hero Kalyāṇavarman is said to have lived in disguise in an inaccessible place called 'Vyādha-Kiṣkindhā' in the vicinity of lake Pampā situated close to the temple or an abode of Caṇḍikā, or goddess Viṅdhyavāsini. There is an appearance of goddess Ekanaṅgā in the drama. In this play, there is also a city named 'Pampā'. N.V. Rao only suggests that the geography of this drama indicates that Rāmāyaṇic Kiṣkindha must be searched for on the northern slopes of Mt. Vindhya. He however did not try further to identify the exact geography of the scenes of action in the drama with places in modern geography, and yet he suggested that the geography of the drama could point at the location of rāmāyaṇic Kiṣkindhā. D.P. Mishra[50] has reviewed the scholarly studies carried out to identify Kiṣkindhā. He notices the mention of *Vyādha-Kiṣkindha* in the play *Kaumudī mahotsava*. He believes that it was the territory of aborigines, like the Pūrikās, the Daśārṇas, the Śabarās of the Vindhyas, and still says that, 'This Kiṣkindha can be easily recognised to be the same as that of *Rāmāyaṇa* and is to be located near modern Malkangiri (Matangagiri), i.e. somewhere at a spot where the boundaries of Bastar, western Orissa and northern Cirkars meet in a valley', as rāmāyaṇic Kiṣkindha was situated in a valley, he argues. But in fact his site for Kiṣkindha is not the one amidst numerous caves and rock shelters. Rai Krisnadas[51] suggests that Mahadeo *pahada* to the south of Bhopal (in district Hoshangabad, M.P.) might have been the *vānara* kingdom of Kiṣkindhā. This site is in Vindhya (or Mt. Ṛkṣa), and to support his theory, he points at places like Bandarabhan, Bankheri etc. in the vicinity. Rai Krisnadas mentions the play *Kaumudī mahotsava* but does not connect the geography of the drama with the abode of Viṅdhyavāsini in actual geography indicated therein. Moreover, his Kiṣkindha is far away from Mt. Citrakūṭa. U.P. Shah[52] in his critical edition of *Kiṣkindhākaṇḍa* refers to *Kaumudī mahotsava* but in conclusion only states though rightly, that Kiṣkindha of Vālmīki was not in Karnataka but to the north of Vindhya, while D.R. Bhandarkar[53], in spite of admission of the fact that these places from this drama are not far from Mt. Citrakūṭa in Banda district in U.P., opines that Rāmāyaṇic Kiṣkindha was far to the south at Anegundi in Karnataka.

In this scenario it is now imperative for our study to identify the places of the scenes of action of the drama with corresponding places in modern geography and further to examine whether the sites identified have any literal or geographical justification for a claim for Rāmāyaṇic Kiṣkindha region, and this has not been done by the above mentioned or other scholars before. The general scene of the drama is the Vindhyan range, to the north of river Narmada and the story in addition also suggests that the hiding place of the exiled prince must have been near Māgadha territory. Paṃpā city and a temple of goddess Viṅdhyavāsini are also important places in the play.

Viṅdhyavāsini Devī

This goddess, mentioned in *'Devī Bhāgavata'*, was a celebrated deity of ancient India and her popularity had crossed the geographical limits of her actual location. The ancient temple of Viṅdhyavāsini [topo-sheet # 63 K/4+8] is situated in the vicinity of Mirzapur in U.P. as was observed by Cunningham during his surveys[54] (see map 1) .

Imperial Gazetteer (volume IX)[55] informs us that when the headman of the Bundela Thakur tribe offered himself to goddess Viṅdhyavāsini, from the drops of his blood that fell on the goddess, his son was born. This local legend is popular in Bundelkhand (including the districts of Jalau, Jhansi, Hamirpur and Banda). Viṅdhyavāsini is supposed to be the daughter of Yaśoda, meaning, she is Śri Kṛśṇa's sister and the goddess is also named Kauśikī[56]. The goddess was specially adored by the *'ṭhuga'* people (bandits). An animal fair takes place annually in the temple area and is called 'Trikona *yatra*' for the three goddesses namely Viṅdhyavāsini or Vindhyeśvarī, Mahākālī or Cāmuṇḍā, and Aṣṭabhujā or Kāli *khoh*. This fair is very popular amongst the locals and pilgrims come from faraway lands to attend it. This whole information about the area around the temple of Viṅdhyavāsini should be further analysed and scrutinised. Mirzapur area seems to be the most probable region for the location of Kiṣkindha as is indicated by the geographical location of this temple as well as other confirming evidences discussed below. *'Imperial Gazetteer of India- Mirzapur'* (Uttar Pradesh, Benaras division)[57] provides very useful information as follows, which must be considered in this connection.

Mirzapur is situated in U.P. between Kaśi or Vārāṇasi (Banaras) and Prayāga (Allahabad) and to the south of both these cities. To the north of Mirzapur are Jaunpur and Banaras, to the east is western Bihar, to the west is Allahabad and to the south of Mirzapur lies district Sonbhadra (U.P.), Reva and Sidhi districts of north-eastern M.P. and Surguja and Korea districts of Chhattisgarh. Mirzapur was known to Ptolemy by the name 'Sagala'[58], as has been recorded by R.C. Majumdar, who compiled the classical accounts of all such travellers. Mirzapur earlier was the capital city of Korea district of Chhattisgarh. The eastern parts of Mirzapur are hilly with many table-lands (topo-sheet #63L/9+13). The valley of river Son spreads to the south of Mirzapur. The main rivers of the landmass are Ganga and Son. *Sāla, Mahuā, Khairā*, Bamboo and *Āsana* are the main trees in the thickly forested land of south Mirzapur and Sonpur areas, rich with wild life including the tiger[59].

At earlier times the south Ganga plain were under the control of Bhāra people. To the west of Mirzapur city, at eight km is a small town called 'Bindhyācalā', with the temple of goddess Viṅdhyavāsini, on a hill nearby. The town of Bindhyācalā was included within the circuit of the ancient city of Paṃpāpura which was the ancient capital of the Bhāra people (near Bindhyācalā). (see map 1). Here one finds extensive occurrence of the remains of ancient city of Paṃpāpura in Bindhyācalā [topo-sheet # 63 K/4+8 and # 63 K/12+16].

The local belief is that there were 150 temples in and around Paṃpāpura. *'Imperial Gazetteer'*[60] informs us that the stone images found there are not of typical Hindū (Aryan?) style, but indicate an aboriginal style. This *Gazetteer* also provides a detailed description and information about Mirzapur city. It tells us that except the south Ganga plain, the rest of this country is hilly with numerous table lands. The Kaimur range, valley of river Son, the hills in Son-valley and Singrauli basin are the physical divisions of Mirzapur. The hills of Mirzapur and Banaras are denuded due to exhaustive axing down of the jungles, but South Mirzapur and Sonpur have some forested land. To the east of Mirzapur are situated the Chunar hills (Cakora *parvata* or *Caraṇādrī* of ancient times). Once beyond these hills was the settlement of Cero people. Some cave paintings found in Kaimur hill range are thought to be around 3000 years old. One of them depicts a rhino and a hunter. This suggests that Chunar area in ancient times must have been an extensive marshy land with thick forests and heavier rainfall. At this date, a vast landmass to the immediate south of Chunar is a 'stoney waste' to the north of river Tons (topo-sheet # 63 G/12+16)

In *Baburnama*[61], Babar writes that near Cunar hills animals like lion, elephants, wild buffalos and even rhinos could be easily seen. Places like Bhadohi, Barhar etc. in the south Ganga plain still carry the marks of old and rich culture of Bhāra people. If more exhaustive archaeological studies and excavations are carried out in this area of south Ganga plain, it may bring to light a shrouded part of ancient geography, culture and history of north India.

A small place called 'Kindiya' is identified with modern Shahajahanpur of Rohilkhand. Kindiya was locally called 'Kanta'. Yule[62] says that this same Kindiya or Kanta is identified with modern Mirzapur on the banks of Ganga. Is Shahajahanpur then same as Mirzapur?

District Gazetteer of Mirzapur[63] informs us that near the confluence of rivers Ganga and Ujla is a place called 'Kāntit',- which is also near Mirzapur and near Bindhyācalā, where one finds innumerable marks of ancient Bhāra culture in the form of remains of ancient constructions and old forts. Interestingly enough, to the east of Mirzapur, at a distance of 15 km, is a place called Bharpura (topo-sheet # G44-Q;#63 K/12; #63 K/16). The above mentioned Gazetteer also notes that the Gaharvar rulers had set their capital city at Paṃpāpura which was near Kāntit. This whole information is of immense value for the present study of the geography of *Rāmāyaṇa*, and to get closer to the geographical position of Sugrīva's Kiṣkindhā. Sardar Vinchurkar's travel account *'Tīrthayātrāprabandh'* (ed. by Lele) [64] cites the following *ślokās*-

jānhavī sarvataḥ puṇyā brahmahatyānivārinī |
tatrāpitraviśeṣeṇa yatra vindhyenasangatā ||

Translated as: River Bhāgīrathī Ganga is holy and offers salvation everywhere, but much more so at a site where it meets Mt.Vindhya.

This information suggests that the 'especially holy site'could be Mirzapur. It is so, because it is in this Chunar-Mirzapur area that river Ganga reaches her southern-most point, from where it takes a north-easterly course to pass by Vārāṇasi. At a nearby spot i.e. near the hills of Chunar, it turns towards the north touching the foothills of Chunar, or the mountain touches the feet of river Ganga, hence the name 'Caraṇādrī', (modern Chunar (see map 1)) '*Skanda Purāṇa* mentions 'Moharapura' at a distance of 22 km from Mirzapur. A.B.L. Awasthi in his book states that at 14 miles from Bindhachala is a place called 'Moherakapura', a place in Dharmāraṇya. He suggests that ancient Kāntipura in U.P. is same as modern Mirzapur. Kāntipurī which was the capital city of Kanti *janapada* mentioned in the epics and *Purāṇās* is identified with modern Mirzapur, Awasthi opines[65]. Kāntipurī is same as Kāntit near Mirzapur and this Kāntit was the capital city of *janapadās* Kanti and Kosālā. (Is the name 'Kāntit' a remembrance of name 'Kiṣkindhā'?). Now, all these evidences suggest that Kiṣkindha of *vānarās* must have been located somewhere in the same area in the vicinity of Mirzapur. Thus it can be logically inferred that the actual geographical location of Kiṣkindha of Vālin and Sugrīva was in south Ganga plain, in Kaimur arm of Mt. Vindhya, somewhere near Mirzapur in the hilly region. If we identify rāmāyaṇic Kiṣkindha with a region to the immediate south of Mirzapur, it also fits well with the purāṇic indications for the land of the Kiṣkindhakās.

It can now be imagined that, at Pañcavaṭī, after realising the fact that Sītā could not be found near Citrakūṭa, Godavari or anywhere in Janasthāna, Rāma with Lakṣmaṇa might have descended from Pañcavaṭī (Reva upland) in southern direction, passed through Krauñcavana (Kahenjua forest) and after getting tipped by Kabandha walked towards north to reach Paṃpā, Mataṅgavana, Ṛṣyamūka as places near Kiṣkindhā. This route must have been from the south-eastern end of Reva plateau, but through the jungles of the plains, i.e. from the northern border of Sidhi district penetrating into Mirzapur district (see map 2).

Kiṣkindhā, described as a cave city[66,67], only means that it must have been a settlement in and around a group of caves situated safely amidst hills making it nearly inaccessible. It might have been at a strategic point as political and military tactics had to be practiced by tribal people of ancient times. It might be for these reasons that it was made the capital or the main dwelling place of *vānara* tribe. We cannot, however, trace any lake or a river bearing the name 'Paṃpā' in modern geography. Nevertheless, it will not be out of place to assume, that a lake or a river bearing the name 'Paṃpā' near the ruined capital Paṃpāpura or somewhere to the south of Mirzapur then existed, which dried up later due to natural causes. (Ṛṣyamūka hill similarly cannot be identified at the moment.)

Vānarās can only be the aborigines living in groups of caves to the south of Mirzpur in rāmāyaṇic times (or from times immemorial as well?). Will it be possible to identify at least approximately the geographical position of the *vānara's* domain (or of Kiṣkindhakās) is a problem to be solved finally. In this connection it must be noted that although Mirzapur area was never thought by scholars to be the *vānara* domain, this area with caves, numerous rock shelters and perennial water sources within easy reach was noticed by researchers as an ideal site for human occupation at any stage of human development. Some archaeological studies have therefore been carried out in the past, in Mirzapur district.

Cockburn[68] had discovered Palaeolithic tools from Singrauli basin of Mirzapur district (1883). Mirzapur district has the northern alluvial plain of the Ganges, table land between Vindhyan to Kaimur ranges and the valley of river Son. It is in the rocky-craggy valley of Son abounding in caves and large rock shelters that rock paintings are chiefly found. They are mentioned in the Imperial gazetteer of India and also in district gazetteer of Mirzapur, based on Cockburn's research[69,70].

Some rock-paintings, noticed by K.N. Dikshit, from three different places of the Mirzapur district appeared in the report of the Lucknow museum in 1918 as memoirs of ASI no. 24, 1998.

Raisahib Manoranjan Ghosh[71], the then curator of Patna museum has given a detailed account of his observations of the primitive rock-paintings, stone implements and other antiquities (including inscriptions of later times) found in Mirzapur and three other places from M.P. In Mirzapur district he found at Likhunia *dari,* a waterfall nearby and rock shelters of large size with paintings and similarly at a place called Kohbar. At Bhaldaria he found a ninth century inscription and three other rock shelters with paintings, and also a large pool with perennial stream by the side of a rock shelter. All these were situated amongst picturesque surroundings of the lower Garai river near Ahraura, which itself is about 40-50 km to south-east of Mirzapur. Other sites of Vijaygarh fort (construction attributed to Koles, an aboriginal tribe) and Mahararia are close to Robertsganj, which is 36 km to south of Ahraura (see map 1). To the south of Ahraura is a place called Madhupur, which reminds us of Sugrīva's leisure garden or *Mahuā* grove 'Madhuvana'. To the north of Ahraura is a place called Mahuabari. The above mentioned archaeological studies carried out so far have revealed that Mirzapur district presents ideal conditions for a stone-age life similar to that of the tribe of *vānarās.* Mirzapur district certainly invites more exhaustive study involving multidisciplinary approach.

To summarise, Vālmīki *Rāmāyaṇa* has provided us with geographical information in the testimony of *vānara* king Sugrīva. We have also explored the area around Mirzapur, Bindhachal, Paṃpāpura, Chunar and Viṅdhyavāsini temple, using for this search the tools of both ancient literature and findings of later times recorded in gazetteers and have arrived at the most believable conjecture regarding the actual geographical location and identification of Rāmāyaṇic Kiṣkindhā.

The present studies have narrowed down the Kiṣkindha region to the southern part of Mirzapur district in south Ganga plain, on the northern slopes of Kaimur ranges, where *sāla* forests dominated. This region is in the valley of river Son and its northern part. *Vānarās* and *rakṣasās* were both aboriginals and *vānarās* are described by Vālmīki as cave-dwellers with most primitive way of life, their food being mostly the forest produce. They seem to have had love for *mahuā* liquor. They fought only with their teeth and nails, stones and parts of *sāla* tree, all being their primitive weapons. Vānarās were experts in mountain warfare (*'parvatayodhinaḥ'*). This suggests that the tribals in this area should be studied with all the aspects including tribal migrations and settlement patterns in this area.

We cannot pass a judgement on the validity of the geographical knowledge of Vālmīki or that of Sugrīva as there have been plenty of later additions mostly borrowed from *Purāṇās* as D.R. Mankad[72] has rightly suggested. Thus, mistakes are not unexpected. In *Kiṣkindhākaṇḍa* we also find many names and descriptions of rivers, mountains and countries based on the purāṇic concept of the division of the globe (*'saptadvīpā vasumatī'*) which seems to have appeared later in *Rāmāyaṇa*. Examples of this are Uttara-*samudra,* Yamā's capital, Vaḍavānala etc. It may be granted that Sugrīva'*s* knowledge of geography was faulty but still it is not necessarily a thing to be ignored and discarded totally. It can be argued that the same imperfect knowledge can be useful to some extent if analysed carefully.

We have already noticed, in *Kiṣkindhākaṇḍa* maximum confusion, disorder, chaos and incoherency about the places situated in southern direction. This could be due to the following reasons. The epic first travelled and spread through oral tradition to a maximum extent towards south. The places described in *Rāmāyaṇa* therefore were appropriated more by south and southern culture and were given new geographical locations. This went on for several centuries. Thus, places to the far south of Mt. Vindhya were listed and included in Sugrīva's list. To add to this, new sites were 'found' in south India and adored as rāmāyaṇic sites and Rāmāyaṇic names were attached to them. Such changes (additions and may be omissions also) were made in *Rāmāyaṇa* and such corruptions were taking place up to the fifth and sixth centuries as well. The same thing still goes on. Epic *Rāmāyaṇa* has crossed the boundaries of India and its appropriation and popularity has reached countries and lands far away from its origin e.g. there is 'Ayodhya' in south-east Asian countries and there is 'Laṅkā' in Ceylon. *Rāmāyaṇa* has many versions within our country itself. Thus if we want to know the 'original' *Rāmāyaṇa*, we cannot start from stories and versions that are prevailing in the faraway lands. It should be on priority to examine minutely what the epic itself (with its corruptions) has to say about the Rāma story; and even then, 'we may still be far away from the original text', as D.R. Mankad has said[73].

References: *Kiṣkindhākaṇḍa* of *Rāmāyaṇa*

1. 7:6:1-59 -By (Prakshipta sarga south recension 16:27-39), 7:36:35
2. *'Gīrvāṇalaghukośa'* p. 141, 158
3. 3:6:16
4. 4:29:1
5. 4:25:37
6. 4:26:1
7. D.R. Mankad: 'Introduction to *Kiṣkindhākaṇḍa* of Vālmīki *Rāmāyaṇa*', c.e. Baroda, (1965), p.35
8. 7:34:23-31
9. 4; 47:7-12
10. 4:40:17-29
11. 4:41:7-45
12. 4:42:6-49
13. D.R. Mankad: op.cit. p.46 (XLVI)
14. Romila Thapar: *'Exile and the Kingdom'* (1978), p.14, 15
15. 1:16:5
16. *'Prācina Sthalakośa',* p: 582, 583
17. *'Tirthasār',* p.380 (quoted by S. Chitrav, *'Prācina Sthalakośa'* 1, p.495)
18. *'Prācina Sthalakośa'* p.494, 495
19. *'Imperial Gazetteer of India',* vol. 13: p.235
20. 'Vālmīki *Rāmāyaṇa*'
21. D.R. Mankad: op.cit. (1965), LVIII p.158
22. Varāhamihira: *'Bṛhatsaṃhitā',* 14:10
23. *'Padma Purāṇa', Adi.*17:210
24. *'Matsya Purāṇa',* 113:53
25. *'Mārkaṇḍeya Purāṇa',* 55:18
26. Moniar Williams: (quoted by *'Prācina Sthalakośa'* p. 494)
27. *'Mbh'. Āraṇyakaparvan.*48:18
28. *Prācina Sthalakośa* p. 494
29. Ibid. p.488 also quoted by S.M.Ali p.168

30. *'Harivaṃśa Sāgaracaritam'*: 1: Adhyāya 10, F.N. no. 210, vol. I and II, c.e. BORI, Poona (ed. 1969/1971)
31. *'Mbh'. Sabhāparvan.* 31:17-By, *Digvijayaparvan*: 2:28, *Pariśiṣṭa* 1:13, 14
32. *'Vāmana Purāṇa'* 14:54, (quoted by *Prācina Sthalakośa* p.488 and S.M. Ali p.168)
33. S. Chaudhari: *'Index to place names in the Varāha Purāṇa'*, (1993) 3
34. Varāhamihira: *'Bṛhatsaṃhitā'*, (quoted by Narla V. Rao, (1990) p.71
35. Ramakumar Rai: *'Vālmīki Rāmakośa',* (1965), (vol. 1:4:41:10); (vol. 1:4:2:14) (Chaukhamba Sanskrit Series, Vārāṇasi)
36. Rajshekhara: (quoted by N.V. Rao, p. 70, 71)
37. D.R. Bhandarkar: *Jha comm.* vol. (1937) p.52
38. *'Imperial Gazetteer',* vol. V. p.373
39. B.C. Law: *'Geographical Essays',* (1937) vol. 1
40. P.V. Kane: JBBRAS, 27:38
41. Patañjali 1:445, 3:96
42. *'Mbh'.Sabhāparvan.* 3:96:1-405, 31:17
43. S.M. Ali: *'The Geography of the Purāṇās'* (1965), p. 168
44. M.V. Kibe: *'Location of Laṅkā'* (1947) p.13, 26
45. Pāṇinī and Patañjali (quoted by U.P. Shah (1975) p. 38)
46. V.S. Agrawala: *'India as known to Pāṇinī'* (1956), p.76
47. U.P. Shah: op.cit. (1975) p.38
48. N.V. Rao: Prologue to his play *'Sītā Josyam'* (1990) p.70, 71
49. Shakuntala R. Shastri: *'Kaumudī mahotsava'* (1952) pp. 25-32
50. D.P. Mishra: 'The Location of 'Kiṣkindhā' *'The Search for Laṅkā'* (1985) p.49 Agam Kala Prakashan, Delhi
51. Rai Krisnadas: *'Rām vanavās ka Bhūgol': Ṛṣyamūka-Kiṣkindhāki Bhaugolic Awasthiti'* Nagarī Pracharini Patrika, 52:4 (quoted by U.P. Shah, op.cit.p.38)
52. U.P. Shah: op.cit.p.36
53. D.R. Bhandarkar: 'Daṇḍakāraṇya', Jha Comm. vol. (1937) pp.47-57, p. 51 footnote 1
54. A. Cunningham: ASIR 1974-75, 75-76 vol. XIII (1904) p.17, 19
55. *'Imperial gazetteer of India'*, vol. 9
56. *'Bhāratiya Sanskṛti Kośa',* (ed. Mahadevshastri Joshi) vol. 8: p.649 *'Imperial Gazetteer'* of Mirzapur, U.P. –Banaras Division (19....)
57 *'Imp. Gazetteer of India'*, (1911) XXVII. (Special issue on Mirzapur)
58. R.C. Majumdar: *'The classical Accounts of India'* (1960), p.372 Firma K.L. Mukhopadhyay Publication, Calcutta.
59. B.C. Law: *'Historical Geography of Ancient India'*, 1954, p.134
60. *'Imperial Gazetteer of India'*, (1911), special issue of Mirzapur XXVII
61. *'Baburnama'* (Quoted in Imp. Gazetteer 1909)

62. Yule: (Quoted by *'Prācina Sthalakośa'*, p.488)
63. *'District Gazetteer of Mirzapur'* vol.XXVII 1909
64. *'Tīrthayātrāprabaṅdh'* (1885/1964) compiled and ed. By Ganeshshastri Lele: Sardar Vinchurkar's all India travel account (of 1770), Deshmukh and co. Pune
65. A.B.L. Awasthi (1976), (quotes N. Dey, p.56, 131) p.108, p. 124 *'Studies in Skanda Purāṇa'*, Parts 1 and 2, Kailash Prakashan, Lucknow, U.P.
66. 4:29:1,
67. 4:26:1
68. Cockburn: JRAI XVII (1988) pp.57-65
69. *'Imperial Gazetteer of India'* vol. XVII, (1908), pp.89-98; Oxford
70. *'District Gazetteer of India'*, [Mirzapur issue] vol. XXVII (1911), pp. 200-203
71. Manoranjan Ghosh: *'Rock Paintings and other Antiquities of Pre-historic and later times'* Memoirs of ASI, no. 24, (1998) Chapter no. 1 p. 1,2; Chapter 4 pp. 15-20
72. D.R. Mankad op.cit. (1965) p. 38
73. Ibid p. 41

§§§

4

ṚKṢABILA AND DAKṢIṆA SĀGARA

We started our journey from Ayodhya through the pages of the epic. After Sītā was abducted by Rāvaṇa, Rāma and Lakṣmaṇa started searching for her. As advised by Kabandha, they formed an alliance with *vānara* head Sugrīva. Sugrīva then sent four different *vānara* groups from Kiṣkindha in quest of Sītā. *Kiṣkindhākaṇḍa* informs us that the groups that had gone in the east, north and west directions came back frustrated and without any success. We will now see how the most efficient group of *vānarās* including Hanumat, Tāra and Añgada progressed and advanced in their search. *Kiṣkindhākaṇḍa* gives a detailed description of their journey.

The *vānarās*, while wandering through the valleys and hills of Mt. Vindhya and trackless forests of Daṇḍakāraṇya, went in the south-west direction[1], and searched those vast and dense forests, in vain. Exhausted, thirsty and dejected they came across an opening in one of the mountains. The *'bila'* (opening or cave) was overshadowed with greenery and shrubs. It was a very large opening from which a variety of water-drenched birds were coming out. The trees, creepers, shrubs, herbs, grass, moss and ferns around were all moist and seeing that the *vānarās* thought that there could be a source of water inside the *bila*. *Vānarās* entered the *bila*, which was pitch dark and scary inside, with many types of birds and wild animals taking their abode in the cavity. Holding each other's hands they walked through carefully. After they had walked a long distance of about one *yojana* they could see light, and as they walked further they came to a delightful place with *sāla, Tāla, Tamāla* trees and creepers etc. The place was a wonderful woodland. The place had streams and lakes and also was furnished with food and materials necessary for living. They were welcomed by a woman ascetic named Svayaṃprabhā. She told them that Mayāsura, the architect of *dānavās,* was specially trained by Uśanā *maharṣi* and the beautiful *bila* called *Ṛkṣabila* was the craftsmanship of Mayāsura. Then his eyes fell on Hemā *Apsarā* (celestial damsel*)* and both lived there like lovers. Indra, in anger, then killed Mayāsura. Hemā, after handing over this place to Svayaṃprabhā went away. Hemā *Apsarā* had a daughter Mandodarī. Her sons Dundubhī (in the form of a buffalo) and Māyāvī, both were killed by Vālin. *Vānarās* were pleased by the hospitality shown by Svayaṃprabhā, and requested her to show them a way out of *Ṛkṣabila.* She then asked them to close their eyes as she expected that they would be wonderstruck when they see light again. She led them out of the *bila* and after they came out, to their surprise, the scene in front was quite different. Svayaṃprabhā said to them-.

eṣaḥ vindhyo giriḥ śrīmānnānādrumalatāyutaḥ |
eṣaḥ prasravaṇaḥ śailaḥ sāgaroyam mahodadhiḥ ||[2]

'This is Mt. Vindhya, rich with a variety of trees and creepers, and this one is Mt. Prasravaṇa and this is the *'sāgara'* with abundance of water.' After she turned back into the *bila*, *vānarās* with their leader Hanumat sat there worrying, at the foothills of Mt. Vindhya on the shore of that *sāgara*.

From the above description it becomes clear that *Ṛkṣabila* was not a large, deep cave through which one could easily come out unassisted but a huge tunnel with another opening at the opposite end of it. *Ṛkṣabila* is of unique and exceptional importance for the geographical study of *Rāmāyaṇa*, and yet the subject has so far been left unstudied. *Rāmāyaṇa* informs us that, from the second opening of *Ṛkṣabila* the *vānarās* could see Mt. Vindhya, (Obviously as the *bila* or tunnel was situated amidst

Vindhyan ranges), so also Mt. Prasravaṇa and a sea at the foothill of Mt. Vindhya.

An exhaustive study of *Ṛkṣabila* was therefore undertaken. Scholars have so far not studied *Ṛkṣabila* from geographical perspective possibly because of the word *'bila'* that is elusive and most scholars have taken it to mean a bear's hiding place, a burrow or a large and long cave where aborigines of Ṛkṣa *janapada* lived. But we have seen that rāmāyaṇic description itself suggests that *Ṛkṣabila* certainly was a tunnel. Where was it situated? The rāmāyaṇic description of *Ṛkṣabila* itself helps us identify the *bila* with a corresponding site in present geography.

As per the instructions given by Sugrīva, *vānarās* going in the south direction were to see Mt. Vindhya to start with, with its thousand peaks and after that they would come across river Narmada, Godavari, Kṛṣṇavenī etc. according to *Kiṣkindhākaṇḍa*. It can be explicitly said that the *vānarās* led by Hanumat, even before they had come to river Narmada, had entered the *Ṛkṣabila*, a part of Mt. Vindhya itself.

It therefore becomes imperative to examine closely the origin of the name *'Ṛkṣabila'*. Word *'Ṛkṣa'* (and not *'ṛśya'* - meaning deer) has the following meanings in Sanskrit - bear, monkey, deer and as an adjective - 'that which is pierced'[3]! The last meaning of the word *'Ṛkṣa'* is indicative. *Kiṣkindhākaṇḍa* does not say that the *bila* was an abode of any of the above mentioned animals. Monkeys and deer never have a *bila* as their habitat. It is therefore logical to accept the meaning of the word *'Ṛkṣabila'* as a *bila* in Mt. Ṛkṣa. (Here *'bila'* denotes a tunnel, explicitly indicated by its description in the epic as I have explained.) This statement is also supported by numerous evidences from ancient literature. 'Ṛkṣa' was said to be one of the seven *kula-parvatas* (*Purāṇās*). There is no agreement whether Ṛkṣa was central and middle part of Mt. Vindhya or Mt. Pariyātra or Mt. Śuktimat. Ṛkṣa therefore will have to be located with the help of the names of rivers issuing from it. Son, Narmada and Mahanadi have their rise in eastern or Maikal ranges of Mt. Vindhya (see *Sthalakośa* list) in Amarkanṭak hill area. Thirty-two km south of Prayāga, river Tamasā (Tons) joins Ganga. It rises in dist.

Reva and flows towards north-east to join Ganga. It has its origin in Mt. Ṛkṣa it is said. Thus, a mountain in district Reva, where Tons has its origin is Ṛkṣa.

According to *Purāṇās* (e.g. *Vāmana Purāṇa*) the list of rivers having their rise in Mt. Ṛkṣa includes Mandākinī, Citrakūṭa, (synonymous with Mandākinī?) Daśārṇa (Dhasan) Son, Mahanadi, Tamasā (Tons), Pippalāvatī, (or Pippalī) Citrotpalā, Śuktimatī (Ken) as main rivers, (*Prācina Sthalakośa*) along with some unidentified rivers. *Prācina Sthalakośa* therefore considers it logical to suggest that: Mt. Vindhya and Ṛkṣa must be continuous mountains. Ancient literature considers *'vindhyapāda'* to include middle part of the present Mt. Satpura, middle part of Vindhya together with all its eastern parts, (water shade area of Son). Here the Maikal ranges (spread in all directions) come together to the east of Mt. Śuktimat (where river Ken has its rise), all this is Mt. Ṛkṣa.

According to Ptolemy, Ṛkṣavanta or Oxenton was the eastern part of Mt. Vindhya. *Prācina Sthalakośa* has taken this as the most rational view while deciding the location of ancient Mt. Ṛkṣa and therefore concludes, that to the south of river Son, Chota Nagpur, Ramgarh, Surguja and other mountainous areas, all together must have been Mt. Ṛkṣavanta of Ptolemy[5]. *Purāṇās* like *Mārkaṇḍeya Purāṇa* informs that Ṛkṣa *parvata* is considered to be the eastern part of Vindhyan ranges that are to the north of Narmada[6]. Now then, can we identify in actual geography around Mt. Ṛkṣa any such exquisite place answering to the epic description of Svayaṃprabhā's *Ṛkṣabila?*

Where is this *Ṛkṣabila* tunnel? A tunnel of this kind is extremely exclusive. To our astonishment there exists such a tunnel in our country in Chhattisgarh state. It is situated in one of the Vindhyan hills named Ramgarh hill in district Surguja, the northernmost district of Chhattisgarh state (Ramgarh - 23^0 40'N and 82^0 24'E). It is around 34 km south-west of Ambikapur (see maps 1 and 2 and photograph 1).

In south India there are a few large and deep caves near Kotamsar, but they being very narrow are not suitable for human habitation. They are of stalactite-stalagmite type, difficult to enter and one cannot pass through them. Moreover, these caves are situated about 18-65 metres below the ground level. They are not situated in Mt. Vindhya and as these caves do not fulfil most of the conditions of *Ṛkṣabila*, they cannot be accepted as Rāmāyaṇic *Ṛkṣabila*. Near Travankore in Kerala, to the south of Mt. Sahyadri and Mt. Malaya, are sites with names like Svayaṃprabhā *tīrtha*, some caves and also Mt. Vindhya and Mt. Mahendra which are believed to be Rāmāyaṇic sites. But this again is a case similar to showing a site of heap of ashes from Vālin's bones near Anegundi. Also no tunnel exists there, and mount Vindhya cannot be shifted to south India.

Rāmāyaṇic *Ṛkṣabila* was neither a valley nor a bear's hole, nor a cave nor merely a steep ridge, nor *durga* (a fort) as few researchers think. T.P. Iyer[7] identifies *Ṛkṣabila* with the south-west end of Kaimur section of the Vindhyan range terminating near Katangi at the twenty-fourth mile on the Jabalapur-Damoh road. The extraordinary cleft or a ridge through which river Kair enters the Sihora *haveli* to the south, is a narrow knife edge. Iyer believes that Svayaṃprabhā led the *vānarās* up the steep slope to the top of the ridge from where she may have pointed out the *Sāgara* below, formed by river Kair where it joins river Hiran to swell its waters. However, Iyer's identification of *Ṛkṣabila* does not satisfy the peculiar conditions of Rāmāyaṇic *Ṛkṣabila.* This site being in the open and not being a perfect shelter or a through tunnel, a pass at Katangi (near Jabalpur) cannot be accepted as *Ṛkṣabila* of *Rāmāyaṇa*. Moreover, no remains or marks of Rāvaṇa's domain are found in that area, as will be discussed in the following pages.

Researchers like D.R. Mankad, or more recently R.K. Shukla have however expressed an entirely different view regarding the location of Rāmāyaṇic *Ṛkṣabila* and the nature of that *bila* as described by Vālmīki. A few more words therefore are necessary here about this issue, so that the present author's notion becomes clear.

Sugrīva does not mention *Ṛkṣabila*. Hanumat and his search group on their way from Kiṣkindha in south direction, come across *Ṛkṣabila* quite accidentally. Later, they explain about this venture to Saṃpātī, who comes to meet them just outside the other opening of the *bila*. There is no mention of it worthy of note in any of the later books of Vālmīki *Rāmāyaṇa*. Svayaṃprabhā's account of her dwelling place in her own words and the detailed description of the '*bila* 'can be found only at this place in *Kiṣkindhākaṇḍa.*

Kiṣkindhākaṇḍa describes *Ṛkṣabila* as ***'tatastasminbile durge nānāpādapasaṅkule'***[8]. *'durga'* or *'durgama'* means, 'difficult to enter' (*Gīrvāṇalaghukośa*) and not mountain fort as suggested by R.K. Shukla[9]. Supporting this is an evidence from *Yuddhakāṇḍa*[10], where the expanse of water body called *'Dakṣiṇa Sāgara'* which was not easily passable for Rāma's army, is described with adjectives '*sudurgam*' and '*durgamargam*'. Shukla gives an example (from the epic) of another *bila,* Malaya *bila,* which is near Kiṣkindhā, the cave settlement of *vānarās*. In this *bila, dānava* Māyāvī had entered when he was chased by Vālin. D.R. Mankad has said that Māyāvī, the son of Mayāsura, when chased by Vālin, must have run away to his own abode, i.e. in such a *bila*, which was constructed by his father Mayāsura. Therefore, that cave or *Malaya bila* itself was *Ṛkṣabila*, which cannot be far away from Kiṣkindhā[11]. R.K. Shukla gives similar argument and states that Māyāvī fled to a *bila* which had to be near Kiṣkindha and that it was *Ṛkṣabila* where Svayaṃprabhā lived. Both these arguments cannot be accepted for the following reasons.

Rāmāyaṇa, while describing the event, clearly states that after Māyāvī entered the *bila,* which was a cave in Malaya *parvata,* Vālin followed him and he too entered that *bila*. Sugrīva following both reached the entrance and as instructed by Vālin, waited there for a very long period for Vālin to come out of the *bila*, ultimately found instead, blood flowing out from the same opening of the *bila*. Thinking it must be dead Vālin's blood, Sugrīva then fixed a huge boulder at the opening of the cave. He then with a sigh of relief returned to Kiṣkindhā, knowing that there was no other opening for that *bila* in that Malaya hill cave, for anyone to escape and both Māyāvī and Vālin must be lying dead inside. After returning, he even declared himself as the lord of Kiṣkindhā. The description clearly indicates that this Malaya *bila* in Mt. Malaya had only one opening. It was only a long cave but not a through tunnel. As we know, Malaya *bila* was not far from Paṃpā or Ṛṣyamūka hill and was only one *yojana* away from Kiṣkindhā[12].

Rāmāyaṇa also states that this Mt. Malaya was adjoining Mt. Ṛṣyamūka. When Sugrīva's aides had the first glimpse of Rāma and Lakṣmaṇa as well armoured strong men, fearing they could be Vālin's men, had fled from Ṛṣyamūka peak to Malaya peak, as these two peaks were adjoining each other. Hanumat then pacifies Sugrīva saying that (like Mt. Ṛṣyamūka) on this great mountain Malaya also there is no fear from Vālin. The verse is-

malayoyam girivaro bhayam nehāsti vālinaḥ |[13]

We also learn from *Kiṣkindhākaṇḍa* that Ṛṣyamūka was the only safe place for Sugrīva where Vālin could not enter. Sage Mataṅga, having his hermitage in Ṛṣyamūka area, had earlier suffered from the bloodshed of a combat between Vālin and Dundubhī (Māyāvī's brother, Mayāsura's second son). This tussle had taken place near Kiṣkindhā, and Kiṣkindha was only one *yojana* away from Ṛṣyamūka hill. This can be said since Vālin had thrown away dying Dundubhī's body a *yojana* away (word *yojana* used in sports since, i.e. 660 feet away) and the blood from Dundubhī's body had splashed in sage Mataṅga's hermitage, which was in Ṛṣyamūka hill area. Sage Mataṅga had therefore prohibited Vālin from approaching Ṛṣyamūka area. This also means that Ṛṣyamūka hill area with Mataṅgāśrama in it and the adjoining Malaya hill both were at a distance of one *yojana* from Kiṣkindhā.

All this proves that *Ṛkṣabila,* where Svayaṃprabhā lived, and Malaya *bila* of Vālin-Māyāvī-Dundubhī combat arena near Kiṣkindha were two distinct caves of different kind. Malaya *bila* had only one opening while *Ṛkṣabila* had two openings. Both these large *bilas* were in Mt. Vindhya is true indeed. However, it is clear that *Ṛkṣabila* was not near Kiṣkindha but Malaya *bila* was. Both these caves were located far apart from each other.

R.K. Shukla further suggests that *Ṛkṣabila* was really a fort as is clear from the statement of Añgada, who proposed to settle there permanently, as 'the place was incapable of being approached and abounded in viands, with variety and excellence, and drinks etc.', he describes it as

'idam hi māyāvihitam sudurgamam
prabhūtavṛkṣodakabhojyapeyam' |[14]

Here also, '**sudurgamam**' means inaccessible and not a fort. Shukla further argues that Svayaṃprabhā explains that it was (a fort) constructed by Mayāsura[15, 16], but the adjectives used here are '**kāñcanam vanam**' (golden grove) and she describes it as '**yenedam kāñcanam divyam nirmitam bhavanottamam**' \|[17]. Thus *Ṛkṣabila* was a 'very richly decorated plush dwelling place' of Svayaṃprabhā as *Rāmāyaṇa* mentions:

'**papraccha kā tvam bhavanam bilam**' |[18]

Meaning, (Hanumat asks her) who she was and whose dwelling place that *bila* was.

'**śāśvataḥ kāmabhogaśca gṛham cedam hiraṇmayam**' |[19]

Translated as, 'it was a dwelling place, a house, a golden grove with everlasting comforts'. There were no stocks of weapons of any kind inside *Ṛkṣabila* and Svayaṃprabhā was the only human being living there. Thus, it is clear that *Ṛkṣabila* could not have been a fort. Shukla further argues that it was a fort based on the use of the word *'guhā'* in this context; *'guhā'* means a cave but at one place it expressly stands for Kiṣkindhā. He quotes-

'**praviveśa guhām ghorām kiṣkindhām rāmaśāsanāt**' |[20]

Meaning, '(Lakṣmaṇa) entered that scary cave Kiṣkindha at Rāma's command', and therefore, *Ṛkṣabila* was a fort (like Kiṣkindhā) he argues. In my opinion, Kiṣkindha was a cave or *'giri-guphā'*. This essentially means that there were many caves in that mountainous region, which were occupied by tribe of *vānarās*. It was an inaccessible place but that does not make it a 'fort' in the sense in which it is commonly used. *Vānarās* did not have even crude weapons as *Rāmāyaṇa* explicitly describes.Such cave dwellers could not construct forts. In dense forests, the caves are occupied by animals as well. Here the word *'guhā' or 'kandara'* is also used for animal habitat e.g. '**śailakandaraṃśca**'[21], '**śailam bahukandaram**'[22], '**simhaśārdūlajusṭāsca guhāśca**'[23], etc. Kiṣkindha might have been situated at a very strategic place from defence point of view and therefore it was the main dwelling place (or the capital) of *vānara* domain. The concept of 'fort' or 'fort city' or 'city protector fort' could not have existed in times when people lived in caves.

In order to lead the *vānarās* out of the *bila,* Svayaṃprabhā asks them to close their eyes. According to R.K. Shukla this means that *Ṛkṣabila* was a fort as it was provided with an artificial defence in the nature of an elementary maze (through which she could lead them out of the *bila*). The reason for this act of hers has already been given. *Rāmāyaṇa* clearly states that *Ṛkṣabila* was a long tunnel of about one *yojana* in length ('**jagmuryojanamantaram**')[24]. The actual length of Ramgarh tunnel is 135 m or 450 feet and this is closer to its Rāmāyaṇic description (here a *yojana* is used in the sense of a Stadium i.e 660 ft). It could not have been a fort, hundred *yojanās* in length as R.K. Shukla opines[25]. If it were hundred *yojanās* in length, then it could not be a fort and also it will be an extreme exaggeration on the part of poet Vālmīki. Also it will be very easily noticeable if such a long *bila*-fort ever existed anywhere. No doubt, *Ṛkṣabila* (or Ramgarh hill identified with it by the present studies) can be called a natural fort because of its high, straightly cut rocky walls, its inaccessibility in general and its water-logged surroundings, but the description of *Ṛkṣabila* given by Vālmīki of its interiors does not suggest that it was a fort. Ramgarh hill might have been used as a fort in later times, but not when Svayaṃprabhā lived there. *Ṛkṣabila* had a variety of trees, water-holes with fishes and lotus flowers, beautiful sitting arrangements, dwelling places, beds, many pleasure giving materials like perfume stocks, food, warm clothing, etc[26]. It is very clear from the poetically exaggerated description from the epic itself that *Ṛkṣabila* is indicated as a rich dwelling place and could not be a fort, at least not in Rāmāyaṇic times. It is discussed in the following pages and it is suggested here, that Svayaṃprabhā's wonderful home *Ṛkṣabila* can be identified with Ramgarh hill tunnel in Surguja district of Chhattisgarh.

RAMGARH HILLS IN SURGUJA (see maps 1 and 2)

Surguja or Kāntara of ancient times is a vast table land at the northernmost corner of Chhattisgarh and is surrounded by hill ranges from north, east and south directions. The southern boundary of dist. Sidhi (MP) touches the north boundary of Surguja. To the west of Surguja are forest-clad districts of Korea and Shahdol. The forests here are thick and impenetrable and even Mughals were unable to reach Surguja. Its local name is 'Dāndora'. Gondvana is the western part of it, whereas the eastern part, Chota Nagpur, was under the rule of Kols. Until 1613, first Raksel Rajputs and later Ceros were the rulers of this area. In A.D. 1758 however, the Marathas subordinated and brought them under Berar rule.

Chhattisgarh is a state comprising of 16 districts. It lies to the east of Madhya Pradesh. Surguja district is in the north-east region of Chhattisgarh. Surguja is a vast table land, on which are numerous hills and plateaus, locally called '*pat*'[27]. The eastern boundary of Surguja is formed by a long winding range of hills and plateaus called Jamirpat, which touches the borders of Bihar and Jharkhand or Chota Nagpur. Palamau district forms the north-eastern boundary of Surguja. Towards the west of Mainpat plateau and to the south-west of village Lakhanpura, an isolated hill of our interest, namely Ramgarh is situated. It is 160 km from Kharsia railway station on the Bengal-Nagpur railway line (see map 1).

Colonel Ouseley[28], a British officer, was the first one to notice Ramgarh hills in 1848. The place of course was known as 'Kāndā Ghuṭrī' to the locals from ancient times. He described the hill (inclusive of the tunnel and caves) to have formed of sandstone type of rock. 'There is a small spring 'Turrā Panī' of fresh water on one side of the hill. The huge tunnel that pierces through the hill opens on the other side in a valley or a basin, which is extremely picturesque and it would have been a vast lake, but for the tunnel through which that small stream flows', he writes. Inside the tunnel Col. Ouseley had noticed the impressions of tiger's paws. In the forests of Surguja, he found all the animals of India, except the rhinoceros. Col. Ouseley had noticed only one cave in Ramgarh hill with a name 'Sītā-Mārī' (and not 'Sītā-Bengrā'). Dalton[29] in 1865 had found the second cave also. Dalton says that –

'As I am standing at the western (end) of Mainpat, which rises majestically from the plain in successive steps ----- and as the eye follows what so much resembles a long coast, the mind is filled with the idea that the ocean must once have existed, where the Sāl trees now wave and this is strengthened when ---- (words unreadable)----to the isolated bluffs having all the features of the mainland, from which they appear to have been cut off, rising abruptly 2000 (feet) above the plains or appearing in --- from the parallel markings on the face of the rock like ------ batteries protecting the coast.'

The hill of Ramgarh is 13 km to the west of Mainpat. The upper portion of Ramgarh hill is very striking, Dalton reports:

'So regular is its form and so abruptly precipitous are its sides. The hill has two arms and they have joined together to form a straight cut high rocky wall (150 feet high) on the face of the hill and have formed a horse-shoe shaped basin below. The basin as is enclosed by a precipitous high wall would be almost inaccessible, had not nature provided an entrance by a natural tunnel through the stone wall'.

As Dalton imagined, the horse-shoe embraces an acre or two of well wooded valley below. The name of the tunnel was 'Hath-phor'. Both Ouseley and Dalton have described the 'Hath-phor' tunnel to be 136 Metres (450 feet) in length.

V. Ball (1873) has given a detailed description[30] of magnificent and extremely beautiful scenery of Mainpat (that can be viewed from Ramgarh hill-top) as well as that of the tunnel. He says that 'the hill is to the west of Lakhanpur at a distance of 6-7 miles away, near village Khudri'. He describes the tunnel to be just a mile away from the village of Udaypur. He says with certainty, that the tunnel is not man-made as there are no marks of human workmanship there. It is naturally formed by trickling of water through sandstone rock of the hill, over a very long period. It seems he is also highly impressed by the incomparable beauty of the valley in which the tunnel opens. He opines that, originally the two caves on the face of the rock must have been only a nature's creation. He describes the tunnel to run through the same arm of the hill, in which both the caves exist.

Beglar and Cunningham (1882)[31], while describing the tunnel, have stated that the two streams flowing through the horse-shoe shaped valley must have combined together at some remote time, to form one single forceful flow of water that must have created the tunnel in one of the arms of Ramgarh hill. Their description of Ramgarh hill and 'Hath-phor' tunnel is quoted below:

.... 'In addition to the objects of interest already enumerated, Ramgarh hill possesses a natural curiosity in the shape of a tunnel through the spur in which the caves exist. A little rivulet rising in and flowing through the valley at the foot of the spur is joined by another which comes from beyond the next spur, and the two combined have forced their way through the spur. It appears from an examination of the valley that it was at some remote period a lake, for this valley has no outlet, except through the tunnel; supposing it to have been a lake, the caves noticed would be most picturesquely situated on its margin. The waters of the lake appear to have eventually forced a passage through the spur by a long tunnel; the tunnel is 450 feet in length, the least dimension of the tunnel being at a point 250 feet from the mouth, where it measures only 16 feet across. The roof which is an irregular curve being here 12 feet above the bed of the Nullah at its highest point. At its entrance the tunnel is 55 feet wide, with a height to the crown of its natural arch of over 100 feet; but it diminishes rapidly, being only 32 feet wide at a distance of 40 feet from the entrance, with a height of about 20 feet, and goes on diminishing gradually to its minimum dimensions, beyond which it increases again, being 35 feet wide and about 16 feet high at 400 feet from the entrance, and 90 feet wide at its exit. A long bench, at a minimum height of about 4 feet above the bed of the *nala*, runs along the whole length of the tunnel, demonstrating that when the pent-up waters first forced a way through the rock, the bed of the *nala* was 4 feet at least (and probably more) higher than now, leaving for the minimum height of arch only 8 feet; but even this would not correctly represent the really small opening which at first allowed exit to the waters, as the passage is obstructed by large boulders projecting from both sides. The material through which the *nala* has forced its way is yellowish coarse-grained sandstone. So far as I could judge in the gloom, granite rock, with roughly rhomboidal plain of cleavage, two magnificent mango trees rising almost from the very bed of the *nala* shade of the entrance, and two equally superb mango trees perform a like orifice at the exit; there are, besides, numerous tall Sakhua trees

Ramgarh hill tunnel Surguja district, Chhattisgarh, India called the 'Hathipole Tunnel' (Image by Manoj Kulkarni)

Fig. 1

Early Indian Astronomer's concept of
Divison of the Globe-Saptadvipa Vasumati

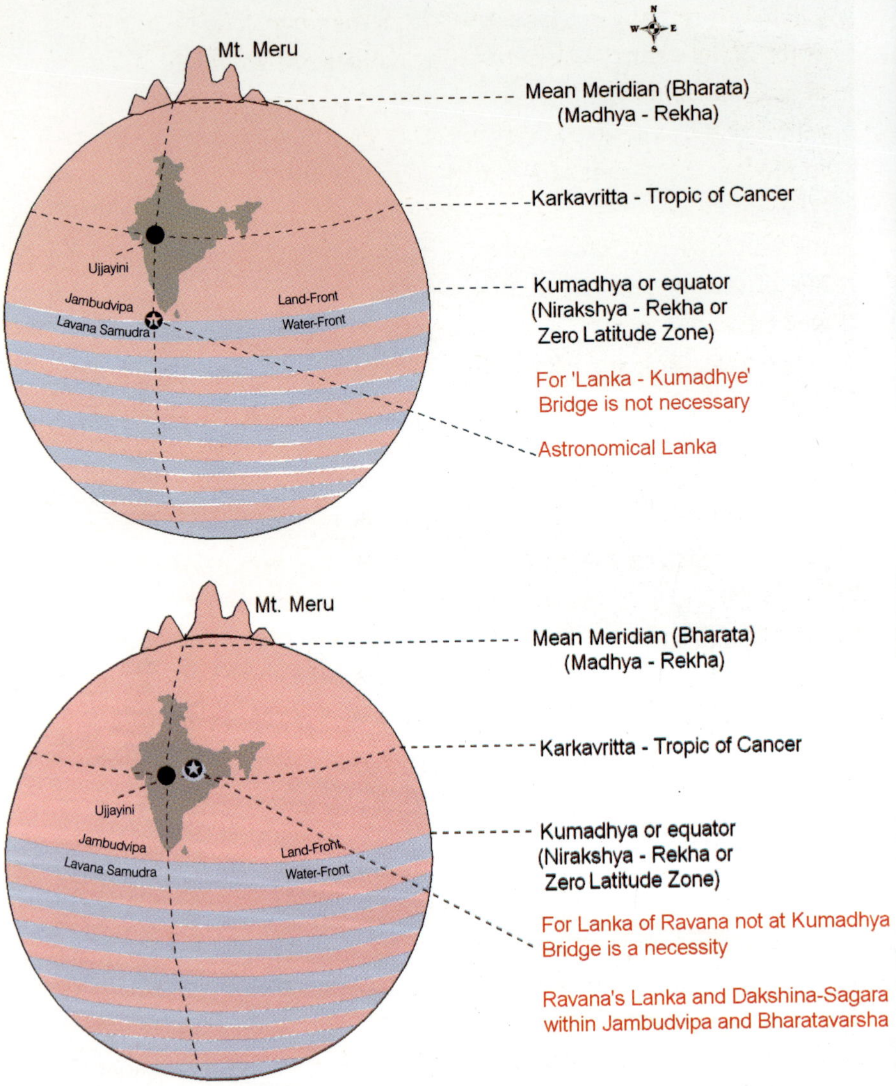

Visualisation of conepts by the author

and other trees all over the valley. The striking and picturesque beauty of the tunnel is charmingly enhanced by the fringe of moss and ferns that hang in fairy clusters from the crown, and haunches of the grand natural arch hiding irregularities and imparting an air of softness to the outline, and a contrast of colour with the dull yellow of the rock which even an artist's pencil may vainly attempt to render. The tunnel runs almost exactly south-east; it is called 'The Hāthphor'. There are some other caves, one in particular on the south side of a spur some distance from the Hāthphor, the only one of several caves there, that are now accessible, and which is well cut and smoothed and almost polished; the others being no longer accessible, and a few in the valley of the Hāthphor itself, but as they are of no special interest, this mention of them I consider sufficient. I have now finished the description of the objects of interest in the hill. Tradition says Sītā used to reside in the'.....etc.

It must be pointed out that 'Hath-phor' or 'Hathi-pol' might not be the original name of the place. The local name of the twin hill as recorded in the topo-sheet is 'Kāndā Ghuṭrī'. (see Topo-sheet#64J/13) The present name seems to be an explanatory name alright, but is definitely of later times. In remote prehistoric times, the name of the tunnel could be different, so also its importance for the locals of that time. In this enquiry, we have therefore attempted to find out, if there is any description of such a unique place in ancient literature (Epic *Rāmāyaṇa* for our enquiry purpose) and also to find a place in actual reality which matches the fictitious description.

Beglar[32] (1894) had suggested that this Ramgarh hill in Surguja is Mt. Citrakūṭa of *Rāmāyaṇa* and not the Citrakūṭa of Bundelkhand the well-known hill, that already enjoys the reputation of being the actual rāmāyaṇic Citrakūṭa of Vālmīki. He further suggested that Mara caves near Ramgarh hill is the site for sage Atrī's hermitage. This will have to be dealt with separately. It is, however, necessary to mention here that most scholars consider Beglar's view completely baseless simply because Ramgarh hill is miles away from Prayāga and river Yamuna.

Beglar had noticed 'Muni *guphā'* and 'Kabīr *cautra'*at Ramgarh hill. The female image and those of Rāma and Lakṣmaṇa on hill-top, all could be of Gupta period in the opinion of Beglar and Cunningham. (1882) Most remarkable thing they found was that the images in ruins were popularly known to be of Rāvaṇa, Mạhirāvaṇa and Meghanāda. All these images were in a hall, carved in stone, and the hall itself was called 'Rāvaṇa *baiṭhakā'*. There were some peculiar incomprehensible stone discs placed at one side. There was a Rāvaṇa image with twenty hands which is also said to be of goddess 'Durgā' and the image opposite to this with eight hands that of Śiva. They noticed one more image of Śiva with two hands holding two snakes and in addition one image of Viṣṇu.

T. Bloch (1903-1904) wrote an article on the 'caves and inscriptions in Ramgarh hill'[33]. He observed that the site of the hill is very popular amongst the locals and pilgrims gather there for the annual fair in large numbers. He observed that the caves exist in the western slope of the northern part of the hill, which forms a long range stretching from north to south, the highest point being at the southern end. The caves are reached through a natural tunnel, 55 metres long, (The actual length is 135 Metres or 450 feet and Bloch seems to have miscalculated) and so high that an elephant can easily pass through it, hence its name 'Hathipol'. At the western end of this tunnel, the slope of the hill forms itself into a crescent, overlooking a thickly wooded valley closed to the west, by a parallel range of the same hill. Both the caves are open to the west. The northern one is called 'Sitabenga cave' and the southern one 'Jogi Mara cave'.

Bloch says that the interior of these caves looks like a theatre and theorises that this is the most ancient theatre of India. He tried to read and study the inscriptions inside. According to Bloch, the inscriptions are written scripts with characters similar to ancient Brahmi script employed in the Aśoka inscriptions. H.L. Shukla[34] (2002), after studying the inscriptions, extended the theory propounded by T. Bloch. He also noticed 'Kabīr *caurā'*, and most importantly, images of 'twenty armed Durgā', eight armed Śiva and Hanumat. It can be argued that before the natural caves were carved out to decorate them for their use as a memento or a sacred place (a temple) or a theatre they might have been in use simply as a dwelling place for generations. Moreover, their theory that the caves were being used as a theatre has been opposed by some other researchers[35].

Our enquiry of Ramgarh hills here is not about the caves or inscriptions found in them. However, the descriptions of the remains of old temples and the possible methods which might have been used to construct them, all suggest that in ancient times Surguja must have been inhabited by people, who were far more advanced than the people presently living in Surguja[36]. Cobden Ramsay[37] L.E.B. a British I.C.S. officer also had visited Ramgarh hills in 1905. He describes the hills as follows-

'The south part of the Mainpat plateau is composed of gneiss and iron-stone with the northern side is a massive wall of sand-stone and it is indented like a coast-line with isolated buffs standing up in front of the cliffs from which they have parted.'

Thus he also seems to have imagined a sea of some kind (an extensive water reservoir) facing the Ramgarh hill. Thus the 'Sea was dotted with smaller mountain peaks.' He has given detailed descriptions of Ramgarh hill, the tunnel, the caves and archaeological remains[38].

It is observed in the present studies that besides this, opposite to Ramgarh hills at a distance of about 3 km, a group of three hills can be seen. In the relevant topo-sheet, No.64 J/13, the hills are shown to be standing facing the horse-shoe shaped valley, below the opening of Ramgarh hill tunnel. They are named 'Lakhan dih *pahārā'* (636 metres.), 'Bhandar dih *pahārā'* (810 Metres.), and the northernmost unnamed hill (636 metres). (Bhaṇḍārī is the name of Kubera!) These hills surrounded by numerous water currents might be habituated, if not now may be sometime in the past. To find such marks on these hills is quite possible and may throw more light on Ramgarh hill findings in general.

To the west of this group of three hills is another group of five minor hills. These are locally called 'Panch bahani *pahārā'*, as also shown in the topo-sheet no. 64J/13 (22° 57'N, 82° 50' E). To this date, no information is available about these two groups of hills facing Ramgarh hill of Surguja.

Reading Cobden Ramsay's account in his own words is a treat and food for thought for anyone interested in studies connected with *Rāmāyaṇa*. His account based on his minute observation is indicative of many interesting facts about the hill as well as about the geographical scenario of *Rāmāyaṇa*. His account from a rare journal therefore is partially reproduced and given below.

Cobden Ramsay's report - 1905:

'Sarguja ledge is reached by the remains of an old gateway, known as the 'Pauri Deori', are met with. Before reaching this gateway the lower range of the hill narrows down into a small ridge which forms the only means of approach to the ledge of rock and the sheer pinnacle towering above it. This ridge is extremely narrow and steep and has apparently long ago been hewn out into steps to render the approach easy. These steps, however, have now nearly entirely worn away. The gateway now consists of two enormous monoliths of stone wedged between fragments of other stones which perhaps formerly composed the arch of the gateway. The image of Gaṇesh mentioned in Hunter's account has now become so worn as to be indistinguishable. On either side of this gateway there lie; strewn about on the face of the hill, huge blocks of cut stone, which probably at one time formed a wall encircling the base of the perpendicular rock above. Passing on through the 'Pauri Deori' and climbing up by a track which eventually ends in a series of staircases in the perpendicular face of the rock, the Kabīr Chaurā (gravestone) of one Dharam Dās is pointed out by the local Baiga. This Dharam Dās is said to have been the last Jogi of the Ramgarh hill, and his body was removed to his house in Korba; but how long ago this was done no one could give me any information. A little further, a huge boulder lies close to the path. On the side turned away from the path this boulder has a small entrance cut in it just large enough for a man to squeeze through into the inside of the boulder, which has been completely hollowed out. This boulder is known as 'Vashistha Guphā' where the spiritual adviser of Ramchandra is supposed to have lived.

Worshippers wending their way to the temples on the summit are alleged to have been mystified by the supernatural utterances proceeding apparently from this solid rock. Facing the entrance in the boulder are found scattered about large hewn stones which apparently formed the walls and roof of a dwelling house, the floor of which is still clearly visible. From this point the pathway commences to ascend the perpendicular face of the rock, and to render the ascent possible regular staircases have been hewn in the face of the rock made by inserting enormous blocks of stones. These steps lead up to the 'Singh Darvaza'. This gateway is built of great masses of stone cut and carved in scroll work. The outer arch of the gateway is still standing, but the inner one has fallen. The remarkable feature of this gateway and all the remains found on this hill is the enormous blocks of stones used to build them. It is almost beyond belief that human hands could have erected them, especially in the case of this gateway, perched as it is on the sheer face of the rock. Inside this gateway there is apparently a modern image of 'Bhairab' though no one can remember when the image was placed there. The Image faces as usual east. From either side of this 'Singh Darvaza' remnants can be traced of a massive stone wall running up the face of the rock to the summit and built out on a crag close to the gateway, are the remains, apparently, of a watch-house from whence the country to north, east and south could be scanned for miles. Leaving the 'Singh Darvaza' a series of stairs or rather what is left of them; known as the 'Gaṇesh Siri' leads to the remains of the 'Rawan Darvaza'. Outside this gateway I observed side by side two Images, one of 'Gaṇesh' and the other of Hanuman. Through this gateway the 'Ravan Darbar' is entered. The floor is still clearly traceable, being made of large blocks, and the blocks forming the walls in some places still standing to the height of a few feet. In the Ravan Darbar there are images of Ravan and his brother Kuṃbhakarṇa and also of dancing girls, a narrow path leads from here to the summit of the hill. Along this path are several stone monoliths standing upright on the hill side, but they are bare of any carving or inscription, and I could learn nothing about them. On the summit of the hill there is a small temple more or less intact. The temple is not remarkable in any way for architectural beauty, but for the enormous blocks of stones used in construction. Outside the temple are images of Mahadeo and Hanuman and within images of Ramchandra and of Janaki, wife of Ramchandra, on his left hand. There are images also of Bharat and Viṣṇu Bhagvan with four hands. The hill cannot be descended on the western side, but it is possible to make one's way some two hundred feet down to a small...' etc.

According to V.D. Jha, Surguja earlier, in the medieval period, was known as Dāndora which became Kāntara and in Gupta period, Surguja was known by the name 'MahāKāntara'. Jha had also recorded in 1973 at Ramgarh hills, the presence of Rāvaṇa *darvājā,* Rāvaṇa *darbāra* and Kabīr *caurā*. Near the *simha* (lion) *darvājā,* he states he noticed one *yakṣa* image. He opines that the work in 'Sītā Bengrā' seems to be influenced by Gupta art and in the medieval period there seems to be a harmony established between *Śaiva* and *Vaiṣṇava* styles in Surguja. Jha suggests the association of this land with the culture of *Rāmāyaṇa* and *Mahābhārata*. However, his studies of rock paintings and stone tools found in river beds and open fields around the area suggest human activities of even earlier time phase. Implements of four stone ages, viz. early, middle, late and new have been recorded in Surguja[39].

If we analyse the observations made by all the above mentioned surveyor-travellers or scholars, we see that five out of eight of them have recorded that they noticed things connected with Rāvaṇa; the images, *baiṭhakā, darvājā, darbāra* etc. Four out of eight have noticed Kabīr *Cabutrā* (see End Note 1). It is also clear that four out of eight people were informed by the locals that the twenty armed figure was not of Rāvaṇa but of Durgā, and out of these same four, three persons noticed images of Rāvaṇa, Mahirāvaṇa, Meghanāda and also Rāvaṇa *darvājā* and Rāvaṇa *darbāra.* Now a problem crops up. At a place, where local tradition is of Rāvaṇa's domination it is unlikely that a Durgā image would be sculpted and therefore, the broken image still showing twenty arms must be a Rāvaṇa image, or if at all, iconographical study proves it to be a Durgā image, it must have entered the scene much later, and originally, there must have been images of Rāvaṇa and his subjects as the local tradition suggests. Needless to say, much research needs to be carried out in this area. Moreover, an image of Durgā, Mahiṣāsurmardini, is to have ten hands traditionally[40], and as we know Aṣṭabhujā is a female deity with eight hands.

One more aspect of the problem needs consideration here. Based on the present studies it is argued here that Ramgarh hill tunnel is the *Ṛkṣabila* of *Rāmāyaṇa*, from where, Laṅkā was 100 *yojanās* away, beyond the 'sea', according to Saṃpātī. Why then on Ramgarh hill are mementos connected with Rāvaṇa? Is Ramgarh hill Rāma's place or Rāvaṇa's? The answer and an explanation can be as follows: *Rāmāyaṇa* says that *Ṛkṣabila* was the creation of Mayāsura, the architect of *dānavās*. (In reality it is unambiguously a wonderful creation of nature.) Before Mayāsura was killed by Indra, Mayāsura's wife Hemā *apsarā* had abandoned that place leaving their child Mandodarī with Mayāsura. Later, Rāvaṇa had asked for Mandodarī's hand in marriage from Mayāsura and had taken her to Laṅkā. After Mayāsura was killed, Svayaṃprabhā, Hemā's friend, had taken *Ṛkṣabila* in her care. *Rāmāyaṇa* clearly says that knowing Rāvaṇa's nature and fearing Rāvaṇa's might, Mayāsura had to agree to Rāvaṇa's proposal of taking Mandodarī away as his wife: Thus, the verse (omitted from C.E.) is-

mayena dānavendreṇa tvadbhayātsakhyamicchatā |
duhitā tava bhāryārthe dattā rākṣasapuṅgava ||[41]

According to the epic, Mayāsura, the architect of *Ṛkṣabila* was Rāvaṇa's father-in-law, and was under his domination. It is therefore reasonable to suppose that, since the whole area surrounding *Ṛkṣabila* was under the influence and command of Rāvaṇa, the lord of the area would naturally be adored by the locals and he would have his marks on the works of craft, traditions, and places and so on. Thus, it can be said that the images of Rāvaṇa and his subjects must be the original creations and in later times images of other deities entered the scene. This state of things invites exhaustive archaeological studies to be done on the material lying on Ramgarh hill which can throw some light on the source, time period of the creation of individual artefacts etc.

In essence, images and mementoes related to Rāvaṇa did exist on Ramgarh hill and this is in accordance with the tradition of generations of the local people, the aborigines, whereas a 'temple' of Rāma on the summit of the hill could be a later addition. The caves in the hill, originally a nature's creation, as judged by scholars, exhibited craft of crude local style initially and then again, in the third to fifth century, another phase seems to have come of craftsmanship, sculpturing and inscriptions.

Ṛkṣabila is neither revisited by *vānarās* nor by Hanumat himself. Accompanied by the *vānara* army, Rāma advances from Kiṣkindha in the south direction towards Laṅkā for war and constructs a link bridge, 100 *yojanās* in length from Mt. Mahendra at the north shore of *dakṣiṇa sāgara* to reach Laṅkā. From the epic it is obvious that Rāma does not come across *Ṛkṣabila* any time in his entire journey.

Geographical features of Ramgarh hill tunnel and the surrounding area:

The tunnel in Ramgarh hill in Surguja is situated in Vindhyan ranges and so was *Ṛkṣabila* of Vālmīki *Rāmāyaṇa*. The immediate beautiful surroundings of Ramgarh hill are thickly forested even today having a great variety of plant life and of course *Sāla* trees dominate (see eye witness accounts). When *vānarās* approached *Ṛkṣabila*, they found birds drenched with water, flying out of the huge opening. The tunnel in Ramgarh hill similarly has a water source both inside and outside. After coming out of *Ṛkṣabila*, Svayaṃprabhā points out Mt. Vindhya and Mt. Prasravaṇa. As we have seen, if Mt. Prasravaṇa can mean any hill with numerous water currents flowing over it in all directions, (see Appendix 3) Ramgarh hill itself can be called 'Prasravaṇa' as the topo-sheet map of the area (No.64J/9+13) clearly shows numerous currents and nullahs flowing over it and forming a watery area of quite a large extent around it. Ramgarh hill tunnel has openings at both the ends and so also *Ṛkṣabila* had as we have argued here, based on the evidences from the epic itself.

As pointed out here, most of the old travel reports say that the horse-shoe shaped basin below Ramgarh hill was in all probability a vast water reservoir in ancient times. This geographical feature was also the most striking one of *Ṛkṣabila* of *Rāmāyaṇa* with *Sāgara* surging at its foothill. The watery area surrounding Ramgarh hill could not be of great depth, and it showed rocks and smaller peaks emerging out of shallow waters, (references of eye witness accounts given), the 'sea' opposite *Ṛkṣabila* also showes a few peaks. The epic description indicates that *Ṛkṣabila* area was under Rāvaṇa's control. To corroborate this we have seen that many old reports like the one by Beglar, Cunningham, Cobden Ramsay and others indicate that there were remains on Ramgarh hill locally known as 'Rāvaṇa *baiṭhakā*', 'Rāvaṇa *darvājā*', 'Rāvaṇa *darbāra*', and images locally assumed as those of Kuṃbhakarṇa, Rāvaṇa and his aides. It is a sad thing that images of Rāvaṇa and his aides, the other *rakṣasās*, or even the spot-names mentioned, are only a thing of the past at Ramgarh hill today. Is Rāvaṇa, an important part of the Rāma story, banished deeper into the forests? No one knows.

Which of these remains or the enormous blocks of stones and other structures and also the broken images was a creation of pre-historic period remains to be further studied and interpreted by archaeologists. Excavations around the hill should throw light on many facets of this problem. For the time being, evidences provided here suggest an entirely new hypothesis, namely that the Ramgarh hill tunnel in Surguja district of Chhattisgarh seems to satisfy all the conditions to claim its identification with *Ṛkṣabila* of *Rāmāyaṇa*. The name *Ṛkṣabila* seems to have been coined by the poet himself. The significance of *Ṛkṣabila* identification is that it is from here that Saṃpātī points to the *vānarās* the direction of Laṅkā only to the north of Ramgarh hill (*Ṛkṣabila*) as will be discussed further.

The group of three small hills (22° 55′ N, 82° 52′ E) [topo-sheet No.64J/13] opposite Ramgarh hills, encircled by numerous water currents, and the 'Panch bahani *pahar*' hills (22° 56′ N, 82° 48′ E) might have been inhabited from ancient times. The locals believe that this area at Devgarh to the west of Ramgarh was where sage Jamadagnī and wife Reṇukā (river Rihand?) had his hermitage where Parśurāma used to come to visit his father (Manoj Kulkarni, personal communication). This entire area certainly awaits much research work to be carried out (also see End Note 2).

According to Saṃpātī's account, not just beyond the water reservoir surging in the basin outside *Ṛkṣabila* hill,but up to a distance of 100 *yojanās* or more and to the north of *Ṛkṣabila* the sea was spread, beyond which Laṅkā was situated. According to the present study there was a lake or an expanse of water to the north of the tunnel and not to its south or east. If we consider the geographical situation and more specifically the orientation of Ramgarh hill, we find that it is a semicircular hill couplet with both its spurs or arms opening towards north, encompassing the valley, with clear indications of an ancient 'sea' (i.e. a large water body) in the basin below. Towards the south, the hill is backed by hilly area. [(see topo- sheet# 64 J/9+13) showing the actual orientation of Ramgarh hill] Obviously, when *vānarās* come out of *Ṛkṣabila* and meet Saṃpātī on the northern slope of that hill, he points out to Laṅkā 100 *yojanās* away towards the north beyond this sea. Laṅkā therefore, should be to the north of the tunnel. Whether this sea in *Ṛkṣabila* basin was *dakṣiṇa sāgara* or not has to be examined now. From the epic it is abundantly clear that *Ṛkṣabila* was to the south of Kiṣkindhā. This would mean that the geographical position of the 'sea' (adjacent to *Ṛkṣabila*) and also the 'south-sea' (or the'*dakṣiṇa sāgara'*) as per Saṃpātī's account, must have been between these two points i.e. Kiṣkindha and the *Ṛkṣabila* (see map 1).

It should be noted here that as per the text, Svayaṃprabhā denotes the vast expanse of water at the foot hill of *Ṛkṣabila* simply as *'sāgara'* ('**sāgaroyam mahodadhiḥ**')[42]. The same *Sāgara* was *dakṣiṇa sāgara* according to Saṃpātī ('**dakṣiṇasyodadhestīre vindhyoyamiti niścitaḥ**' **|**)[43] and beyond which at a distance of 100 *yojanās* was Laṅkā which Saṃpātī could actually see with his specially powerful vision. Initially Saṃpātī says[44], that he himself had seen Rāvaṇa carrying away Sītā ('**hriyamāṇa mayā dṛṣṭā rāvaṇena durātmanā**'). But later he explains that he had really known it only by knowledge of it, by *jñānacakṣu* ('**jñānena khalu paśyāmi**')[45]. He further says that he had heard about it from Supārśva who, after flying a long distance from Saṃpātī's abode or from *Ṛkṣabila,* had actually seen Rāvaṇa carrying away Sītā at Mahendra *dvāra* and at Rāvaṇa's request had made way for him to pass and proceed towards Laṅkā.

Thus, regarding the location of *dakṣiṇa sāgara* there seems to be a contradiction in Saṃpātī's account. It can be inferred from the above that *'sāgara'* in Supārśva's account could be *Dakṣiṇa Sāgara* surrounding Laṅkā. The one surging at the foothill of *Ṛkṣabila* was simply *'sāgara'*, meaning a vast expanse of water. A careful scrutiny of these accounts also makes it clear that Hanumat did not cross this sea which touched the foot hills of *Ṛkṣabila*. The epic makes this fact even more clear in *Kiṣkindhākaṇḍa*. It is evident from the description[46] that *vānarās,* after taking a hint from Saṃpātī, leave that spot at the foothills of *Ṛkṣabila* and walk through forests to reach the north shore of another sea which is much larger, described as the one that could contain the reflection of entire *dyūloka* within its waters, and that was *dakṣiṇa sāgara* with Mt. Mahendra on its northern shore. This is in accordance with our inference that neither *dakṣiṇa sāgara* nor Mt. Mahendra set with it was located anywhere near *Ṛkṣabila* of Svayaṃprabhā and for this reason, both these sites, i. e. *dakṣiṇa sāgara* and Mt. Mahendra with its pass, were naturally not within the view of Svayaṃprabhā, Saṃpātī or Hanumat's group of *vānarās*, is very clear from the epic itself.

U.P. Shah feels that the expanse of water at the foothills of Vālmīki's *Riksabila* was the *'dakṣiṇa sāgara'* as he considers only a part of Saṃpātī's account[47]. D.R. Mankad suggests that Mt. Mahendra, a hill or a part of it, was close to this (end) hill of Vindhya (meaning *Ṛkṣabila* hill)[48]. However, this interpretation which supports U.P. Shah's notion is not tenable as is clear from the discussion above.

Thus, *dakṣiṇa sāgara* and Mt. Mahendra were not near *Ṛkṣabila. Rāmāyaṇa* makes it abundantly clear that Mt. Mahendra set in the sea by sage Agastya, was close to the north shore of *Dakṣiṇa Sāgara.* (1) Rāma and the *vānara* army after descending Mt. Mahendra were still on the north shore of *dakṣiṇa sāgara.* (2) Saramā consoles Sītā by informing that Rāma having crossed the sea has now reached the south shore, at the gates of Laṅkā. The verse is-

uttīrya sāgaram rāmaḥ saha vānarasenayā |
sanniviṣṭaḥ samudrasya tīramāsādya dakṣiṇam ||[49]

It appears that *vānarās* entered *Ṛkṣabila* (Ramgarh hill of present studies) from its south-eastern end, (from an easier ascent, from Udaypur village of the present in district Surguja), then later, after coming out of Riksabila, taking a hint from Saṃpātī, they first turned towards south, (as *Rāmāyaṇa* says towards Abhijit *nakṣatra,* a constellation) since to the north there was the 'sea'. They then took a U-turn and walked through forested hilly region towards the north shore of *dakṣiṇa sāgara* (see map 2).

'dakṣiṇasya sāmudrasya samāsādyottarām diśam'[50] After this, they ascended Mt. Mahendra from where Hanumat took his first leap towards Laṅkā, in south direction. He then crossed *'Dakṣiṇa Sāgara',* entered *Laṅkā* and finally returned with the good news about Sītā back to Mt. Mahendra where *vānarās* were waiting for him. As per the description in the epic, from here they all go back to Kiṣkindhā, via 'Madhuvana' where they drink *mahuā* liquor, sing and dance, celebrating the success of their mission with uproar. Madhuvana was Sugrīva's reserved forest, a part of *vānara* domain, and so might not have been far from Kiṣkindha and hence the route and the country were familiar to the returning search party of Hanumat (see map 2).

Location and the Nature of South Sea:

Again, to find a solution to this problem a perusal of ancient literature is necessary. *Mahābhārata* as well as *Purāṇās* give traces of information through stories, remarks and descriptions, finally gathering a sea of information about the 'south sea'.

After being blessed by Brahmā with many boons and favours, Rāvaṇa boastfully moving around, goes to Kiṣkindha and in his conceit challenges Vālin who at that time had gone for his evening prayers at 'south sea' or *dakṣiṇa sāgara*. Description here in *Uttarakāṇḍa*[51] of four 'samudrās' seems to be based on the fanciful conception of the division of the globe as pointed out earlier. *Sundarakāṇḍa* gives a dialogue between Sītā and Hanumat[52] which describes the south sea in following words, **'śatayojana vistīrṇaḥ sāgaro makarālayaḥ'**. Meaning, it (*dakṣiṇa sāgara*) is 100 *yojanās* in extent and a home of crocodiles. In this context it should be noted that researchers who firmly believe that Laṅkā of *Rāmāyaṇa* was somewhere in eastern M.P. also suggest that *dakṣiṇa sāgara* in *Rāmāyaṇa* in all probability must have been a vast expanse of water, the extent or scope of which was known and was not a boundless sea. This point has been discussed by Hiralal[53]. It is then more reasonable to believe that *dakṣiṇa sāgara* was one such huge, marshy water reservoir where crocodiles predominated as predators. We will now have to see if this theory can be validated by evidences from the epics or other sources.

After Rāvaṇa is killed, Rāma returns to Ayodhya in Puṣpak *vimāna*. Kālidāsa describes *dakṣiṇa sāgara*, which Rāma points out to Sītā, describing it thus:

dūrādayaścakranibhasya tanvī tamāltālīvanarajinīlā |
ābhāti velā lavaṇamburāśerdhārārnibaddheva kalaṅkarekhā ||[54]

Translated as: From a distance this salt water body looks like an iron wheel with a thin dark rim and because of the lining of trees like *Tāla* and *Tamāla* and so on, the shore line looks like a wheel rim darkened by rust. Kālidāsa, although is of a much later time, seems to have followed the original *Rāmāyaṇa* tradition.

Pulastya's pilgrimage[55] mentions a list of *tīrthās* he visited, in the order of their occurrence as follows:

Puṣkara *tīrtha* → Jambūmārga → Agastya *sarovara* → Kaṇva's hermitage → Dharmāraṇya → Yayātipatana *tīrtha* → Mahākāla (Ujjayini?) → Koṭī *tīrtha* → Bhadra *vaṭa tīrtha* → Narmada → 'south sea' → Carmanvati (Chambal river of Malva) → Arbuda mountain (Mt. Abu.) etc. This information suggests that the 'south sea' was located between the valley of river Chambal of Malva and the water shade area to the north of river Narmada, although this order seems chaotic and not in accordance with the geographical positions of some of the known sites.

The description in *vanaparvan* of *Mahābhārata*[56] further lists the places, the order being, Kālanjar → Citrakūṭa → Mandākinī → to the south Jyeṣṭha *sthāna* and a water body having the waters of all the four seas together, *samudrakūpa,* (this could be referring to the lotus-earth theory) → Śṛṅgaverapura → Ganga → Prayāga with Agastya's hermitage → Hiraṇyabindu *tīrtha* of Mt. Kālanjar → Mahendra mountain of Paraśurāma Bhārgava (Mt. Mahendra being the sacrificial ground of Brahmā) → Maṇikarṇika lake with Bhāgīrathī (Brahmaśāla at Vārāṇasi!) → Mataṅgakedāra. Thus this list indirectly suggests the location of *dakṣiṇa sāgara* to be in south Ganga plain where Bhāgīrathī Ganga sunk herself in a lake or sea as will be explained in the next chapter (the location of Mt. Mahendra is an unsolved problem at the moment (see Appendix G)).

Hanumat takes off

From Mt. Mahendra Hanumat takes his first leap southwards towards Laṅkā. *Sundarakāṇḍa* (*sarga* 1) states that Hanumat comes across the first obstacle namely that of *nāgamātā* Surasā. She is referred to as *'dākṣāyaṇī'*[57] and also as *'rāmaviṣayavāsinī'*[58] by Hanumat (*viṣaya = deśa,* a country). These names are interesting. As she widens her mouth, Hanumat enters it and comes out of it, the way moon comes out of Rāhu's mouth in a lunar eclipse (as per popular belief). Hanumat on his way is again caught and pulled by his shadow, by another *rākṣasī* named Saiṃhikā.

The description clearly indicates that Aṅgārakā, initially referred to by Sugrīva, is the same as Saiṃhikā[59]. Saiṃhikā is the wife of a *dānava*, called 'Vipraciti'. Vātāpī and his brother Ilvala and the pair Rāhu-Ketu also are Saiṃhikeyās. Saiṃhikā is the sister of *dānavās* Hiraṇyakaśipū and Hiraṇyākṣa. Hiraṇyakaśipū is recreated as Rāvaṇa and Hiraṇyākṣa as Kuṃbhakarṇa (Rāvaṇa's brother). Thus Saiṃhikā is closely related to Rāvaṇa. The 'flight' of Hanumat, an expert jumper ('**plavatāmuttamo**'), and especially his overcoming the obstacles could be an allegorical description of an eclipsed moon. Hanumat is described as an expert jumper and although the word *'uddāṇa'* means aviation or flight, it also means a jump, leap, bound or a hop (see appendix B).

As Hanumat was jumping across the sea, *dakṣiṇa sāgara* thought to himself that he ('south sea') always held the Ikṣvākus in high esteem and therefore:

sāhāyyam vānarendrasya yadi nāham hanūmataḥ |
kariṣyāmi bhaviṣyāmi sarvavācyo vivakṣatām ||[60]

Meaning, 'if *dakṣiṇa sāgara,* at this point of time, does not offer help or oblige Hanumat, any person having the power of speech would speak ill of him and it would be a shameful thing. He will be worthy of slander'. Thinking thus, *dakṣiṇa sāgara* said to mount Maināka (that was submerged in the waters of the south sea,) that he should come out of the sea waters, so that Hanumat can descend on its top and rest for a while, which will make his further task easier. The 'south sea' also said about Mt. Maināka that the king of gods Indra had commissioned Mt. Maināka to deter the *asurās*, having their dwelling place in *pātāla*. Maināka could extend itself on all sides and thus emerged from the waters of the south sea to make a resting place for Hanumat. However, Hanumat, in order to avoid delay, declined his request politely and continued to get across the sea non-stop.

Mount Maināka gives his own reasons for being desirous of helping Hanumat (Sundarakāṇḍa). He refers to Hanumat as supreme son of wind god Vāyu, to whom he feels obliged. Maināka explains that in *Kṛtayuga*, all the mountains had wings and they could fly. Fearing that they may fall, Indra then cut down the wings of all the mountains with his *'vajra'*. At that time Vāyu blew Maināka out in the sky and then dropped him in 'south sea'. Thus he saved Maināka with his wings intact[61]. Maināka is imagined to be a mountain capable of movement while all the rest are stationary. (Maināka was the son of Mt. Himalaya and Mena and Mt. Krauñca was the son of Mt. Maināka.) Mt. Maināka was immersed at the centre of *dakṣiṇa sāgara* ('**punarmadhyena Sāgaram**')[62]. Mt. Maināka is also called 'Sunabha', 'Hiraṇyanābha' or 'Sanuṣu' (see Appendix G).

Sundarakāṇḍa informs us that Hanumat gets across the sea and reaches the shore beyond. He sees the forests of Mt. Malaya and then descends on a hill-top named 'Laṃba' which was one of the wonderfully rich peaks of Mt. Trikūṭa. Thus-

tataḥ sa lambasya gireḥ samruddheḥ |
vicitrakūṭe nipapāta kūṭe ||[63]

Hanumat, as he was standing on Laṃba peak, could get glimpses of Laṅkā, situated on the adjacent peak of Mt. Trikūṭa. (It may be noted here that Laṃba is another name of Khara *rakṣasa,* Rāvaṇa's cousin brother.)

It can be seen that, Trikūṭa *parvata* was with numerous wonderful and strange looking peaks, one of them being Laṃba peak. The above description indicates many peaks of Trikūṭa *parvata*. It does not suggest Trikūṭa to have only three peaks. Emphasis on its numerous and strange looking peaks is indicative. Of course the name of the mountain was not Vicitrakūṭa but only Trikūṭa.

Sundarakāṇḍa describes Laṃba in the following words; having many high peaks it looked like clouds hanging down from the sky. The verse is -

'sa laṃba śikhare laṃbe laṃbatoyadasannidhe' |[64]

There is good reason to believe that this vivid description might help further to identify Laṃba and Trikūṭa mountains in their actual geographical locations. Hanumat observes Laṅkā to be **'sa nagāgre ca tām laṅkām'**|[65] or, **'girirmūrghni sthitām Laṅkām'**|[66], meaning, Laṅkā was a hill-top settlement of Rāvaṇa.

Hanumat found that the north gate of Laṅkā was sky-high like Mt. Kailāsa[67]. This description can be taken to mean that the north peak was the highest point on Trikūṭa *parvata*. Laṅkā was situated on a hill-top has been mentioned repeatedly at various places in *Rāmāyaṇa.* Laṅkā, meaning a high land, is a word from Munda language according to Sankalia[68]. Hanumat reaches back to Mt. Mahendra and declares that after all the ado he has finaly found Sītā. *Vānarās,* highly delighted then go to Madhuvana grove/ forest near Kiṣkindha and celebrate their success in the mission.

Now, all have gathered together in Kiṣkindhā. Under Sugrīva's guidance, they get ready for war. The battle will be fought in Laṅkā. Rāma with all the armies and generals advances in south direction towards Laṅkā. Hanumat makes things clear by saying, '*dakṣiṇa sāgara* which I crossed to reach Laṅkā has a long shore. Boating or navigation is out of question and there are no indication marks in that sea to understand distances'. Thus:

sthitāpāre samudrasya dūrapārasya rāghava |
naupathaścāpi nāstyatra nirāddeśaśca sarvataḥ ||[69]

Hanumat also explains that there are four ramparts and measures around Laṅkā city. The first one with weaponry, the second defence is of the streams and rivers which moat Laṅkā, the third defence is of mountains encircling it (this description is interesting and is of geographical significance) and the fourth is the one artificially constructed, all making the city of Laṅkā completely inaccessible, he explains. Although the task was considered to be extremely arduous and challenging, determined to find a solution for the hard problem of crossing the sea, the huge *vānara* army of Sugrīva and Rāma marched towards south.

A *śloka* in *Yuddhakāṇḍa* curiously indicates that Rāma's *vānara* army in their march from Kiṣkindha to Laṅkā in the south direction, was descending the mountain ridges and at some point they observed that the rivers were flowing in an unnatural way[70]. G. Ramdas feels that here the poet is describing a mountain ridge that separated the rivers flowing northwards from those that flowed southwards, a phenomenon the geographers call water parting[71]. This could be applied to the area discussed in this chapter as a part of future studies. However, the river directions could also be from east to west and west to east. It can only be said at this moment that the *vānara* army may have been descending down some Kaimur range running from west to north-east.

Yuddhakāṇḍa says that they came across Mt. *Sahyadri*![72] There is no mention of Mt. Vindhya, and rivers Narmada and Son, before the mention of Mt. Sahyadri. One can say that this could be a case of later addition. This is so, since even if Anegundi of Mysore is Kiṣkindha and Ceylon is Laṅkā as per the popular belief, it is incomprehensible to suppose that Rāma and others can come across Mt. Sahyadri between Anegundi and Ceylon. Moreover, Sahyadri and Mt. Mahendra (of Orissa!) cannot be put together. Interestingly, in the description of the flora and variety of trees at Mt. Sahyadri and Mt. Malaya, *Sāla* trees are not mentioned at all!

Rāma then ascended Mt. Mahendra, from where he overlooked the sea (*Dakṣiṇa Sāgara*) crowded with aquatic animals like fish and turtles etc. *Vānara* army chief Nīla had the *vānara* army encamped on the shores of that roaring sea[73]. Needless to say, this was the north shore of *Dakṣiṇa Sāgara*. Laṅkā was vulnerable and approachable only from the north has been indicated in various ways in *Rāmāyaṇa*. The battle field was near the northern gate of Laṅkā. This in turn suggests that Laṅkā highland was inaccessible from the south, vulnerable from the north and that too by constructing a bridge over the sea waters.

After surveying, Rāma with his army, descended from Mt. Mahendra and entered the forest on the north shore. They could not view the shore on the other side, where they wanted to reach. The vast expanse of water was heavily infested with dreadful crocodiles of enormous size, is what *Rāmāyaṇa* describes.

In Laṅkā, the wise man Bibhīṣaṇa's advice to Rāvaṇa was that he should give Sītā back to Rāma, since wedging war with Rāma and Sugrīva would be to Rāma's advantage. Hearing this, Rāvaṇa vehemently condemned Bibhīṣaṇa, who then left Rāvaṇa's court and came to join Rāma's party and stood on high land on the north shore, where all were sitting worried and helpless ('**uttaram tīramīsādya khastha eva vyatiṣṭhata**')[74]. Rāma, guessing Bibhīṣaṇa's desire to help him, assured him that Rāma will make Bibhīṣaṇa the king of Laṅkā. Hanumat and Sugrīva then asked Bibhīṣaṇa, 'How can we, along with this huge army, get across this boundless and profound sea that is the abode of Varuṇa?' The army should get across speedily to avoid being attacked by ferocious crocodiles, they felt. Hearing this Bibhīṣaṇa suggested, "Rāma, you the descendant of Raghu (Rāma's ancestor), should surrender to the sea. This boundless sea has been unearthed by the sons of king Sagara (also Rāma's ancestor) by his command. This sea therefore would help Rāma willingly". Thus,

evamuktastu dharmajñaḥ pratyuvāca bibhīṣaṇaḥ |
samudram rāghavo rājā śaraṇam gantumarhati ||
khānitaḥ sagareṇayamaprameyo mahodadhiḥ |
kartumarhati rāmasya jñāteḥ kāryam mahodadhiḥ ||[75]

This feat of Rāma's ancestors has been mentioned and praised in Mahābhārata, *Raghuvaṃśa* of much later times and also in *Purāṇās* etc. In this connection, *Raghuvaṃśa* of Kālidāsa gives the following verse:

guroryiyakṣoḥ kapilena medhye rasātalam saṅkramite turaṅge |
tadarthamurvīmavadārayadbhiḥ pūrvaḥ kilāyam parivardhito naḥ ||[76]

Meaning - The 'south sea' says, 'When our adorable king Sagara had commenced horse sacrifice, the released horse was taken away by Kapila to *rasātala*. Then, while searching for that lost horse, our ancestors, king Sagara's sons, had dug out the earth and that resulted in enlarging the sphere of this 'sea', extending its dimensions. King Sagara is therefore respectable for me.'

We have seen earlier, that the sea wanted to help Rāma and as it was his very strong and sincere desire, at that point of time he had only requested Mt. Maināka to rise from the sea waters and make a resting place for Hanumat (*Sundarakāṇḍa*). *Dakṣiṇa-Sāgara* feels greatly indebted and says-

ahamikṣvākunāthena sagareṇa vivardhitaḥ |
ikṣvākusacivaścayam nāvasīditumarhati ||[77]

Meaning - The lord of Ikṣvākus, king Sagara and his sons, have extended my sphere and therefore Hanumat, an aide of Ikṣvākus, should be helped in carrying out his mission so that he does not get exhausted.

This is how the sea had thought according to *Rāmāyaṇa*. It can be seen that Vālmīki or the *Rāmāyaṇakaras* in their poetic venture have personified both Mt. Maināka and *dakṣiṇa sāgara,* who expressly justify their earnest desire to help Rāma. It now becomes necessary to find out the reason behind this proposition and also explanation given by the sea, the *dakṣiṇa sāgara*. Now, to search for this 'reason' we will have to go back to the stories and legends connected with Rāma's ancestors, i.e. stories connected with personalities from Ikṣvāku lineage. Such stories can be found in Vālmīki *Rāmāyaṇa* itself or they may be found in some other form and versions in other sources of ancient literature.

In the next chapter we will investigate the rāmāyaṇic concept of '*dakṣiṇa sāgara*' and where Vālmīki places it.

References: *Ṛkṣabila* and *Dakṣiṇa Sāgara*

1. 4:49:1-By
2. 4:52:12
3. *'Gīrvāṇalaghukośa'* J.V. Oak, Jamshedpur Bihar, 1960, p.129
4. *'Vāmana Purāṇa' Adhyāya* 13:24-27, Kalyan series Geeta Press Gorakhpur, (1982)
5. Ptolemy: [(by R.C. Majumdar *'The Classical Accounts of India'* (1960) p. 380]
6. *'Mārkaṇḍeya Purāṇa'*: 54:24, 25

7. T.P. Iyer: *'Rāmāyaṇa and Laṅkā'* Bangalore (1940), p.55
8. 4:49:16
9. R.K. Shukla: *'The Geography of the Rāmāyaṇa'* (2003), p.183, Koshal Book Depot publ. Delhi
10. 6:4:80
11. D.R. Mankad: 'Introduction to critical edition of *Kiṣkindhākaṇḍa* of Vālmīki *Rāmāyaṇa'* c.e. Baroda (1965), p. 59
12. 4:9:5-21
13. 4:2:14-By
14. 4:52:32
15. 4:50:10
16. 4:50:11
17. Ibid.
18. 4:49:32
19. 4:50:15
20. 4:32:1
21. 4:48:13
22. 4:48:19
23. 4:49:2
24. 4:49:16
25. R.K. Shukla: op.cit. p.183
26. 4:49:9-29
27. *'Encyclopaedia of District Gazetteers'*: vol. V. (ed. S.C. Bhatt)
28. J.R. Ouseley: 'On the antiquities of Surguja and its neighbourhood' JASB, vol. XVII, pt. 1, (1848) pp. 65-68
29. Dalton: JASB, vol. XXXIV, pt. 1, (1865) pp. 45-49, pt.2, pp. 25-27
30. V. Ball: *'Indian Antiquary'* (1873) 2, pp. 243-246
31. Beglar and Cunningham: ASIR, XIII, (1882) pp. 20-31
32. Beglar: JRAS, (1894) pp. 39-40
33. T. Bloch: *'Ramgarh hill caves and inscriptions',* (1903-04) ASIR, pp. 123-131
34. H.L. Shukla: *'Archaeology of the Indian Cave Theatre: A Study of Ramgarh Hill of Chhattisgarh'* (2002) B.R. Publishing Corp. Delhi
35. Hiralal: (quotes from Bergess, *'Ind. Antiq'.* vol. XXXIV, (1916) p. 197 ff) in 'Descriptive list of inscriptions in the C.P. and Berar'
36. W.W. Hunter *'Statistical account of Bengal',* vol. XVII, (1877), London, pp. 221-240
37. Cobden Ramsay L.E.B. *'Statistical account of Bengal',* vol. XVII (1905): pp 231-240
38. *'Imp. Gazetteer of Surguja'* (1905), 'Chhattisgarh and Feudatory states,' pp. 230-233
39. V.D. Jha: *'Investigations into Archaeology of Surguja',* (1973); pp. 67-73

40. *'Devīkośa'* (quoted by *'Bhāratīya Sanskriti Kośa'*, vol. 7, p. 256)
41. 6:7:6 By
42. 4:52:12
43. 4:59:7
44. 4:57:15
45. 4:57:24
46. 4:62:15
47. U.P. Shah: op.cit. p. 32
48. D.R. Mankad: op.cit. p. 60, 61
49. 6:24:14
50. 4:63:4
51. 7:34:24-31
52. 5:34:7
53. Hiralal 'The situation of Rāvaṇa's Laṅkā', Jha comm.vol. (1937), Pune, pp.157, 158
54. *'Raghuvaṃśa'* 13:15 [G.R. Nandargikar (1982), p. 402] MLBD Publication, Delhi
55. *'Mbh'. Vanaparvan. Ara.* 3:80:60-73, also see 3:85
56. *'Mbh'. vanaparvan.* 3:87:2
57. 5:1:153
58. 5:1:140 (also see entry 140)
59. 5:1:166-176
60. 5:1:76
61. 5:1:108-112
62. 5: 55:8, 9
63. 5:1:189
64. 5:3:1
65. 5:2:8
66. 5:2:18
67. 5:2: 23
68. H.D. Sankalia: *'Rāmāyaṇa in historical perspective'* (1973) p. 51
69. 6:3:20
70. 6:4:foot note 75
71. Ramdas G. 'Rāvaṇa's Laṅkā' IHQ (1928) p. 342
72. 6:4:55, 56
73. 6:4:64; 6:5:1
74. 6:11:8
75. 6: 13:13, 14
76. *'Raghuvaṃśa'*: 13: 3 [ed. and tr. by M.R. Kale (1972), MLBD Publication, Delhi
77. 5:1: 77

End Notes:

(1) *KABĪR CABUTRĀ*: The famed Amarkanṭak hill has many interesting sites on it or in the vicinity. A noticeable spot is called Kabīr *cabutrā*. It is believed by some to be the grave of famous saint Kabīr. Kabīr *panthīs* (followers) hold a fair on this spot annually, which is attended by innumerable pilgrims. Such Kabīr *cabutrās* are also to be found in many other places like Bandhavgarh, Mandla, Kavardha, and many other districts of Chhattisgarh and M.P. But, there are some spots simply known as *'caurā'* or *'cabutrā'* and not necessarily 'Kabīr *cabutrā'*. In reality, the grave site of any saint or a towering personality should be only at one place. The word *'cabutrā'* is peculiar. Are there such *cabutrās* for other saints?

Pundit V.S. Agrawala explains in his [*'Ancient Indian Folk Cults'* (1970), pp.165-199] that such *cabutrās* are to be found in almost every village of Madhya Pradesh (p. 186), Uttar Pradesh etc. He suggests that these are actually places of *yakṣās* e. g. Bīr, Brahmā, or of *yakṣādhipatī* Kubera. It is therefore possible that some of these *cabutrās* or *caurās* could be in reality *yakṣa sthānās.*

Now, if we go through the biography of Saint Kabīr, (Keay F.E.1931/1995, *'Kabīr and his followers'* Association Press, YMCA/OUP Calcutta) we find that Kabīr died in 1518, in Uttar Pradesh in Maghar (modern Sant Kabirnagar) near Gorakhpur. His famous disciple and a founder leader of the Chhattisgarh section of the Kabīr-*pantha,* was one Dharam Dās. About the *cabutrā* at Ramgarh hill in Surguja, Cobden Ramsay (1905), when he visited Ramgarh hill in 1905, said the following: 'In the perpendicular face of the rock, the Kabīr *Chaurā* (grave-stone) of one Dharam Dās is pointed out by the local *baiga*. This Dharam Dās is said to have been the last *jogi* of the Ramgarh hill and his body was removed to his house in Korba, but how long ago this was done no one could give me any information...'

Therefore it can be said that Kabīr *cabutrā* at Amarkanṭak is not a grave-stone of saint Kabīr as is wrongly believed by people at large and also by some scholars. Dharam Dās, Kabīr's disciple, might have lived and died at Ramgarh Hill in Surguja, in one of the caves, which therefore might have come to be known as 'Jogi Mara', (Mara meaning cave).

(2) PAÑCĀPSARĀS-*TĪRTHA* AND *NĀRI-TĪRTHA*: Udaypur district of Chota Nagpur has a holy water spot or *tīrtha* comprising of five smaller sites. Their names are: Kapu, Bandhanpur, Vanjiamba, Ponri etc. (The fifth name is missing from the list.) These sites are believed to be the place of five *apsarās* (celestial damsels) of *Rāmāyaṇa*, the name being Pañcapsara *tīrtha* (see list of ancient monuments in the Chota Nagpur

division). Some of these spots are mentioned by Cunningham [ASIR, vol. 8 (1874-76) pp. 57-61]

There are *pañcatīrthās* (five water tanks or *kuṇḍās*) elsewhere in India, e. g. near Haridvar, Chennai etc. Similar *pañcatīrthās* are found in Gokarṇa in south India but the one mentioned above seems to be of special significance, obviously due to its geographical location, which is Chota Nagpur in Vindhya mountain ranges.

Arjuna had visited a place occupied by five *apsarās* (their names being Vargā, Saurameyī, Samicī, Budbuda and Latā) transformed into crocodiles as a result of the curse of a sage. Arjuna then conferred upon them a boon by which they regained their original form and the place became famous as 'Nāritīrtha' (*'Mbh'. Adi.* 1:208:1-21) *Mahābhārata* says that these five *tīrthās,* which were on the shore of swampy and marshy *dakṣiṇa sāgara* (**dakṣine sāgarānūpe**) were totally abandoned by sages and hermits, fearing the existence of those crocodiles there. This story reminds us of the Pañcāpsaras *tīrtha* story of sage Maṇḍakarṇī of *Rāmāyaṇa*, which is also a place of five *apsarās,* although sage Maṇḍakarṇī's pleasure resort was devoid of crocodiles! *Mahābhārata* legend involves crocodiles. (We find that the crocodiles crowd *Rāmāyaṇa*, and the related places are swampy wetlands of *Dakṣiṇa Sāgara* and Chota Nagpur area! The cursed *apsarās* had seduced a sage). Coming back to the story of Nāritīrtha, *('Skanda Purāṇa', Maheśvara-Kumārikā Khaṇḍā,* Chapter:1, p.72 Geeta Press) gives the names of these five *tīrthās* as, Agastya *tīrtha,* Saubhadra *tīrtha,* Pauloma *tīrtha,* Kārandhama *tīrtha* and Bhāradvāja *tīrtha,* all comprising to one Nāritīrtha. When Pāṇḍavās later visit Nāritīrtha, their approach route is given as, Mahendra *parvata* → Godavari → Draviḍa *deśa* → Agastya *tīrtha* and → Nāritīrtha. These places indicate regions of south eastern India. Could this be a case where legends from both the epics have got mixed up?

In my opinion, 'Panch bahani' *pahārā,* (shown in the topo-sheet# 64 J/13), (which are minor hills and not water spots) needs to be investigated with further exploration and study of the local legends, for the remains of ancient monuments, marks of human habitation, etc. The relevant topo-sheet actually shows a group of five small hills with the name of the group given as 'Panch bahani' *pahārā*.

(3) MOUNT PRASRAVAṆA: *Rāmāyaṇa* mentions four different Prasravaṇa mountains, and in addition, one more, Mt. Plakṣa Prasravaṇa, in the Himalayas, a source of river Sarasvatī as mentioned elsewhere in ancient literature.

[A.] Bhṛgu Prasravaṇa, where Ikṣvāku king Sagara practised penance to please sage Bhṛgu (1:37:10). This was in the Himalayas.

[B.] It is said that the second one was near Pañcavaṭī, Jaṭāyu's abode was on this Prasravaṇa hill ('**godāvarīm janasthānāmimām prasravaṇa girim**' | (3:60:14)). Nandalal Dey (p.159) mentions this to be near Aurangabad, on the banks of south Godavari in Maharashtra. However, the present study suggests that this Prasravaṇa hill should be looked for in the vicinity of Mt. Citrakūṭa and river *gupta* Godavari, not far from Reva table-land, somewhere near Godā *pahārā* area, where Pañcavaṭī is placed by present studies. Cunningham has suggested that Mt. Citrakūṭa itself can be Vālmīki's Mt. Prasravaṇa. (Cunningham. ASIR, vol. XXI, 1883-1884)

[C] The third one was outside *Ṛkṣabila* as pointed out by Svayaṃprabhā to Hanumat's search party (4: 52:12). The present study indicates that this Mt. Prasravaṇa should be identified with Ramgarh hill itself in Surguja district of Chhattisgarh. The relevant topo-sheet map (#64 J/9+13), shows many rivulets and nullahs in the surrounding landscape.

[D] The fourth Mt. Prasravaṇa, also called Mt. Mālyavān, was near Kiṣkindha where Rāma and Lakṣmaṇa stayed during the four monsoon months ('**bahudṛśyadarīkuñje tasminprasravaṇe girau**' | (4:26:5; 4:6:10)). Nandalal Dey (p.159) places this in south India, near Anegundi in Mysore state (presently Karanataka), on the banks of river Tungabhadra, consequential to the notion that Kiṣkindha can be identified with Anegundi. However, the present study suggests that, this Prasravanagiri should be looked for in U.P. amidst Mirzapur hills where Kiṣkindha should be placed.

Thus, the epic itself suggests that the geographical locations and the identity of all these four or five Prasravaṇa hills was not the same, strengthening the possibility that the word 'Prasravaṇa' (meaning any hill with numerous streams and currents flowing over it in all directions) seems to have been used simply as an explanatory common noun by poet Vālmīki.

§§§

5

THE BIRTH STORY OF DAKṢIṆA SĀGARA

In the previous chapter we have seen that Vālmīki prepares the background for the acceptance of the truth regarding the birth story of *dakṣiṇa sāgara*. This starts from *Kiṣkindhākaṇḍa* itself and later in *Yuddhakāṇḍa* the truth strikes us with a bang. It is also realised that many connected threads of this truth are scattered through ancient literature as well. Various aspects of this truth have already been indicated and brought to light in earlier pages. How to interpret them will be considered here, to be followed by geographical justification. However, it is necessary to discover the literary justification first. In this chapter therefore we will see how *dakṣiṇa sāgara* was created, its background and the reasons for its creation. What is mentioned about this in Vālmīki *Rāmāyaṇa* and other sources of ancient literature?

The story of king Sagara appears in *Bālakāṇḍa*, as narrated by sage Viśvāmitra. When one gets to the root and details of the story its geographical significance is revealed. This story from the epic itself has not been noticed and interpreted earlier by scholars as a remarkable and convincing evidence for understanding ramayankara's notion of *dakṣiṇa sāgara* and for identifying the most probable location of *dakṣiṇa sāgara*. This story with its important details is therefore given in the following pages. The story in *Bālakāṇḍa*[1] goes like this:

King Daśaratha of Ayodhya performed *'Aśvamedha' yajña* (horse sacrifice) and *'Putrakāmeṣṭī' yajña* and got four sons as a favour from sage Ṛśyaśṛṅga. After educating the sons in all kinds of skills and knowledge, as Daśaratha was thinking of marrying them off, sage Viśvāmitra appeared in his court. At his request Daśaratha had to send his two sons, Rāma and Lakṣmaṇa to protect the sage's *yajña.* The three men proceeded by the south bank of river Śarayu, till they came across the confluence of rivers Śarayu and Ganga. The next day they navigated Ganga and came to the south bank of Ganga. The description here suggests[2], that they crossed Ganga near modern Chapra. Then they entered the southern forests, Tāṭakāvana (Malada Karuṣa *deśa*) a region ruled by Tāṭakā *yakṣī* (see chapter 2 on Daṇḍakāraṇya and map 2). After Tāṭakā is killed they entered Siddhāśrama area the domain of Mārīca and his consort Kālakā, from where Mārīca is driven away by Rāma and Lakṣmaṇa.

After this, they come to the north bank of river Son. Thus it seems that, they initially entered Tāṭakāvana, then walked southwards to enter Kālakāvana and reached Siddhāśrama in the vicinity. Sage Viśvāmitra tells them that his Siddhāśrama was in the same area. They do not cross river Sumāgadhī or Son, but instead walk back a long distance to reach the banks of river Ganga[4]. On their way they get the glimpses of city Girivrajā or Vasumatī near the right banks of river Son. Rāma, Lakṣmaṇa and sage Viśvāmitra take a night halt on the southern or right banks of river Ganga. Rāma requests the sage to explain how Ganga descended from Mt. Himalaya and became a river flowing by three ways in three different directions[5]. Viśvāmitra then narrates the story of *'tripathaga'* Ganga which goes like this[6].

Ages ago king Sagara, a descendant of Ikṣvāku line and the son of king Bāhu was ruling over Ayodhya. Sagara was nurtured by sage Aurva. King Sagara, with his two queens Keśini, the daughter of king of Vidarbha, and the younger one Sumati, daughter of Ariṣṭanemi, went to Himalayas and practiced penance at Mt. Bhṛgu-Prasravaṇa to get a son. [The brother of Sumati was Suparṇa or 'Garuḍa' (king of birds).] By the blessings of sage Bhṛgu, Sagara got sixty thousand sons from queen Sumati and only one son from Keśini to continue the lineage. *Purāṇās* like *Vāyu, Matsya* and *Brāhmāṇḍa* also have these stanzas. Keśini's only son was named Asaṃañja. As Asaṃañja was wicked and immoral, king Sagara expelled him from the city of Ayodhya. Asaṃañja's son Aṃśumana however was virtuous and popular.

Later, mighty king Sagara commenced Aśvamedha *yajña* or a horse sacrifice, the sacrificial ground being the land between Mt. Himalaya and Mt. Vindhya as that was the best land for performing sacrifices. Aṃśumana, the grandson of Sagara was guarding the horse. The sixty thousand princes in charge of the horse allowed it to stray (as was the custom). It was stealthily taken away by Indra to '*pātāla*' (to the lower regions) and was kept in the vicinity of hermitage of sage Kapila who was then engaged in devotion.

Seeing this obstacle in the sacrifice, Sagara asked his sons to go and if necessary search deep into the earth and bring back the horse. Enthused by their father's command the army of princes started to search, each one of them searching one *yojana,* but in vain. They then tried to make their way using tridents, *vajrās* and other instruments by digging deep through the earth. They dug out sixty thousand *yojanās* of *rasātala* and caused suffering and destruction all over. The distressed *gandharvās*, gods, *asurās*, *pannagas* and *rakṣasās* went to Brahmā and complained that, king Sagara's princes are committing violence towards innocent people. Brahmā consoled and pacified them all by saying that as the entire land or earth is sage Kapila's consort, his anger will turn those thoughtless beings into ashes. The pacified gods and others then went back.

The princes came back and told their father that they could not find the horse. King Sagara was annoyed and asked them to try again. The princes started to dig out the *rasātala,* only to find the four *dik-gajās* (imaginary elephants which hold and balance the earth on their heads) in all four directions[7]. It was only when they turned towards the *īśanya* (north-east) direction they saw mighty sage Kapila. They also saw the horse grazing nearby. The princes rushed on sage Kapila in fury, raising their weapons and instruments, thinking him to be the culprit and an obstacle in the horse sacrifice. Then just by the gaze of raged Kapila all those sons of king Sagara were scorched to heaps of ashes. King Sagara, awaiting his sons to return with the horse, then commanded that his grandson Aṃśumana should find, with better weapons and instruments, the whereabouts of his uncles and the horse thief. Aṃśumana then started and came to a spot from where his uncles had made their way through the earth. The *'dik-gajās'* blessed him. He then came at the site where Kapila had scorched his forefathers to ashes. Aṃśumana also saw the horse browsing nearby.

Aṃśumana was grieving. He could not find water anywhere around to perform the death rites of his uncles. Seeing him desperate, Garuḍa (his grandfather and queen Sumati's brother) approached and said to him, 'O mightiest! Do not grieve, for this annihilation of your forefathers will contribute to the welfare of people at large' (the verse is given below). Garuḍa said that the men were burnt down by the wrath of Kapila, who was no ordinary sage and Aṃśumana therefore should offer libation not with ordinary water. (It should be noted here that Garuḍa, being the knowledgeable authority on death rites is the adviser here (see *Garuḍa Purāṇa*)). He consoled Aṃśumana by saying:

mā śucaḥ puruṣavyāghra vadhoyam lokasammataḥ |
kapilenāprameyeṇa dagdhā hīme mahābalaḥ |
salilam nārhasi prājña datumeṣām hi laukikam ||[8]

Garuḍa further said that their death rites therefore should be performed with the waters of river Ganga. When their ashes are soaked with Ganga waters, they will find their final abode in heaven. On Garuḍa's instructions Aṃśumana took back the horse and king Sagara completed his horse sacrifice. King Sagara, however, could not find a remedial way to bring Ganga waters down from heaven (Himalayan heights) for the salvation of his sons.

Sagara's grandson Aṃśumana practiced penance in Mt. Himalaya but without success and died there. Aṃśumana's son Dilip also planned to bring Ganga down but failed. Dilip's son Bhagīratha was then crowned. He had no son and therefore he handed over the empire to his ministers and decided to devote himself to the cause of his forefathers. Bhagīratha went to Gokarṇa and practiced arduous penance. Brahmā, pleased by his prayers blessed him, but said that the earth could never bear those torrents of Ganga coming down with speed and Śiva alone can hold the river on his head. Thus, Śiva now appears in this story of Rāma's ancestors and has an important role to play.

Bhagīratha again engaged himself in devotion and penance to please Śiva. Pleased by Bhagīratha's devotion, the god of the mountains, trident wielding Śiva held on his head the furious Ganga in her descent from Himalayan heights. Proud Ganga thought she could push down Śiva in *pātāla*. Angry Śiva kept the river on his head and kept her wandering until her pride was tamed. Ganga found no way to reach earth.

Then many seasons passed as Bhagīratha waited in expectation. Then his terrible penance began. Śiva for the sake of the hermit let the river loose from the locks and tangles of his hair. Ganga set free by God Śiva, sank into Bindu *sarovara*, and from Ganga waters seven noble rivers emerged. Out of these seven Ganga currents, three, namely Lhādinī, Pāvanī and Nalinī, sought the eastern side, Su-Cakṣu, Sītā and mighty Sindhu sped with their waters to the west and the seventh flowed where Bhagīratha led her. Mighty river Ganga started flowing with three currents in three different directions. Thus she became '*tripathaga* Ganga'. Ganga descended from the sky on to Himalayas (Śiva's head) and from there she appeared on earth. The story following this is more important for our purpose.

After this incident Ganga again followed Bhagīratha's chariot and with him reached the site where the sons of king Sagara had dug up through the earth to form a ditch or a *kūpa* (a well) and from there Ganga reached *rasātala*[9]. Bhagīratha then noticed the ashes of his forefathers. Ganga soaked the ashes with her holiest and pure waters, and Sagara's sons finally reached their heavenly abode. After hearing this story of king Sagara from Viśvāmitra, the three men crossed river Ganga and reached the hermitage of sage Gautama and Ahalyā. This can be convincingly identified with Ahalyaghat near Baxar, though acccording to the local tradition it is shown at the southern bank of Ganga still in Ganga-Son doab in northern Bihar (see Map 1). *Bālakāṇḍa* here gives the story of deliverance of Ahalyā by Rāma[10]. After this they proceeded towards Viśāla city (the city was set by Ikṣvāku's son Viśāla, and hence the name). The next day they walked the way and reached the city of Mithilā of king Janaka. Daśaratha's four sons then got married in this city.

We have seen before that, according to the epic, Mt. Maināka, since it was obliged by wind god Vāyu, wanted to help Hanumat, the son of Vāyu, in appreciation. *Dakṣiṇa sāgara* also 'indebted to Ikṣvākus', expressed his gratitude and an urge to help Ikṣvāku blood - Rāma. Where did this event take place? We must therefore identify the general area of *dakṣiṇa sāgara* that will satisfy the conditions laid in the epic in the context of location of Laṅkā since Laṅkā was beyond this very same *dakṣiṇa sāgara* according to the Rāmāyaṇa itself. In this connection it is necessary to find out how sage Agastya is related to the problem of location of *dakṣiṇa sāgara* and Laṅkā. Here *Mahābhārata* comes to our aid. An account from *Agastyopākhyāna* of *Mahābhārata* gives an extremely interesting legend. Agastya's mastery, command and prowess are described by three legends[11]:

(1) A triumph over Indra *(Indravijaya)*

(2) Overpowering Mt. Vindhya *(Vindhyavijaya)*

(3) Winning over the sea *(Samudravijaya)*

For the sake of Yudhiṣṭhira, Sage Lomaśa narrates an account, and the story of Samudravijaya goes like this -

Long ago in *Kṛtayuga,* Kālakeyās, a community of *daityās,* were living in lands adjacent to the 'sea'. These Kāleyās or Kālakeyās, Paulomās and Nivātakavacās had their original home in (Aśmanagara? or) Hiraṇyapura. They were frightful, aggressive and combative. They were dependants of Vṛtra. In the war between gods and demons, Indra then annihilated Vṛtra. Humbled down and frightened Kālakeyās then took shelter by the sea that was infested with fish of many kinds and dreadful crocodiles.

Later, the Kāleyās or Kālakeyās again started creating obstacles in *yajñas* and assaulting people practicing penances[12]. All the gods then went to resourceful Viṣṇu, who told them a trick. The tactic was that if gods somehow succeed in drying or depleting and shrinking the sea, by which the Kālakeya *daityās* had taken shelter, only then the Kālakeyās would perish. Viṣṇu further said that wise sage Agastya alone can consume and absorb the entire sea waters. All the gods then went to the hermitage of Agastya. They worshipped and praised him. They mentioned that Agastya had once dethroned king Nahusa. Agastya had also humbled down Mt. Vindhya (see End Note 1). Now, Agastya was their only saviour!

The anxious gods ran to Agastya and pleaded for mercy. Hearing their complaints and grievances against Kālakeyās, sage Agastya went to the sea and he completely consumed that vast sea, drying up its waters along with its aquatic life. This was Agastya's *samudravijaya.* Delighted, the gods then brought about extermination and downfall of Kālakeya *daityās.* Kālakeyās who could save themselves from destruction dug through the earth and started living in '*pātāla*.'

After this victory over the Kālakeyās, the gods again praised Agastya and pleaded, 'O mighty savior Agastya! Please release the sea waters that you have consumed, back into this landmass.' Hearing these words Agastya said to the gods that he had already digested all the waters and hence the gods should try to find an alternative. The gods were stunned and dejected. They then went to Viṣṇu and then to Brahmā, who calmed them down, saying, 'O gods, you may all now go assured and tension free, wherever you want to go. After a long time from now, when king Bhagīratha will need to perform the death rites of his forefathers, he will give back this sea its original form', (of a great and vast water reservoir). Hearing this, the satisfied gods went back and waited for the right time to come[13]. After this Lomaśa tells Yudhiṣṭhira the story of king Sagara[14, 15] from *Bālakāṇḍa* which we have already seen.

There are a few variations in the story of king Sagara, given in Vālmīki *Rāmāyaṇa* and *Mahābhārata*. According to *Mahābhārata* the 'sea' in which the sacrificial horse vanished, was a sea without water and so looked deathly. This particular feature of the 'sea' indicates that the region was arid, dry and perched in Sagara's times. Most importantly, this also explains why Aṃśumana could not find any water source nearby to perform the death rites and why Garuḍa consoled him by commenting that the horrible death of his uncles would in future benefit people at large (when Ganga waters would reach that perched land as a consequence of arduous efforts by king Bhagīratha).

Mahābhārata also mentions that, when king Sagara'*s* sons went again in search of the horse, they found the earth shattered. They approached the site of the broken earth and started to excavate that sea with '*hala*' and '*śūla*' as instruments. (Interestingly, *Mahābhārata* states that the instruments used were plough blades and pick-axes.) By this the sea-land was getting split and torn and the creatures in it were distressed. The princes of king Sagara went in *īśanya* (north-east) direction where ultimately they saw the horse (It is noteworthy that a particular direction is mentioned in both the epics).

The story of king Sagara

Vālmīki Rāmāyaṇa informs us that, king Sagara whose sons excavated the south sea or *dakṣiṇa sāgara* was a great king in Ikṣvāku lineage. Whenever he used to go on an expedition, his sons used to accompany him. The verse is-

yeṣhām sa sagaro nāma sāgaro yena khānitaḥ |
ṣaṣṭiḥ putrasahasrāṇi yam yāntam paryavārayam ||[16]

Not only in *Bālakāṇḍa* but also in *Ayodhyākāṇḍa,* while delineating Ikṣvāku genealogy to Rāma, sage Vasiṣṭḥa says-

sa rājā sagaro nāma yaḥ samudramakhānayat |
iṣṭvā parvaṇi vegena trāsayantamimāḥ prajāḥ ||[17]

Meaning, king Sagara commenced his *yajña* in '*parvakāla*'. He then got the land mass at the sea exhumed by his sons and the bang of their operation distressed the people.

Kālidāsa in his *Raghuvaṃśa* says the following:

tadarthamurvīmavadārayadbhiḥ pūrvaḥ kilāyam
parivardhito naḥ |[18]

The story of king Sagara also echoes in *Purāṇās.* In *Viṣṇu Purāṇa*[19], it is unambiguously stated that, the landmass that was dug out (unearthed) and excavated was itself reckoned by king Sagara as his own son, as his own creation and for this very reason that land mass watered by river Ganga came to be known as son of king Sagara and therefore Sāgara (**sagaraputra** = Sāgara). *Brahmā Purāṇa*[20] delineates the lineage of *sūryavaṃśa*. It says that after Ganga was brought down the same waters worshiped king Sagara and seeing that, pleased king Sagara gave it the name 'Sāgara'. *Vāyu purāṇa*[21] tells us that the sacrificial horse of king Sagara was stolen in *dakṣiṇa-samudra prānta* (south sea area) and when Sagara's sons excavated the earth at that site and after Ganga was brought down there, the whole land up to the sea (meaning that exhumed south sea) was enriched with prosperity. *Harivaṃśa* tells us:

sa tam deśam tadā putraiḥ khanayāmāsa pārthivaḥ |
āseduste tatastatra khanyamāne mahārṇave ||[22]

Means: 'It is known to the people that our forefathers who excavated the sea have also extended that sea.

Sagara story given in *Harivaṃśa* is dotted with more information. The father of Sagara, Bāhu, had been dethroned by Haihayas and Tālajañghas. Later, mighty king Sagara annihilated those enemies. He also punished those who had assisted his enemies. They were Yavanas, Khaśas, Pāradas, Pallavas and Kāmbojas. Sagara forced them to change their way of dressing and hair styles although they were all (assumed) *kṣatriyas*. This suggests that in pre-Sagara times the above mentioned 'invaders' had overpowered the Ikṣvāku rulers, namely king Bāhu of Ayodhya.

Here it is said that Sagara's horse was taken away from *āgneya* (south-east) seashore, **'samudre pūrvadakṣiṇe'**[23]. When his sons dug up the land, excavated a huge landmass and made a large ditch as expansive as a sea, then they saw the horse and sage Kapila. From the wrath of Kapila, only four of Sagara's sons were saved. They were Bṛhatketū, Suketū, Dharmaratha and Pañcajana. King Sagara was blessed and favoured by the sage, who said that 'the lineage and fame of Ikṣvākus will remain forever and the sea itself will become his son'[24]. Thus, Sāgara or that vast expanse of water, became the son of king Sagara, who was responsible for its creation.

Samudra or sea, thus obliged, then came into being and he worshipped the king. Pleased by his devotion, king Sagara reckoned that sea as his own son and gave him the name 'Sāgara'. This very Sāgara, 'the sea' of Sagara's story is *'dakṣiṇa sāgara'* obviously situated in south Ganga plain touching the foot of Mt. Vindhya and 100 *yojanās* beyond which, Laṅkā was situated. Thus, obliged by Rāma's ancestors, as explained by the numerous stories from different sources given in chapters 4 and 5, this very Sāgara, as a gesture of gratitude, wanted to help Rāma reach Laṅkā. Thus, king Sagara and his sons along with their lineage descendent, king Bhagīratha were all responsible for the creation of *dakṣiṇa sāgara* and then for filling it with Ganga waters. This exhumed *dakṣiṇa sāgara* was situated in a region where originally Kālakeya *daityās* were living, as we can now infer. Identifying the general area of this south sea is pivotal in our search for *dakṣiṇa sāgara* and also for Laṅkā and not the sea around far away island Ceylon. Most importantly, this is suggested by Vālmīki *Rāmāyaṇa* itself as can be safely inferred from the above discussion.

Thus, in conclusion, it can be said that *dakṣiṇa sāgara* was indeed a water reservoir of huge expanse, exhumed from earth as the analysis of information and evidences gathered tells us. It is possible that this Ganga water reservoir became salty by natural causes or it might not have been salty at all in all probability. It is also logical to infer that this *dakṣiṇa sāgara* was situated in south Ganga plain, to the south of river Ganga and so was called *dakṣiṇa sāgara*. According to the geographical concepts of *Rāmāyaṇa*, the notion regarding the division of the globe was very peculiar, based on which *Rāmāyaṇa* also mentions, '*uttara samudra*'[25]. It can therefore be argued that the *sāgara* that was unearthed to the south of Ayodhya and to the south of river Ganga around Laṅkā was naturally called '*dakṣiṇa sāgara*'. Also, perhaps for the same reason it was sometimes called *Lavaṇa samudra, Kṣara samudra* etc., although according to its birth-story it was filled with Ganga waters (such names could be borrowed from the purāṇic conception of *saptadvīpā pṛithvī* wherein *lavaṇa samudra* is imagined to be situated to the immediate south of Jambūdvīpā). This fact, when forgotten, must have helped in shifting both *dakṣiṇa sāgara* and Rāvaṇa's Laṅkā out of *Bhāratavarṣa* up to Ceylon. The waters from the same *dakṣiṇa sāgara* area had been consumed and dried out by sage Agastya and only then the gods had exterminated the displaced Kālakeyās.

However, the 'south sea', presumed to be situated to the south of Kiṣkindha (identified with Mirzapur region), where Vālin used to go for his evening prayers was not *dakṣiṇa sāgara* around Laṅkā. Thus it can now be theorised that, based on his knowledge of 'geographical reality', Vālmīki's own concept of *'dakṣiṇa sāgara'* was that it was a vast expance of water in a landmass, which originally was the homeland of Kālakeyās.

Much has been talked about *Bālakāṇḍa* and *Uttarakāṇḍa* being later additions and that through such additions Bhārgavas have tried to show their superiority. *Mahābhārata*[26] and *Purāṇās* consider epic poet Vālmīki as a Bhārgava. D.R. Mankad[27], in a different context has not noticed the connection between the Sagara story and the creation legend as well as the location of *'dakṣiṇa sāgara'* and still says that the story of king Sagara does not form an integral and essential part of the original kernel of Rāma's story and these lines therefore, very likely, are taken from different sources and added later on. Same is the case with Janaka's genealogy and Diti and Indra story etc. he says.

Remarks made by U.P. Shah[28] in this connection are noteworthy - 'What we can however say is that all the portions of *Uttarakāṇḍa* do not form a homogenous unit with other *Kāṇḍās*, and were added later is clear from 'some obvious contradictions' (occurring in *Uttarakāṇḍa*). But these are problems of 'higher criticism'.

From an examination of the story of creation of *dakṣiṇa sāgara* by Rāma's ancestors, the helping role of Mt. Maināka obliged by Hanumat's father Vāyu, the extension of the *Gaṅgāvatarana* story with an indirect suggestion of it being an effort of Ikṣvākus to irrigate a land-mass which originally was a region occupied by Kālakeyās, what appears is that all these episodes are interwoven very skilfully. All important threads of the story are scattered not only through *Bālakāṇḍa* and *Uttarakāṇḍa*, but also through *Ayodhyākāṇḍa, Sundarakāṇḍa* and *Yuddhakāṇḍa* and undoubtedly present a kind of an inevitable interconnectedness. King Sagara story especially can be examined in this perspective and in the context of the present effort at locating *dakṣiṇa sāgara* and Laṅkā. This story should not be looked at as an extraneous thing. King Sagara story and *dakṣiṇa sāgara* (exhumed by King Sagara's 60000 sons), are mentioned by Jain version of *Rāmāyaṇa* (In *Sandhi* V of *Paumacariyam* by Vimalasuri of early A.D. centuries)[29]. In the whole scenario, however, the Mahendra *parvata,* Bhārgava Paraśurāma's favourite abode, does appear a misfit in the main backdrop of the happenings. The reasons for this will be discussed later in this book (see Appendix G). And further, even if it is so, it cannot be denied that the later part of the King Sagara story, i.e. of king Bhagīratha and *Gaṅgāvatarana,* about which we are concerned here, provides a clue to the scenario of pre-Rāma days. It is suggested that the weaving in of these legends 'could be explained by arguing that they were linked to the personalities belonging to the Ikṣvāku or *sūryavaṃśa* lineage'[30] as Romila Thapar has said.

From an examination of King Sagara story, a few things can be inferred regarding the Rāmāyaṇic notion of *dakṣiṇa sāgara*. Consequential to this is a fact which becomes apparent: Rāvaṇa's Laṅkā was bounded by this south sea, and was adjacent to the south shore of it, is what *Rāmāyaṇa* says. (A) *Dakṣiṇa sāgara* around Laṅkā was within Jambūdvīpā (and hence within *Bhāratavarṣa*). (B) This south sea was artificially made, a work of human hands and the bridge constructed over it to reach Laṅkā too was a work of human hands, Rāma's army. (C) This sea was created by the ancestors of Rāma. (D) *Dakṣiṇa sāgara* was not boundless but was spread over a definable area. (E) In all probability it was filled with Ganga waters (and not salty water), and was somewhere in south Ganga plain. (There are number of Ganga canals in south Ganga plain ending in large reservoirs but of modern origin. It can be imagined that similar efforts were made in ancient times also.)

It is now necessary to find the original home of Kālakeyās—*Mahādānavasaṅkula,* which later became the home of dreadful crocodiles, **'sāgaro makarālayaḥ'**, for that would indicate the most believable location of the famed '*dakṣiṇa sāgara',* adjacent to Laṅkā of Rāvaṇa.

Who were Kāleyās (Kālakeya) or Kālakhañja daityās ?

Kālakeyās have been mentioned a number of times in both the epics, in *Purāṇās* or elsewhere. This Kāleya tribe was living in Aśmanagara of *rasātala* (or Hiraṇyapura). They were also called Paulomās. *Vanaparvan* of *Mahābhārata* informs that Arjuna had brought down the destruction of Kālakeyās[31]. Kāleyās and Paulomās together were called Nivatakavcas. According to Vālmīki *Rāmāyaṇa*, Rāvaṇa had confronted them and in that war, Śūrpaṇakha's husband, *'Kālakeyādhipatī'* Viddyutjjiva, was killed at Rāvaṇa's hands inadvertantly[32]. Thus we get a sea of evidences, gathered from the epics and other ancient literature sources, which makes it abundantly clear that the geographical position of *dakṣiṇa sāgara*, in other words the original land of Kālakeyās might have been in close proximity of Rāvaṇa's Laṅkā, and to the north of Laṅkā. This can be said on the basis of delineation of events and their chronology indicated therein.

There were frequent wars between gods and *rakṣasās*. What was the cause of these conflicts? It could be the control over land, water or both. The conflicts were between (1) Gods and Kālakeyās (took place in northern part of south Ganga plain in pre-Sagara times) (2) Indra and Vṛtra (took place in Ganga Son *doab*-northern part) (3) Agastya and Viśvāmitra and Tāṭakā *yakṣī* (took place in Ganga-Son *doab*-southern part and (4) Rāma and Rāvaṇa [took place, further south, still in Ganga plain in north-eastern Vindhya or Kaimur ranges. Thus, a movement can be marked, i.e. from north, towards south-east, then towards south-west and from there towards southern land mass touching the Singrauli basin adjacent to the Son valley, as can be inferred from the discussion that follows.

Mārīca was the son of Tāṭakā, who was ruling over Karuṣas. Kālakā was Mārīca's wife. Their dwelling place was Malada and Karuṣa *deśa* and the land to its south. *Rāmāyaṇa* tells us that Mārīca and Kālakā had 14,000 sons who were called 'Kālakeyās', **'kālakeyāḥ iti khyātāḥ sahasraṇi caturdaśāḥ'** |[33]. They are mentioned in Mahābhārata as well. This reminds us of the fact that Khara and Dūṣaṇa were stationed at the outskirts of Janasthāna with an army of 14000 *rakṣasās,* who were annihilated by Rāma.

Thus their quantitative description matches with that of Mārīca-Kālakeyās. Moreover it can be argued that they must have been in fact the sons/subjects of Kālakā and Mārīca and must have been Kālakeyās. This can be said since after Mārīca was driven away from Tāṭakāvana and Kālakāvana, Vidyujjiva, Śūrpaṇakha's husband must have become the headman of Kālakeyās or 'Kālakeyādhipatī' as is mentioned and later after Vidyujjiva's death, Śūrpaṇakha, when defaced by Lakṣmaṇa, is consoled by Rāvaṇa, who sends her to Daṇḍakāraṇya under the patronage of Khara, who is then the commander of the same 14000 Kālakeyās, it can easily be inferred. This inference leads us to an important conclusion that the outskirts of Janasthāna were very close to the domain of Kālakeyās and also Mārīcasthāna.

Uttarakāṇḍa[34] gives other details of Rāvaṇa's wanderings, which suggest that Rāvaṇa assisted by Mārīca and others, conquered the Nāgā people of Bhogāvatī, Nivātakavacās of Maṇimayī and also Kālakeyās of Aśmanagara (the domain of Bali *daitya*, where Viṣṇu in Vāmana incarnation had conquered him, in the region of Siddhāśrama, according to *Bālakāṇḍa*). The delineation indicates that the same place, Aśmanagara, was also the domain of Hiraṇyakaśipū, the grandfather of Bali.

Medieval literature tells us that 'Kair' ('Kaimur-hill range') was another name of Karuṣa *deśa*[35] i.e. Bundelkhand-Bagelkhand and Reva state. It is also said that it was a *janapada* located in the *īśanya diśa* (north-east) of Mt. Vindhya. These people were living between the lands of Cedi and Māgadha or the land between rivers Son and Ken. Pāṇinī says that they were good fighters and lived in inaccessible parts of Mt. Vindhya and were resenting the Vedic Aryan culture. *Mahābhārata* tells us that Karuṣa king was Dantavaktra[36]. Both the epics make it abundantly clear that the king of Kālakeyās or Kālakhañjās, was Śūrpaṇakha's husband, Kālakeya Vidyujjiva.

In conclusion, Hiraṇyapura, or Aśmanagara, Tāṭakāvana, Mārīca's abode, dwelling place of Kālakā and Kālakeyās, are all the places which must be located in the vicinity of each other and also of Daṇḍakāraṇya, Janasthāna and Pañcavaṭī (see map 1). Even today in north-eastern Madhya Pradesh, near the confluence of rivers Son and Rihand (Reṇū), is a village called 'Kalakapur' (in the map it is near Daltonganj in district Surguja). In summary, Kāleyās (or Kālakeyās) were an ancient non-Aryan community, living in the forests of north-eastern slopes of Mt. Vindhya. It can be inferred from the above discussion that *dakṣiṇa sāgara* was a man-made sea of huge dimensions and a remarkable confirmation has been found about the identification of the site in a region which was originally the home of Kālakeyās in the north-eastern part of Son valley and Kaimur scarp. Can the two names Asmanagar and Hiraṇyapura give any clue? From the above discussion we can infer that we have been able to demarcate the general boundaries of the original home of Kālakeyās.

Coming back to the story of Rāma, *Dakṣiṇa* Sāgara then advised Rāma (see End Note 2), that Nala *vānara* the gifted craftsman, should construct a bridge over the sea and the sea will hold it and no ferocious crocodiles shall attack till *vānara* army has crossed it. Then *vānarās* charged with exuberant spirits, entered the forests around and collected woods and logs from *Sāla* and a variety of other trees. Using all those trees and rocks, the *vānarās* constructed in five days the bridge (10 *yojanās* X 100 *yojanās*) that touched the opposite shore. Both Rāma and Hanumat mention that navigation was impossible in *dakṣiṇa sāgara.* This whole description suggests various physical features, characteristics and nature of the sea that was *dakṣiṇa sāgara.* Although expansive and vast in dimensions, *dakṣiṇa sāgara* must have been very shallow, not allowing navigation. Thus a bridge was the only choice. The sea waters must have been dotted with rocks and crags (mountain peaks). It also must be a muddy, swampy and marshy wetlands crowded with crocodiles. *Rāmāyaṇa* at various places mentions that the main hurdle in crossing the sea was the ferocious crocodiles in it (see Appendix A) and this important characteristic of *Dakṣiṇa Sāgara* suggests that it must have been located amidst thickly forested area.

Having crossed the sea, Rāma's army reached the far bank and encamped on the southern shore of *dakṣiṇa sāgara.* They all ascended Mt. Suvela. Rāma overlooked Laṅkā situated on the hill-top of Mt. Trikūṭa and noticed *rakṣasa* king Rāvaṇa sitting there, the two hills being very close. *Rāmāyaṇa* mentions that from Suvela peak Rāma could view some minute details of Laṅkā. This obviously indicates that Suvela and Trikūṭa, both must be the peaks of a single mountain range. *Gīrvāṇalaghukośa* states[37], that Trikūṭa is just another name for Suvela. Thus, after crossing over the sea if Rāma's *vānara* army has reached that most inaccessible and nebulous *rakṣasa sthāna,* Laṅkā, we must find out where Vālmīki had imagined it to be situated. Can we find a place in actual geography that not only answers the description of Rāvaṇa's Laṅkā given in the epic but also is geographically connected with other major sites like Daṇḍakāraṇya, Pañcavaṭī or Kiṣkindhā? This most important aspect will be dealt with in the next chapter.

The Return Journey from Laṅkā to Ayodhya

After Laṅkā war was over, Rāma told Bibhīṣaṇa to make arrangements for their return journey to Ayodhya. Rāma does not say that the way is a distant one, he says,

ayoddhyāmāyato hyeṣaḥ panthaḥ paramadurgamaḥ |[38]

Meaning, The route to Ayodhya is arduous and tough. Thus, the above description makes it clear that it was a walkway ('**panthaḥ**'), rough route on land. Rāma and some others started their return journey to Ayodhya, this time with grandeur, in Puṣpak *Vimāna*. The present author has shown with conclusive evidences that Puṣpak *Vimāna* could not have been an air-craft but was a huge and heavily decorated palanquin (see appendix F).

As Puṣpak departs from Laṅkā, Rāma points out to Sītā various places and sites on the land below as they overlook from Puṣpak *Vimāna*. The description appears in the fascicule 3, second half of *Yuddhakāṇḍa*[39]. Rāma had made his journey on foot to Laṅkā. While the return journey is on, Rāma points out to Sītā the following places in order:

The battleground of Laṅkā situated near the north gate of Laṅkā → *lavaṇarṇava* (salt water sea) and the bridge over it → Golden mountain Hiraṇyanābha or Mt. Maināka submerged in *Dakṣiṇa Sāgara*[40] → Śiva *tīrtha* (see End Note 3) → Kiṣkindha (at this spot on Sītā's wish the *vānara* women are picked up) → Ṛṣyamūka *parvata*

→ Lake *Paṃpā* → Mataṅgavana and Śabarī hermitage → place where Kabandha was killed by Rāma and Lakṣmaṇa → Janasthāna and the huge *vaṭavṛkṣa* (Banyan tree named Subhadra-*vaṭa* as we have seen earlier) → the place where Jaṭāyu was killed → Pañcavaṭī and *parṇakuṭī* → river Godavari → Agastya's hermitage → Śarabhaṅga's hermitage → Atrī's hermitage and the place where Virādha was killed → Citrakūṭa *parvata* → river Yamuna → Bhāradvāja's hermitage → river Ganga → Śṛṅgaverapura → *niṣād* king Guhā's abode → Ayodhya.

Curiously, in this list there is no mention of river Narmada or Mt. Mahendra though Mt Maināka is mentioned. Similarly, there is no mention of any place from south India either. The present studies have identified all the important rāmāyaṇic sites to the north of Vindhyan ranges.

References: Birth Story Of *Dakṣiṇa-Sāgara*

1. 1:38; 1:43
2. 1:23:10
3. 1:33: 12
4. 1:31:5-8
5. 1: 34:10
6. 1: *sargās* 38-43
7. 1: 39:12
8. 1:40: 17, 18, 19
9. 1:42:23, Entry: no. 934
10. 1:48: 1-22
11. *'Mbh'. Vanaparvan. Tirth.* 3:94

12 Ibid .3:101:1-10

13. Ibid. 3:104:1-4
14. Ibid. 3:104-108
15. Ibid. 3:105:24
16. 1:5:2
17. 2:102:19
18. *'Raghuvaṃśa'*, 13:3
19. *'Viṣṇu Purāṇa'*, 35
20. *'Brahmā Purāṇa'*, 5: part: 2
21. *'Vāyu Purāṇa'*, 54

22. *'Harivaṃśa', 'Sagarotpattī',* 14:23-26
23. Ibid. *Purvardha:* 1:14:22
24. Ibid. *Purvardha:* 1:14:23-30
25. 4:43:54 -By
26. *'Mbh'. Shantiparvan.*57:40
27. D.R. Mankad: *'Introduction to Kiṣkindhākaṇḍa'* (1965), p. 38,
28. U.P. Shah: *'Introduction to Uttarakāṇḍa'* (1975) p. 52, 53
29. *'Paumacariyam'* of Vimalasuri (ed. and publ. by H. Jacobi Sandhi V, (tr. Hindi by Vora Shantilal) B.R. Publication Corporation Delhi
30. Romila Thapar: *'Exile and the Kingdom',* (1978) p. 4
31. *'Mbh'. Vanaparvan. Ara. Yakṣayuddhaparvan* Adhyāya 170:1-70, 3:77:73-74
32. 7:23:1-12 and 7:23: entry no. 443
33. 7: 23:15, 7:23: entry no. 443
34. 7:12:2
35. *'Prācina Sthalakośa'* (S. Chitrav.), p. 377
36. Mbh. Sabhā. Mantraparvan: 2:13:10, 12
37. *'Gīrvāṇalaghukośa',* p.636
38. 6:109:7
39. 6:111:1-39, part II, Fascicule III
40. 6:111:12

End notes:

(1) VINDHYA VIJAYA OF AGASTYA: The legend about Mt. Vindhya is narrated by Lomaśa (*Mbh. Sabhā.Vana.*3:102:10-14) Great Mt. Meru stood high and bright and the sun as usual was revolving around Mt. Meru. Seeing this, jealous Mt. Vindhya said to Sūrya (the Sun), that Sūrya should revolve round Mt. Vindhya too. Hearing his words Sūrya said that, he only follows the rules made by the 'Creator'. Annoyed and jealous, Mt. Vindhya then started to grow (of its own) becoming an obstacle for the sun, moon and the constellations. This blocked the sunlight to north of Mt. Vindhya and people were distressed. Sage Agastya then went to Mt. Vindhya and said he wished to go to south for a cause and Mt.Vindhya should make way and humble down till Agastya returns. Mt. Vindhya obeyed and, stopped growing. Agastya then crossed over the mountain but never returned, thus bringing Mt. Vindhya to his knees. Obviously, in this narrative there is an implication of a natural geographical phenomenon.

(2) DRUMAKULYA AND MARUKĀNTĀRA: Viewing the expansive sea with surging waters, Rāma worshipped the sea for three consecutive nights (6:1; 14:7). When Rāma was angered he stringed and stretched his bow, the ocean arose himself. He promised Rāma that though the sea was vast and incapable of being crossed and as he could not deprive his waters abounding in crocodiles, he would instead suggest a remedy (6:15:6).

Then Rāma said that the stretched arrow of his, must accomplish the end intended and the sea should tell where Rāma should let it light. The place Drumakulya, to the north of *dakṣiṇa sāgara* was the abode of Abhīrās (Dasyus), where the arrow hit, was celebrated on earth as 'Marukāntāra'. The word *'druma'* means tree or a Banyan tree, Parijata tree or *purohita* of Gandharavas, Kubera's devotee, king of Kinnaras, Kubera, etc. (*'Gīrvāṇalaghukośa'* p.248 and *'Prācina Caritrakośa'* p.306).

According to *'Bhāratiya Sanskṛti Kośa'* (9:p671), river Sarasvatī and Sarasvān sea were Abhīra's Drumakulya. Drumakulya is mentioned in Arjuna's north expedition (*'Mbh'. Sabhā.* 2:25:1). According to *Mahābhārata*, Kimpuruṣavarṣa was a country of the north-east. The king of this country was named 'Drumaputra'.

Marukāntāra is said to be located between river Narmada and Bhrgukaccha (Bharuch) [A.B.L. Awasthi *'Studies in Skanda Purāṇa'* (1976) p.173]. Awasthi says that one Kantaravana is in the vicinity of Kanṭakacala, river Paṃpā and Godavari. There is a mention of MahāKāntara near Kosālā country in the Allahabad inscription of Samudragupta (*Select Inscriptions* vol. I, D.C. Sarkar p.250).

B.C. Mazumdar [*'Orissa in the making'* (1925) p.189] opines that, MahāKāntara may lie between Ganjam and Chhattisgarh or between Raipur and Sambalpur to the north of Mahanadi of Orissa. It was under the command of a Gond headman Vyāghrarāja, who was overthrown by Samudragupta. The domain of this Vyāghrarāja was located to the west of Jharkhand. Sahadeva had conquered MahāKāntara in his south expedition as *Mahābhārata* informs us and the Kantaraka people lived near river Vena it says. This river Vena must be Vainganga of M.P.

According to Rajim inscription, Jagapala (during the reign of Kalacuri king Prithvidev II of Sripura), had conquered Kāntara which could be located between rivers Raptī and Paruṣṇī of Madhya Pradesh [P.K. Bhattacharya *'Historical geography of M.P. from early records'* (1977), p.18, 277]. On the banks of river Tapi is a Śiva *sthāna* called 'Kāntareśvara'. Kāntara was a land-mass situated in eastern M.P.

and was thickly forested, as can be inferred from the above evidences and indications.

'Prācina Sthalakośa' gives routes used in ancient India. According to the order given → Ayodhya → Pāṭaliputra (Patna) → Tamralipti (Tamluk) → Mahanadi → Chhattisgarh → Raipur → Māgadha → Kaliṅga → north-eastern Maharashtra → south Kosālā, was the route used by sage Agastya, Rāma(?), king Nala and during emperor Aśoka's Kaliṅga expedition. The same route was also taken in emperor Samduragupta's expedition. He had advanced and turned towards the west to conquer the tribal king Vyāghrarāja of MahāKāntara. From this it becomes clear that MahāKāntara was a land that extended in the plain of Mahanadi, Chhattisgarh, Raipur etc. The present area of Surguja was denominated as Kāntara during the *Mahābhārata* period which later came to be known as MahāKāntara in the Gupta age according to V.D. Jha [*'Investigations into the Archaeology of Surguja'* (1973)].

It can be imagined that, to the north of *dakṣiṇa sāgara* the land had been under the command of Druma or Kubera and there was a spot where subterranean water gushed out. The area first dried up and later was enriched because of the same water source as Rāma conferred a boon. The description is given in 6:22:37-40- By:

tasmāttadbāṇapāten apaḥ kukṣiṣvaśoṣayat |
vikhyātam triṣulokeṣu marukāntarameva ca || (6:22:37-By)

The word *'kāntara'* means (1) an expansive forest, (2) hurdled road (3) burrow and (4) drought condition. (V.S. Apte's *'Sanskrit-English dictionary'* 1978) *'marusthala'* means dry, deserted land and therefore the name Marukāntāra is definitely meaningful and explanatory.

(3) MAHADEVA *TĪRTHA*: *Rāmāyaṇa* mentions this Śiva *sthāna*, which is pointed out by Rāma to Sītā from Puṣpak *Vimāna* while returning from Laṅkā to Ayadhya. He points out the half-submerged Mt. Maināka, then the area where the *vānara* army had encamped on the north shore of *dakṣiṇa sāgara,* (no mention of Mt. Mahendra!) and then Rāma says:

atta pūrvam mahadevaḥ prasādamakarodvibhuḥ |
etattu dṛśyate tīrtham sāgarasya mahātmanaḥ || (6:111:entry 3395)

Meaning, 'at this place, I had earlier received blessings from lord Śiva-Mahadeva'. After this, Puṣpak reaches Kiṣkindhā. Śiva's ninth *jyotirliṅga* form was for Rāvaṇa at Vaidyanatha (at Citabhūmī) is mentioned.It may also be noted that Kālidāsa in his *Raghuvaṃśa* refers to a Śiva *sthāna*, named Gokarṇa situated on the sea shore of *dakṣiṇa sāgara* (*'Raghuvaṃśa'*:8:33). This may well could be a later addition. Actual location of a Śiva *sthāna* on the north shore of south sea is a matter of speculation.

(4) BHAGĪRATHA: Ikṣvāku king Sagara and all his descendents, with the exception of Bhagīratha, could not find a way to bring river Ganga down from Himalayan heights. It was arduous penance, resourcefulness and patience that gave Bhagīratha success. It is believed that river Ganga that was going northwards was manoeuvred and brought down towards south by king Bhagīratha. From thereon, any effort and achievement of that magnitude is called *'Bhagīratha'* efforts. This *'vidyā'* (knowledge, skill and technique) was also called *'Bhagīratha vidyā'*, (in which there are six ways described, the most difficult one was to pass one water current over another it is said!) In present terms *'Bhagīratha vidyā'* can be called ultimate irrigation technology! Some modern engineers believe that, Ganga, as it descends from its origin up to a very long distance, flows through a canal constructed in ancient times and this, if proved, corroborates with the mythical story of *Gaṅgāvatarana* by king Bhagīratha [D.G. Godse *'Mātāval'*-Marathi, (1981) Popular Prakashan, Mumbai]. It can be imagined that the story of *Gaṅgāvatarana* seems to reflect continuous, persistent efforts of three generations of Ikṣvākus to irrigate some parched landmass in their territory by constructing canals in order to channelise Ganga waters.

§§§

6

IDENTIFICATION OF RĀVAṆA'S LAṄKĀ

In previous chapters, results of the present studies are discussed and Daṇḍakāraṇya, Janasthāna and Pañcavaṭī within it on Reva plateau have been identified giving convincing evidences. It is argued that *vānara* kingdom of Kiṣkindha must have been around Mirzapur area, in a hilly region of south Gangā plain, which is around 100 km from Reva-Pañcavaṭī. The southernmost site of action of the Rāma *katha*, *Ṛkṣabila* has been identified with Ramgarh hill, dist. Surguja, (in Chhattisgarh state) which points at the direction of Laṅkā to be to the north of this site. *Rāmāyaṇa* tells us that Kiṣkindha was the northernmost starting point from where Rāma, Lakṣmaṇa and Sugrīva with *vānara* army advanced in the south direction towards Laṅkā and came up to the north shore of *Dakṣiṇa Sāgara*, where Mt. Mahendra was set with one of its spurs thrust into the sea waters. It is from here that they had to construct a bridge to cross those waters to reach Laṅkā! In the previous chapter with ample evidences, from the epic itself or elsewhere, it has been inferred that Vālmīki had imagined *Dakṣiṇa Sāgara* to be situated in south Ganga plain. The present studies suggest that, given the topography of south Ganga plain, we find the position to be as under. *Dakṣiṇa Sāgara* could be bound by Mirzapur hills, Reva plateau, and river Son with her south-west as well as north-eastern bound currents. Consequential to these results obtained from the present studies it becomes obvious that we should look for Rāvaṇa's Laṅkā to the south of this *Dakṣiṇa Sāgara*. This region would be the southernmost part of district Mirzapur, Sonbhadra (U.P.) and north-eastern part of M.P. comprising of Reva, Sidhi and Surguja districts of north Chhattisgarh (see map 1).

M.V. Kibe argued that, Rāvaṇa's Laṅkā was in Amarkanṭak hill area (Shahdol district in eastern M.P.). T.P. Iyer's theory was that it could be on 'Indrana' hill near Jabalpur in M.P. Both these important propositions brought the domain of search for Laṅkā well within the boundaries of India. Unreal and absurd theories identifying Rāvaṇa's Laṅkā with places outside India crumbled down by these two theories, which were supported by few other scholars supplying some more dependable pieces of evidence. Such studies directed the attention of researchers towards a particular region, i.e. Madhya Pradesh in the map of India. Thus, these theories compelled researchers to think as to why the neighbouring island Ceylon is regarded as Rāvaṇa's Laṅkā for the last thousand years or more and why it is unacceptable for the thinking mind.

Now the next question that arises is, when can it be said with certainty that Laṅkā could be nowhere else but in north-eastern M.P.? How can one pinpoint and identify the possible location of Laṅkā area? If that is achieved, the next step can be taken. That step will be to undertake a thorough study of the area, the survey of its present occupants, their customs and traditions, archaeological examination of deposits, excavations in the region, geological survey of the area and so on. If Kibe's Amarkanṭak theory and Iyer's Indrana theory are examined in the light of the data that is gathered here from the text and actual 'site searching' on Google, which is possible only now, their sites do not seem to satisfy certain conditions, to be identified as probable sites with a claim for Laṅkā. Most importantly, if according to the epic, description and its interpretation done here, *Dakṣiṇa Sāgara* was to the north of *Ṛkṣabila*, or in south Ganga plain, the sites identified by both scholars lay to the north-west of Ramgarh-*Ṛkṣabila,* and not to its north. Identification of Ramgarh hill tunnel with *Ṛkṣabila* is perfectly in conformity with the data from the text. Moreover,

Laṅkā should be within the Daṇḍakāraṇya boundaries but not far away from Tāṭakāvana or Pañcavaṭī plateau, which the present studies identify with enough confidence, from where Indrana site is away. In addition to this, both Amarkanṭaka and Indrana sites are not situated in an inaccessible hilly area.

Laṅkā should not be away from Pañcavaṭī, which in turn should be at a small distance from Citrakūṭa and river Godavari issuing out from a nearby hill, or river Gadva issuing out from Godā *pahārā*. Pañcavaṭī should necessarily be an elevated vast table-land only slightly away from Citrakūṭa. We discussed these important pre-conditions in previous chapters. The descriptions from the epic supply us with clear evidences which connect all these sites with one another and help in identifying them in relation to each other. If viewed and studied by using modern technique of satellite imaging (in Google Earth), where and which is a site that most faithfully answers the rāmāyaṇic description of Vālmīki's and Rāvaṇa's Laṅkā? The present author has therefore searched for such a site as a first step by way of geographical and topographical studies and by satellite imaging, since it was found that especially the site of Pañcavaṭī could be dependably identified on Reva plateau using satellite imaging.

Viśvakarma had told *rakṣasās* that there are two mountains namely Trikūṭa and Suvela, adjacent to each other. The middle peak of Trikūṭa is so high that it looks like a cloud dangling from the sky. The shape of Laṅkā is very regular as if chipped and chiselled from all four sides, '**taṅkacchinna caturdiśī**', making it inaccessible even for birds[1]. On the table-land of that hill-top, stands the city of Laṅkā, his best creation. It is thirty *yojanās* in width and 100 *yojanās* in length. In *Rāmāyaṇa*, Laṅkā is described as a hill-top city surrounded by a sea ('**samudra parighānāyam**'[2]). It had four concentric moats, four massive gates and mechanical contrivances to deter invaders by means of fire, water and stones. The *rakṣasās* were told that they should make that wonderfully inaccessible city their abode. Hearing all this the *rakṣasās* happily made Laṅkā their home. Later on, however, because of fear of Viṣṇu, they abandoned Laṅkā and started living in *rasātala*.

Vālmīki seldom describes Rāvaṇa's Laṅkā to be a *'dvīpā'* or a *'deśa'*, but more often as a city or rather a settlement. Moreover, *'dvīpā'* does not necessarily mean an island in an ocean, viz. a land-mass surrounded by sea, but could be parts of land too, it is believed, i.e. Jambūdvīpā, Śakadvīpā, Krauñcadvīpā etc. Rāvaṇa's Laṅkā was in an area surrounded by watery and swampy region. There was thick *Sāla* forest where Laṅkā existed and within Madhya Pradesh such areas can be easily marked and identified. Most of the hilly *Sāla* forest areas lie to the east of the mid-point of M.P., which is Jabalpur. Laṅkā was (most importantly) inaccessible, situated within hilly area, like a natural fort that protects from invaders. Rāvaṇa's Laṅkā is called *'laṅkādurgam'*[3], which here means difficult to enter.

Thus, Laṅkā was situated on a high hill-top, '**sa nagagre ca tam laṅkām**', '**girirmūrghni sthitām laṅkām**'[4]. Where in north-eastern Madhya Pradesh can we find a place which will fit in well with the above description of Rāvaṇa's abode given in the epic?

We therefore have to turn towards the north-eastern part of M.P. The old district gazetteers of Satna, Reva, Panna, and Sidhi, inform us that the northern districts of Madhya Pradesh and those of present Chhattisgarh state, namely Surguja, Korea, Chang Bhakar, are especially more hilly, with many peaks, table-lands and plateaus. The extraordinarily thickly forested areas in these districts are still unexplored even today. The district gazetteers of British period are a rich source of the oldest possible written information about these districts. The north-eastern corner of Madhya Pradesh has districts Reva and Sidhi together, whereas Surguja is the northernmost district of the adjoining state of Chhattisgarh. Adjoining these are the districts of Mirzapur and Sonbhadra of U.P. (see map 1) and district Palamau of Chota Nagpur division. In the context of defining Laṅkā area, the relevance and importance of Cunningham's report on Ramgarh hill and Mara (village and caves in Siddhi district) was realised by the present author (after 135 years of its publication in 1874-75) and therefore was taken as a starting point for locating Laṅkā. Curiously though, Cunningham had neither looked at his own observations from this angle nor had linked the site of Mara caves with Rāvaṇa's domain. Beglar had wrongly identified Ramgarh hill at Surguja with Citrakūṭa of *Rāmāyaṇa* and Mara with the hermitage of Atrī. Cunningham had expressed disagreement with Beglar's view[5] of linking Ramgarh hill with Citrakūṭa. Cunningham believed Citrakūṭa of Bundelkhand could itself be Vālmīki's Mt. Citrakūṭa and Mt. Prasravaṇa as well on account of numerous streams and cascades flowing over it. Moreover, Citrakūṭa of Bundelkhand still further corresponds with the Citrakūṭa of Vālmīki in the various hues of its rocks from which it has derived its name and therefore, Beglar's view is not acceptable is what Cunningham has stated, an opinion shared by the present author.

He has further commented regarding Begler's view, which is that Mara could be Atrī's hermitage. It can also be inferred that according to the epic, (1) Atrī's hermitage was close to Citrakūṭa. (2) Anasūyā had comforted Sītā with gifts and kind words before the trio entered thicker forest, suggesting that Atrī hermitage must have been close to Citrakūṭa. (3) Begler based his inference only on one line non-specific description of the route used by the sages.

Mara Caves –While going through the district gazetteers of eastern M.P. it was realised that if we are searching for Rāvaṇa's abode, Mara caves is a site in Sidhi district which should be considered on priority. This was so, since Singrauli basin (see map 1) of Sidhi district had remained unstudied from this angle, of identifying this area with any of the rāmāyaṇic sites. Whilst on a tour of south-eastern provinces, Beglar and Cunningham in 1874-75 had visited Mara caves, as another interesting place in the vicinity of Ramgarh hills of Surguja (Ramgarh 22^{0} 53'N, 82^{0} 5'E, Mand or Mara 23^{0} 55'N, 82^{0} 31'E). The records of their observations suggest that in the context of our present study, this area seems to be most important and pivotal in this search for Rāvaṇa's Laṅkā. The present author therefore visited the site personally.

Near the north-eastern corner of Surguja and near the boundary of Uttar Pradesh a dam is constructed in 1962 on river Rihand (Reṇū). To the west of back waters of this dam called 'Govind Vallabh Pant Sagar,' is a place called 'Waidhan' (the district head quarters of Singrauli) and to the south-west of Waidhan at a distance of about 35 km is village Mand, Manda, Mada, Madha or Mara[6]. Variations found in the name of this site are quite puzzling. [Curiously, a series of names are applied to Sri Laṅkā (Ceylon) directly and indirectly referred to in *Dipavaṃśa*. In the earliest times the names Oja, Vara and Manda are used[7]].

Near this village are three groups of caves on hills and are called 'Mara Guphā'. The three groups are known locally by the names: (1) Baradari Mara (2) Chevari Mara and (3) Rāvaṇa Mara. It is easily noticeable that the distances as given by Beglar and Cunningham or by the gazetteer or in any other maps between Mara village and Mara caves and their actual placements in most maps do not match e.g. the distance between Mara village and Mara caves is shown to be more than 10 km in most maps! To the west of Mara village stands a conglomeration of high hills. On top of one of the hills are remains of a temple like structure. The hill is literally honeycombed with caves[8], as described by Beglar and Cunningham.

(1) In the group of 'Baradari *guphā'*, one particular cave named 'Kacheri *guphā*' consists of a longish room. Adjacent to the back wall of it, is a raised platform or a dais which is strangely called 'king's throne'. In the same group there is one more famous cave and the local legend is that 'Alha' (of the legendary love couple 'Alha-Udal') was confined there but he escaped. Reva state gazetteer says that the caves of all the three groups could be of fifth century.

(2) The second group called 'Chevari Mara' are situated at a distance of 1.5 km. from Baradari Mara caves. They lie on the banks of Pisauli nullah (at present locally called Savli *nadi*) and river Mayar. The place is enchantingly picturesque. Nearby on the banks of the nullah, on the slope of the plateau near the boundaries of rivers Gopad and Myar, stand the third group of caves.

(3) Rāvaṇa Mara Caves: Beglar and Cunningham write in their report as follows-

'On the opposite side of the valley, not immediately opposite to Chevari Mara, but to its south-east about half a mile and a good distance from the *nala*, are the caves known as 'Rāvaṇa Mara'. The caves here are large and were profusely ornamented, though the weather, acting on the coarse-grained easily-friable sandstone, has long ago destroyed a great portion and damaged all. The most important of the caves here is the Rāvaṇa Mara (Rāvaṇa's cave), this indeed gives its name to the whole group of caves. The cave is a large one, consisting first of a long pillared hall, behind which is another, on either side of which is a doorway leading into a chamber. The back wall of this hall is pierced by three openings leading into three chambers which do not communicate with each other. In the centre chamber a hole has been bored through the right-hand corner of the back wall, and communicates with the next cave. In this chamber also is a bench four feet high along the whole length of the west or right hand wall of the chamber: it undoubtedly enshrined statues once, and from the figure of Gaṇeśa over the entrance, it is clear that the statues were Śaivic. The entrance is profusely sculptured, but the sculpture is now worn out and, so far as can be made out, the design appears to have been poor, and the execution coarse. A throne three feet one inch square, occupies the centre of the room, and doubtless seemed as a support to a *liṅgam* and *argha*, which have long disappeared. On the wall at the back in the centre is sculptured a single large lotus flower. The other chambers are quite plain, nor are the entrances to them profusely sculptured; contrary to general custom, the back wall of the second hall, in which are the openings into the chambers, is not ornamented with pilasters in correspondence to the pillars in the front row, but has two niches in two of the spaces between three doors; the pillars in the front row of the first hall are quite plain, though provided with the usual bracket capital and C, but the inner row of pillars is profusely ornamented, not merely with sculptures but with numerous mouldings, and they possess the usual conventional *kuṃbha* shaped capitals below the bracket capitals. The '*kuṃbha*' however, is very short and from Cunningham's researches, it appears that the *kuṃbhās* were not introduced into architecture until the Gupta period; and the earlier ones are all shorter than those we see so frequently in Indian architecture of the ninth century and later. On this ground, and bearing in mind also the evidence as to age furnished by the cave at Chevari Mara, one is inclined, with some confidence, to ascribe this cave to the fifth century of our era.

The front hall of this cave is adorned with two large pieces of sculptures which occupy niches of nearly the entire extent of the side-walls. Of these, the one to the east or left hand represents a twenty armed male figure, (image on cover) with several subordinate figures elaborately sculptured. The design is not spirited, but clumsy, as indeed is inevitable when 20 arms have to be represented issuing out of one pair of shoulder blades. This figure is popularly known as Rāvaṇa, hence the name of the cave; but there can be little doubt that the figure, is meant for Śiva. Facing it, on the opposite wall is sculptured the figure of a ten-armed female, evidently Pārvati. In front of the cave is the usual level platform. Details of plan and section can be ascertained much better by a reference to the plates than by any description! (Rāvaṇa Mara cave plan plates from Beglar and Cunningham's report of tours in the south-eastern provinces, 1874-75 & 1875-76, a rare journal article in ASIR, vol. XIII, 1882. A plate is lithographed at the Surveyor General's Office, Calcutta 1881.) Close to this is another small cave, but of no special interest, and still another of two rooms, the veranda, or front hall, being supported by two pillars and two pilasters; but neither of this is of any special interest. I must note, as a remarkable circumstance, that I saw no tanks, wells or springs close to these caves and was told that water had to be brought from the *nala*, which runs past the Chevari Mara caves nearly half a mile off.

About a mile west (slightly north) from Baradari Mara, and near the Mara Jharia river, is another group of caves, known as 'Byah Mara' (marriage caves). There are four principle caves and a few small ones on the side of the hill to the right of the *nala*. The hill, for some distance, is cut into fine level terraces and the caves are dug into two tiers etc. These Byah Mara caves are located at a distance of about 1.6 km to the north- west of Baradari Mara caves and local belief associates them with the wedding of Alha-udal (a legendary love couple) as a popular legend.'

This report of Mara caves by Beglar and Cunningham is extremely important, and gives a very detailed account of Mara caves and also of Ramgarh hill (as we have seen in chapter 4), as these sites appeared in 1874-76. Their last remark is of significance and therefore is given below in their own words-

'It now remains to find out, what the original name of the place was, the name of the present village Mara, being evidently conferred by the existence close to it of these caves, will not help us in the least in this enquiry, and we must turn to ancient Hindū literature for the purpose. Although the evidence of caves proves it to have been a place of importance from the fourth century, it does not follow that it was not a place of note earlier'.

This comment is a key guide in this study and happily, it proved to be so! Cunningham's report indicates that Singrauli basin of Sidhi district should be explored in the context of search for Laṅkā, it was realised.

Sidhi district (Geographical)-

While describing the physical features of Sidhi, the district Gazetteer gives the following important information: 'The precipitous fall of the Kaimur range together with the parallel course of river Son, is formidable obstruction in free communication between Sidhi and Reva and Sidhi and Mirzapur. Any communication line has to be sought through the passes and wind-gaps, important among which are Baghwar, Gaddi, Mohania, Jati Sarai, Kamarji, Baragaon, Bhaghor, Bichi, Kasda and Khurar.' However, it is also mentioned, that in the lower valley, river Son is merely a waste of sand, during the greater part of the year, an insignificant stream that is fordable nearly everywhere. It is therefore possible to imagine that Rāvaṇa could have crossed the dry sandy bed of river Son, and/or through one of such passes while travelling in his ass drawn cart, from Laṅkā to Pañcavaṭī, (i.e. from Mara in Sidhi to Hanumanā or Devtālāb on Reva plateau) which is at a distance of around 90 km river Son is mentioned by name Sumāgadhī in *Bālakāṇḍa*, a presumed later addition and as śoṇa in *Kiṣkindhākaṇḍa* (map 1).

The district of Sidhi has three subdivisions: (1) Land between rivers Gopad and Banas, (2) Deosar or north-eastern (3) Singrauli subdivision of the south-east. District Sidhi has its northern boundary aligned with the southern boundary of Reva, Mirzapur and Sonbhadra districts while its south boundary touches Surguja district of Chhattisgarh (see map 1).

Kaimur range blocks the northern banks of river Son which rises near Amarkanṭak, flows towards north-west, then turns to the east flowing via Kaimur scarp and proceeds by the northern boundary of Sidhi district. It takes a north-easterly turn where it is joined by river north Koel or Karmanāśā (see End Note 1) and then its bed widens enormously before it joins river Ganga above Patna in Bihar.

Son is joined from the west by smaller (northern) Mahanadi, Banas, Gopad and Johilla. Rivers Rihand, Kanhar and north Koel join it on the right bank before it enters the lower plains of the Ganga.

RIHAND: River Rihand flows through the south-eastern plain of Sidhi district in Singrauli *tehsil.* Rising from the hills of Surguja, it maintains a general north-easterly course and meets river Son in district Sonbhadra of U.P. at Agori Khas, an important ancient settlement and a place of archaeological interest (see map 1). The river has been dammed and the reservoir has submerged the plain up to around 40-50 kilometres from Waidhan to Renukut, both in U.P. and M.P. This dam on Rihand was constructed in 1962 and is named 'Govind Vallabh Pant Sagar' (GVP Sagar of maps). Kachan and Mear (Myar) are effluents which unite to south of Singrauli (Waidhan) before joining river Rihand from the western side. Cunningham's extremely important report describes various ancient pilgrim routes and places, where he noticed some remains of archaeological interest[9]. 'Jabalpur-Allahabad Road and Jabalpur-Mirzapur Road meet at Mangaon (Managavan) in district Reva, (see map 1) a branch crosses the Vindhyan range at Gaddi *ghat*, then crossing Son near Chandrehi, it travels up to Maholi and then bifurcates into two, one branch going towards Chota Nagpur through Kakarsiha and Mara, while the other proceeds via Sohagpur towards Amarkanṭak. This appears to have been the principal pilgrim road from Prayag and Vārāṇasi to Rameshvar. From the abundance of old ruins on these routes it is safe to infer that they were in use from the earliest times' -Cunningham states.

There were passes of Kosda *ghat* and Karrar *ghat* (both in Sidhi) and Silpi *ghat* of Mirzapur, (see topo-sheet # 63 L/10+14) which provided communication lines from north to south and connected Vārāṇasi, Chunar with places like Baghia, Juraundha,

Barauli, Kusmava, Saipur and Mara of Sidhi district. (The distance between Mirzapur and Mara is 125-130 km.) The pilgrim road further traversed Sonhut in Surguja to Seorinarayan (in Bilaspur) and passed on to Cuttack in the east and Rameshvar in south. Saipur was also a meeting point of another road which traversed, through the passes near Agori Khas, where rivers Son and Rihand meet. Cunningham describes Agori Khas-

'After the Khol *ghat* the kaimur range no longer forms a ridge, but merges into the high tableland, the opposite slopes of which run down to the Son on one side and to the Ganges on the other. Near the foot of the northern slope, close to Mirzapur is the famous temple of Viṅdhyavāsini Devi.........' etc. This geography would of course suggest a strange fact and that is, for Bhagīratha to bring Ganga waters towards south would mean (a) either to dig very deep into the earth or (b) to bring it via the land from where it will naturally flow towards south by the law of gravitation. Can we find any trace of historical truth in the Bhagīratha legend any time? Till then we can safely infer that as per Vālmīki's notion, *dakṣiṇa sāgara* was in south Ganga plain and it must have existed in remote times, in a landmass, which was to the north of Laṅkā and was also spread around Laṅkā.

With a strong suspicion that there could be such a place at a site indicated by the description in *Rāmāyaṇa* and that it could be situated in Singrauli basin, that entire area was scanned by using satellite imagery. A singular spot was noticed with its striking topography. It was found to match the epic description of Laṅkā wonderfully, as discussed in the following pages and hence could be said to be the target site of this study. The relevant topo-sheet (# 64 I/ 9+13) revealed that the name of the largest settlement / a village on that hill-top is Betdaha. Down below to its south-east in low lying area are situated both Rāvaṇa Mara and other Mara caves and Mara village. River Rihand flows from south to north by its eastern side. The present author visited Mara caves, Mara village, hilly as well as the low lying area to the east of Mara and also Rihand, the Obra dam and area up to Renukut, which is in dist. Sonbhadra, the north-eastern tip of the back-waters of the dam. Prior to the observations made are presented, an explanation regarding one point is necessary here. According to the present studies, (1) *Dakṣiṇa sāgara* has been located with enough confidence in south Ganga plain in accordance with king Sagara's story from the epic. (2) It was observed that Singrauli basin is a vast area and around Mara-conglomaration of hills, i.e. Betdaha group of hills, there is a low lying area as can be seen in Google satellite image. Apart from the back water area of Rihand dam this entire area shows innumerable water reservoirs, a place called 'Samundar' and many nullahs and rivers around it even today.

This would mean that we have located two sites for *dakṣiṇa sāgara.* The south Ganga plain is separated by the precipitous Kaimur scarp and river Son, both running parallel to each other and from west to north-east. Then, which one was *dakṣiṇa sāgara?* Secondly, was there a vast expanse of water around Mara in the times of Rāma? And even if it were so, was the bridge really necessary? Why the *vānara* army could not have travelled around the sea to reach Laṅkā? These questions need to be answered with the help of our findings.

We know that the distance between Mirzapur (Kiṣkindhā) and Betdaha group of hills (Laṅkā) or from Ahraura to Mara group of hills (see map 1) is around 130 km. The whole area bound by these two points is forested and full of rivers, lakes, nullhas, marshes and swampy water logged areas as is indicated by satellite images of this area. Till king Sagara's times however, the south Ganga plain or some compact area in it (perhaps including the stony waste region to the south of Mirzapur hills?) seems to have been a perched land mass as Sagara's story indicates, and Ikṣvākus wanted to bring Ganga waters down, right there in a region where originally Kālakeyās had their settlements. That would broadly be the area of *dakṣiṇa sāgara*! A remarkable confirmation has been found for the identification of the general area of *dakṣiṇa sāgara* although the exact location cannot be pinpointed at the moment. One possibility is that poet Vālmīki did not have to stretch his imagination too far in visualising vast expanses of water around Betdaha group of hills (since its topography clearly indicates that it is situated well within the Singrauli basin), right up to south Ganga plain, intersected by large rivers like Son, Rihand, Belan, Adwa and Kahenjua, the forest covered hills, ridges and plateaus amidst Kaimur ranges. However, there exists another possibility. The geographical positioning and the topography of this group of hills and the area around it fits in very well with the Rāmāyaṇic description of Laṅkā area. The literary and geographical justification have been produced for this identification. Then, did Vālmīki describe Betdaha hill-top to be Laṅkā which the poet imagined was surrounded by the waters of *dakṣiṇa sāgara* and described it in that way? In other words, the poet might have simply used the name of *dakṣiṇa sāgara* for small and large water bodies around Betdaha. These two considerations are dealt with here and are to be kept in mind. The third question is about the necessity of a bridge. This can be answered if we imagine Betdaha group of hills to be surrounded by marshes and forests crowded with a number of large herbivorous animals and predators as well and large water bodies infested with predators like crocodiles. This point certainly invites biologists and archaeologists to undertake further research in the target area suggested by the present studies.

From Google imagery it can be seen that for Rāma's army coming from north it would be impossible to know how large the expanse of water was to the east and west of Betdaha-Laṅkā. From the north shore, the shore opposite could not be seen. Hanumat makes it clear that there were no identification marks to know the distances. The description in *Yuddhakāṇḍa* suggests that the battle ground was at the north gate of Laṅkā. Starting from Kiṣkindhā, Rāma's army had marched taking a south direction, it is said. This in turn supports an idea that Laṅkā highland was inaccessible from the southern end and was more easily accessible only from the north and that too by constructing a bridge joining rocks emerging out of the south sea waters. In case of Batdaha group of hills too, the south direction is backed by crowding of numerous ranges of high hills with height more than 2500 ft above see level (or more than 1000 feet above the ground level area around). The only access seemed to be from the north, the only direction in which the sea was dotted with rocks and crags (as can be easily seen in Google image) which they might have thought could be joined to construct a causeway over those impassable terrifying marshes and at this very juncture poet Vālmīki gives Mt. Mahendra and Mt. Maināka a role to play! Thus, it can be said that because of the peculiar topography of the area and the characteristic nature of the 'sea', constructing a bridge was not only necessary but was the only way out. The huge *vānara* army naturally avoided traversing a long distance around the waters for bypassing the sea through an unknown territory. It should be noted that all the rivers flowing through this region are not navigable. This corroborates well with Hanumat's description of *dakṣiṇa sāgara*.

Visit to Mara--

From Waidhan at the north-western tip of GVP sagar (see map 1) the present author travelled to reach Mara village and the caves via a lake called Makarohar. The description of the Mara and other caves will not be repeated here. The network of high hills in which the caves exist was found to be uniformly narrowing towards the apex and hence difficult to ascend. Perhaps for this reason the locals on the eastern side of it had no information about any settlements existing high up on this or any other neighbouring hills. In fact an aged farmer stated categorically that there is no communication between them (those living for generations in the low-lying area and Mara village) and those living high up in the mountains. However, it was felt that the foothills of these mountains could be reached from the western side and the hill tops may be approachable from the western side from places like Ajgarbura, Rajmelan, Samundar, Kakarsiha, Kamarji etc. Google imaging confirmed that from places like Kamarji and Ajgarbura there are approaches, roads reaching right up to the foot of this group of hills on which Betdaha is situated. It seems the hills can be explored more easily from the west from Ajgarbura and not from the east, Mara side. The entire area around Mara group of caves was found to be covered with yellowish sand, the result of weathering of sand-stone type of rocks all around.

Interestingly, satellite imaging of Betdaha area shows a place 'Samundar' its name indicating a large body of water (existing in remote past) to the west of this group of hills. Sites like Samundar (topo-sheet # 63 L / at 23^{0} 27' N;82^{0} 23′ E), Devsar, Sajapani, Balai *tāla*, Purani *tāla*, all being most probably large water reservoirs, as can be judged from their names, are shown to the west of Betdaha in the map of Sidhi district. The catchment area of Govind Vallabh Pant Sagar dam to the east of Mara is vast, spread from west to north-east and has submerged the plain, low-lying area upto 40-50 km from Waidhan, both in Uttar Pradesh and Madhya Pradesh, touching a place called Renukut (or Reṇukeśvara) [$24^0 11'$ N, $83^0 01'$ E] (elev. 1316 feet). The catchment area of the dam must have been a low-lying region even before the dam was constructed, and still exhibits watery areas rivulets and nullahs around the dam as well as around the hill-top settlement of Betdaha.

The name of this hill-top settlement/village, given in topo-sheet #.64I/9+13 is Betdaha, which is at the centre of this approximately square plain area. It can be better described as a small hill-top tableland in the shape of a pomfret fish! Bansi and Nangva are the names given of two other smaller settlements close to Betdaha. Betdaha is also shown in ordinary maps but the name appears in a corrupted form as 'Basiberdaha' which obviously is a combination of Bansi and Betdaha (the locals at Mara down below had not heard of these names). Amidst the high hills crowding towards the south of Betdaha (higher peaks with heights of > 800 m) are many other smaller settlements as can be seen in Google imagery. Betdaha group of hills is separated from the south bound extension of the crowd of hills by a narrow valley through which a large river meanders (river Mayar). Betdaha group of hills therefore appears like an island somewhat triangular in shape. This entire network of thickly wooded hills with the inclusion of Betdaha covers a distance from north to south (Betdaha to Ramgarh hill, Surguja) of 130 km and from west to east (river Banas to river Rihand) of more than 100 km. Thus, this hilly region covers a total area of more than 13000 square km. The hills to western side of Betdaha descend more gradually whereas eastern side hills have a more abrupt descend standing as an inaccessible high wall. Betdaha hill-top settlement seems to have an approximately square shape covering an area of about 10 square km in Google image. One large river can be seen flowing east-west which traverses through the settlement. On this hill-top can be seen lush green fields and scattered houses here and there. Edging of the lush green settlement is hilly, clad with dense forests. Four or five hill ridges or long narrow elevations radiating in all four directions, can be seen which look like routes or walkways (foot tracks) joining the upper settlement with the lower land at the foothills. This corroborates the description in *Yuddhakāṇḍa*[10] of Laṅkā, which had four accesses through the ditches or moats surrounding it. The hills around this settlement have heights ranging from 575 to 757 metres and the land at the foothills is at 333 metres from the sea level. Thus, it is a settlement 300-400 m (i.e. more than 1000 feet) higher than the base level low-land, with a natural rampart of hills around it corroborating the epic description of Laṅkā.

Towards the south, this settlement is backed by innumerable ranges of high hills (of average height 545 to 757 metres) crowding around it for miles together making it inaccessible from the south. Towards its west and east large and small watery areas can be seen, as mentioned above.

The hills crowding around this site narrow down to form a long ridge proceeding towards north and then ending in interspersed groups of smaller hills or isolated hills and large rocks spread all over. Thus, the hill-top settlement seems accessible only from the north. This again corroborates very well with the description of Laṅkā given in the epic; inaccessible, situated on hill-top and surrounded by hills, to the base of which is a vast low-lying area, with literally innumerable water bodies, nullahs and rivers. This low land area must have been covered with thick *Sāla* forest with large and small water bodies amidst it in ancient times as could be sensed from local geography and the present flora. However, more investigation is needed regarding this point.

Recently Betdaha hill-top settlement was visited by author's friend who provided her with following interesting information about the local aborigines and other recent settlers there, the deities they worship etc. along with a number of site photographs (Dr Mukul K. Sinha, New Delhi - personal communication).

From Singrauli railway station there is a motorable road from Rajmelan village to the north of Betdaha right up to Nangva and Betdaha (Recently M/s Reliance Power Structures have constructed power transmission towers on the hill-top plateau.)

The original settlers of Betdaha seem to be Gonds, Kharwars etc. They worship mainly female deities, (fertility goddesses?). An unusually tall Śiva-liṅga is also there. A broken square shaped pillar with engraved script on it also exists there.

An interesting folk tale popular amongst locals indicates an ancient connection between Nangvagarh settlers with Mada settlers down below in the east, Rani Kumbhal being the connecting link.

Kumāradāsa[11] (fifth century), the royal poet of Siṃhala-*dvīpā,* describes Mt. Suvela and the ocean nearby in his '*Jānakīharaṇa*'. He says that 'the ocean (*dakṣiṇa sāgara*) was also a place of refuge for hundreds of mountains which were frightened of Śakra (Indra).' Kālidāsa, in his *Raghuvaṃśa*[12] gives another literary evidence by saying that Mt. Maināka and its smaller peaks, were emerging out of the waters of *dakṣiṇa sāgara* and that these were the refuge mountains escaped from Indra's *vajra* which clipped off the wings of other mountains. Thus, *dakṣiṇa sāgara* was apparently dotted with mountain peaks as Hanumat, while crossing the sea, was offered a seat by Mt Maināka, to rest on one of its peaks. Interestingly, these descriptions get quite faithfully reflected in and agree with Gazeetter descriptions, Google satellite images and eye-witness accounts given here.

The present studies suggest that this Betdaha hill-top settlement is a site clearly much more inaccessible than any other site suggested with a claim for Laṅkā. Rāvaṇa Mara and other caves situated on the spur and a narrow terrace, with a width of about 15 to 30 metres running along the circumference of the hill are easily approachable being at a height of only about 15 metres or so from the motorable road below and hence must be only a representation or an identification mark of the upper, precipitous scrap, not so easily accessible hill-top settlement, the target site of Rāvaṇa's Laṅkā as proposed by the present studies. The latitude and longitude of both the places are given below. Betdaha lies to the north-west of Mara village as can be seen from topo-sheet # 64 I/1+5 and parts of 64 I/9+13 (see map 1).

Betdaha : 23^0 56′ 12″ N to 23^0 57′ 45″ N
82^0 22′ 34″ E to 82^0 24′ 11″ E

Mara : 23^0 55′N, 82^0 31′E

The most important thing of note is the two twenty-armed male figures carved in stone on the walls of two chambers one above the other in Rāvaṇa Mara caves. To find a Rāvaṇa image in hill caves of which the geographical location and topographical features quite faithfully match the description of Rāvaṇa's Laṅkā in the epic is extremely important. Both the Rāvaṇa images are more or less similar and show Rāvaṇa supporting with his twenty hands Mt. Kailāsa forming a seat for much smaller images of Śiva and Pārvati than his own. The large images of Rāvaṇa here are given prominence as if to show his might and local importance (image on cover). The image carved on the opposite wall thought to be of Hanumat by the locals as it is coated with vermilion is in fact of Śiva holding in his hands his usual attributes. Beglar and Cunningham had indeed noticed and have made a mention of many images including the one of Rāvaṇa and his aides, not only here but also at Ramgarh hill, but had not produced the photographs. We are now able to produce the photographs here, in this book. (Sadly, mementoes of Rāvaṇa, images of Rāvaṇa, Kuṃbhakarṇa, Meghanāda etc. of which reports were made by Cobden Ramsay and others, names of spots like Rāvaṇa *darvājā* and Rāvaṇa *darbāra* etc. which are mentioned in travel and survey reports of the nineteenth century seem to have become only a thing of the past at Ramgarh hill at Surguja in Chhattisgarh.)

Along with this, some more interesting observations which have been made need a mention here. As of this date, Mara caves have images of Gaṇeśa, Śaṅkara, Hanumat, Buddha ?, Śiva, Pārvati and *liṅgās*, (phallus icon representing Śiva), all mixed up, lying in ruined, abandoned condition. In Biyah Mara cave, which is locked by weeds and mud, locals believe Paraśurāma's *'farsā'* or *'parśū'* (hand axe) is kept. Was Jāmadajña Paraśurāma Bhārgava connected with this area in some way? Why the main river of the district is given the name 'Rihand' (or 'Renu' - Paraśurāma's mother?) In addition to this, the local legend of Alha-Udal wedding having taken place here is still alive! The aborigines living in the area today are chiefly Gonds, Munda, Bhil, Chirva, Kharwar, Kol, Pankia and Biyar tribes. They worship *Nim-Bagia, Bada Deva* and Rāma.

It is interesting that there is a village named 'Makarohar' on the route from Waidhan to Mara (topo-sheet # 64 I/9 + 13). Place names indicating an area with prevalence of crocodiles there in the past are found in district Sidhi, Sonbhadra etc. Makarohar village is shown in maps to the south-west of Rihand dam. There is a pond of more than 2 hectares of catchment area. The present author visited Makarohar. According to local information, up to nineteen eighties there were crocodiles in this pond, which many years back was a much larger water body. There is a Śiva temple near the pond.

Around 3 km from Makarohar, is a waterfall on river Rihand called 'Rakas-Gandi' (also shown in topo-sheet #64I/ 9+13, part-2) Another place called 'Lakṣmaṇa Pav' is similarly associated with a legend about *rakṣasās*. A place named 'Raksa-hut' situated at the north-eastern tip of Sidhi district and Kalakapur in the north-eastern corner of district Surguja all suggest that *rakṣasās* in local cultural traditions must have been associated with this land from remote past and even today. Thus, in conclusion it can be said that it was possible to propose and identify the probable location for Laṅkā by using both topographical studies and Google imagery as this area favourably satisfies the conditions for a claim for Laṅkā quite faithfully. The geography and topography of the hill-top settlement is very much in accordance with the data gathered from the text and this is also supported by topo-sheets and Google satellite imagery evidence. With this geographical justification it can be concluded that this site meets a maximum number of criteria as compared to any other site in this area or any other site proposed by previous studies. This area in Singrauli basin, with conglomeration of hills might have been Rāvaṇa's Laṅkā as imagined by Vālmīki.

All these four sites (Kiṣkindhā, *dakṣiṇa sāgara*, *Ṛkṣabila* and Laṅkā) are more or less on a north-south straight line, i.e. in front of each other. (1) Mirzapur and some compact area to its south, where king Sagara's sons might have dug up the earth and *dakṣiṇa sāgara* was exhumed, or rather extended. (2) Ramgarh hill with its two arms encompassing a vast expanse of water (in ancient times) to its north. (3) Betdaha, the high hill-top settlement of Laṅkā and (4) the low land region around Betdaha group of hills (see map 1).

By present study six sites are considered as probable rāmāyaṇic sites, including Rāvaṇa's Laṅkā. Let us now check their degrees of latitude and longitude.

(1) Citrakūṭa Hill: $25^0\ 10'$ N
(for Citrakūṭa) $80^0\ 51'$ E

(2) District Reva Plateau $24^0\ 30'$ N
(for Pañcavaṭī) $81^0\ 18'$ E

(3) Mirzapur Area $25^0\ 8'\ 51''$ N
(for Kiṣkindhā) $82^0\ 33'\ 48''$ E

(4) Ramgarh Hills $22^0\ 53'\ 35''$ N
(for Ṛkṣabila) $82^0\ 54'\ 57''$ E

(5) Govind Vallabh Pant Sagar Dam near the confluence of rivers Son and Rihand (low-lying area near Betdaha and Mara)
$24^0\ 11'$ N to $24^0\ 12'$ N
$82^0\ 39'\ 54''$ E to 83^0 E

(6:1) Betdaha at hill-top $23^0 56'\ 12''$ N to $23^0 57'\ 45''$ N
$82^0\ 22'\ 34''$ E to $82^0\ 24'\ 11''$ E

and

(6:2) Mara Caves $23^0 54'\ 55''$ N
(For Rāvaṇa's Laṅkā) $82^0 23'\ 32''$ E

It should also be noted that sites 3, 4, 5 and 6 are roughly on the same longitude (of course with some variation), with remarkable connectedness (see map 1).

Thus from present studies it is implicit that the probable sites of *Ṛkṣabila,* Laṅkā and Kiṣkindha (Mirzapur hills), but not Mt. Citrakūṭa and Pañcavaṭī, are the sites which come more or less on the same longitude i.e. all are in one, north-south direction on a vertical line, in succession as they are described by Vālmīki in Saṃpāti's account. Then *dakṣiṇa sāgara* also should lie on the same longitude line since it was in between *Ṛkṣabila* and Kiṣkindhā, and adjoining Laṅkā as the epic describes. It is probable that the *Sāgara* could be situated to the south of Mirzapur, in south Ganga plain, or near the confluence of Son and Rihand, it being a water body with vast expanse, supposedly a watershed region of both the rivers with their numerous small tributaries. Thus the most convincing geographical position of Rāvaṇa's Laṅkā, the *'Sāgara'* around it and the man-made *dakṣiṇa sāgara* have been discussed in this chapter. These studies provide a strong argument for this area for a claim for Vālmīki's Laṅkā and a strong case for further archaeological, geological and other expertly investigations as well. The question remains as regards the identification of tribes of *vānarās* living during the times of Vālmīki, which inhabited Mirzapur hilly area and the tribes of *'rakṣasās'* inhabiting the vast thickly forested area of the network of hills to south of Singrauli basin bounded east-west by rivers Rihand and Banas, extended north-south from Betdaha up to the northern border of district Surguja or Ramgarh hill.

M.V. Kibe in one of his articles has referred to a story of one 'Virabhadra', the story having been composed in A.D. 1643. This Virabhadra is the grandson of king Virabhanu of Baghelkhand in Reva state. This work in Sanskrit praises Virabhadra. The story refers to Laṅkā of Bibhīṣaṇa, situated to the west of forest-lands of Kirāta, Rohitas, and most importantly Singrauli. This appears to be the traces of remembrance of the abode of Rāvaṇa. Rohtas is to the north of the confluence of rivers Son and north Koel (in Ganga-Son *doab*), near Nauhatta in western Bihar. The studies presented in this book have identified Rāvaṇa's Laṅkā with Betdaha group of hills and Mara area in district Sidhi (former Reva state) which is to the south-west of both Rohtas and Singrauli. Kirātās were the residents of eastern Vindhya. If according to Ptolemy, Kirātās were residing by Mt. Meandros, it would mean that Ptolemy, in spite of his limited knowledge was referring to Mt. Mahendra and Kirātās of Orissa. Even in that situation Betdaha (Laṅkā) lies to the west of Kirāta land. Kibe's observation[13] also provides supporting evidence for our identification of the general area of Rāvaṇa's abode (these Sanskrit works in manuscript form are in the collection of Reva state, Kibe informs). All told, we seem to have arrived at Rāvaṇa's abode and with all the evidences presented here it is proposed to identify Rāvaṇa's nebulous city Laṅkā with Betdaha, the hill-top settlement in district Sidhi of north-eastern Madhya Pradesh of India.

This study also makes it clear that the 'original' *Rāmāyaṇa* of Vālmīki does not supply any evidence which could suggest that Vālmīki's (and Rāvaṇa's) Laṅkā was anywhere to the south of Mt.Vindhya or as far as Ceylon. The history of the name 'Laṅkā' as applied to Ceylon in the last 2000 years has been discussed in chapter 8 of this book establishing an obvious fact that Ceylon has nothing to do with Vālmīki's Laṅkā. Mara caves are not dated before fifth century A.D. and therefore are not chronologically associated with the period of rāmāyaṇic events, but along with some other evidences presented in this book only indicate a strong influence of the epic over the region. In addition to this, and most importantly, the geography and the topography of this region correspond closely to the description of Laṅkā in the epic, thus making this compact area an interesting site for *Rāmāyaṇa* studies. In addition to this the geographical position of the proposed site for Laṅkā vis a vis the rest of the proposed rāmāyaṇic sites like Pañcavaṭī, Kiṣkindhā, Ṛkṣaila and *dakṣiṇa sāgara* makes the entire connectivity a dependable and definable compact area, thus making it an interesting locale for further studies.

References: Identification Of Rāvaṇa's Laṅkā

1. 7: 5:21
2. 7:3:29
3. 7:5:24
4. 5:2:8, 5:2:18
5. A. Cunningham: ASIR (Reva, Bundelkhand, Malva and Gwalior) vol.XXI (1883-84)

6. *'Imp. Gazetteer of India',* Districts Sidhi (1994) and Reva vol. IV (1907)
7. Romila Thapar: *'The Rāmāyaṇa: Theme and variation',* [from collected works 'Cultural pasts'](2000), p.678
8. Begler and Cunningham: ASIR vol. XIII (1882) pp. 31-55 (*Report of tours in the south-eastern Provinces,* 1874-75; 1875-76)
9. A. Cunningham: ASIR vol. XIII, pp.6-11, 14-16
10. 6:3:15, 16, 19- 22
11. Kumāradāsa: *'Jānakīharaṇa'* canto. 14: V: 84(quoted by Godakumbura 'Laṅkā of the Classical Indian writres' in All India oriental conference proceedings 27, (1976) pp. 294-391
12. *'Raghuvaṃśa'*13:7, (ed. And tr. By M.R. Kale), (1972), MLBD Publication, Delhi
13. M.V. Kibe: *'Location of Laṅkā in Amarkanṭaka in modern literature' 'New Indian Antiquary',* April-June 1946, No.I pp.91-93

End Notes:

(1) RIVER KARMANĀŚĀ: S.M. Ali [*'The Geography of the Purāṇās'* (1966), p.160] identifies this river with Karamodā or Karatoyā (belonging to the Bundelkhand region) of Purāṇās, but most other evidences place it in eastern Vindhya in Kaimur ranges. Karmanāśā, North Koel or Kokila, all these names represent the same river. (S. Chitrav. *'Prācina Sthalakośa'* p. 386, 599; Asian researches 14.402) Literally Kokila and Koel both mean the same bird, Indian Cuckoo. River Karmanāśā issues out in the Kaimur range of Mt. Vindhya, and flows through the district of Palamau. It flows past the western boundary of Bihar, a few kilometres through south-eastern Mirzapur and joins river Son at Chaus village in Ara district (see map 1). According to a local legend it is identified with river Kokila, or north Koel which joins river Son at a place called 'Daśaṣīṣanātha' (not shown in maps), which is a *śivaliṅga sthāna* (*'Tirth'.*p.158, cited by S. Chitrav in *'Prācina Sthalakośa'* p.386) and established there by Rāvaṇa, hence the name.

It is 'Kommenses' of Arian (Indica-4, Mc Crindle p.191, Cunningham ASIR 1.1) or Karmoda of *'Mārkaṇḍeya Purāṇa'* (54:187:22). The popular belief is that it has its origin from Triśaṅkū's saliva or Rāvaṇa's urine. Near the confluence of north Koel and Son, the flow of the later river widens enormously and turns towards north-east to join river Ganga. Thus it can be imagined that Son and Karmanāśā would form a natural eastern boundary of the territory under Rāvaṇa's command. (Vālmīki does not mention this river). According to *'Vāyu Purāṇa',* (*'Vāyu'.*

88.173) it is an unholy and a cursed river and a local legend marks it as a river which washes away one's virtuous actions, hence the name.
karmanāśāt jalasparśāt punaḥ saṃskāramarhati | (*Tirthasāra* (quoted by Ganesh Shastri Lele in 'Tīrthayātrāprabaṅdh' p. 91))
Nandalal Dey writes about a place called Baidyanātha, (*'Geographical Dictionary of Ancient and Medieval India'* entry: Citabhūmī p.50) as follows: Baidyanātha or Deoghar in the Santhal Pargana (Bihar) is one of the twelve great *jyotirliṅgās* of Mahadeva, in the ninth incarnation, assumed to have been established by Rāvaṇa. The temple close by of Pārvati is said to be one of the fifty-two *pīṭhās*, called 'Hardāpīṭha' as Satī's heart fell at this place. Baidyanātha is called Paṃpāpuri or Palu-gaon. (Distortion of *'Paralipura'* or *'Parali-grama'* of the *'Śiva Purāṇa'*). At this place, 'Haritakivana', (ancient name of Baidyanātha) Rāvaṇa,in order to relieve himself, kept the Śiva *liṅga* down and retired to the north-eastern corner of Deoghar called Harlājuḍi (distortion of Haritakivana) and the result was river Karmanāśā flowing to the north of Harlājuḍi. Interestingly, there is a hill named Trikūṭa nearby.

(2) RIVER VAITARAṆĪ: - The lower part of the above mentioned river Kokila or north Koel is known by the name Vaitaraṇī, or south Koel (Asian researches 14.402). While Sītā is forcibly being carried away by Rāvaṇa from Pañcavaṭī to Laṅkā, anguished Sītā utters words:
'nadīm vaitaraṇīm ghorām rudhiraughanivāhinīm |
khaḍgapatravanam caiva bhīmām paśyasi rāvaṇa' || (3:51:18)
Meaning: 'O Rāvaṇa! You will be seeing (in a dream) the terrible river Vaitaraṇī carrying blood instead of water and also the horrifying forest laden with razor-sharp leaves......' From this description it seems that Sītā only points out to Rāvaṇa the forthcoming danger of his death by creating a vision of a dream with signs like river of blood and trees with razor-sharp leaves as a result of his evil deeds. It appears that in reality they do not pass by river Vaitaraṇī. Sītā sees five *vānarās*, sitting on a hillock below, and throws down her ornaments as a message to be carried to Rāma. These must be the hills to the south of Kiṣkindha (or Mirzapur hills by present studies). Rāvaṇa then crosses river (or lake) Paṃpā and turns towards Laṅkā. It should also be noted that, in his earlier journey from Laṅkā to Pañcavaṭī via Mārīca *sthāna*, Rāvaṇa does not come across river Vaitaraṇī.
South Koel (Vaitaraṇī) does not enjoy the reputation of a holy river. After issuing out in Keonzargarh (eastern region of Mt. Vindhya) in western Orissa, Vaitaraṇī flows through Kaliṅga-*deśa* and joins river

Brahmanī before joining the eastern sea. It is assumed to be the river of god of death, Yamā. Crossing river Vaitaraṇī means reaching the hell. The river is described in *'Mahābhārata'* in *Vaitaraṇīvṛtta* (*'Mbh' Ara. Tirth.* 114, 4,13).

River Vaitaraṇī flows along the boundary of Jajpur district of Orissa. Jajpur is identified with Yayātipur and is near Viraja *tīrtha* (*'Brahmavai'.* 4.2). River Vaitaraṇī is then joined by river Brahmanī. *Mahābhārata* mentions that near the sea-shore, to the north, it forms a land mass, most suitable for *'vedī'* (a place for performing a sacrifice), named 'Svayāṃbhubhavana'. Kāśyapa created this land called Kaliṅga-*deśa* to the north of Mahendragiri (*'Mbh'. Ara.* Tirth. 114:17-26). This land actually forms an island as can be seen in the maps. Mt. Mahendra is in district Gajapati, to the south of Ganjam.

(3) *LAVAṆA PARAGAṆA*: Lavaṇāsura was a *rakṣasa* living in *Madhuvana*. He was the son of Madhu *daitya* and Kuṃbhīnasī (Rāvaṇa's mother Kaikasi's sister and Sumālī's daughter). He was gifted by Rudra with a *'śūla'* (a weapon) that had immortalised him. Rāma's brother Śatrughna killed him using a trick. He was informed that not in summer but in rainy season Lavaṇāsura can be killed. This could be actually a suggestion of a natural phenomenon. In any water reservoir the proportion of *lavaṇa* (salts) would be lessened in rains and water would evaporate and become more salty in summer. Thus, the story of Lavaṇāsura appears to be allegorical. Uttarakāṇḍa, a presumed later addition mentions that Śatrughna changed the name of *Madhuvana* to 'Śūrasena' *deśa* (country) and the capital city *Madhura* became 'Mathura', (*'Prācina Caritra Kosa',* p. 942).

At a few places in *Rāmāyaṇa, Dakṣiṇa Sāgara* is described as *'lavaṇāṃbudhi'* (salty water sea) [*'lavaṇāṃbudhi'* can also mean a salty water reservoir (ASIR, vol. II, p. 308)]. Rai Krisnadas (*'Rām vanavās ka bhūgol'* Nagarī Pracharini Patrika, 54:2, 4, 117) has referred to a Lavaṇa *paragaṇa* to the south of Amarkanṭak, which is reminiscent of the *'lavaṇāṃbhās'* of *Rāmāyaṇa*, he believes. Another meaning of the word *'lavaṇa'* is 'land-mass at a lower level than the surrounding area, a basin,' and therefore naturally would turn into a large water reservoir. Lemna (or *Lavaṇa*) is also mentioned in Raipur district of Chhattisgarh [Hiralal: *'Descriptive list of inscriptions in central provinces and Berar'* (1916) entry: 2, 02, p.148 Govt. Press, Nagpur].

In an inscription found near Bilaspur (M.P.) of Kalacuri king Ratnadeo, the temple of Lavaṇeśvara is mentioned. Interestingly, though, the same place according to local belief is associated with *rakṣasās* Khara and Dūṣaṇa.

There are rivers with names like Lavaṇa or Lun. Ptolemy described 'Luni'. There is a place called Lavaṇa *nagara*. In a copper plate of A.D. 1080 one 'Lavaṇakara' is mentioned. This place was situated in Reva state, far away from any ocean [N.V. Rao (1990) p.62]. It can be imagined that Lavaṇaṃbhus or *Dakṣiṇa Sāgara* around Laṅkā or some of its parts could be such salty water bodies. However, the name Lavaṇa samudra could also have been taken by the poet from ancient concept of *kṣara samudra* being to the south of Jambūdvīpā.

§§§

7

LATITUDE AND LONGITUDE OF LAṄKĀ

The derivation of the name of mountain 'Vindhya' is from a geographical phenomenon. In ancient times and in rāmāyaṇic age, Mt. Vindhya was the south boundary of Āryāvarta. The highest peaks of Mt. Vindhya are only slightly away from the line of the tropic of Cancer or Karkavṛitta. It therefore seems, as if the progress of the sun in northern direction is blocked by the mountain and so the east-west mountain range was famed as Vindhya, meaning 'Hunter'. The most elevated hill ranges of Vindhya are found to run from a point that lies between Chota Nagpur and north Surguja, to the east, to another that is situated somewhere near Ujjayini, towards the west.

One more piece of information is noteworthy in this connection. The whole mountainous region between Kaśi (Vārāṇasi) and Birbhum in Bihar was known as 'Karka Khaṇḍā', the south boundary of this region being river Vaitaraṇī of south Bihar[1].

Pāṇḍava's brother Karṇa (mythical son of the sun-god Sūrya) had taken out a victory march. The description of his travel mentions this same region as Arka Khaṇḍā (*arka* meaning Sūrya). Apart from Karṇa's role for name's sake, it was also called Karka Khaṇḍā because the line of the tropic of Cancer (*karkavṛtta*) passes through this region.

Avantī khaṇḍā of *Skanda Purāṇa* gives one story which is curious and worthy of consideration in the context of the location of Laṅkā. It seems as if the story underlines the illusory line joining Laṅkā and Ujjayini. The story tells us how the pilgrimage named Hanumatkeśvara got established[2]. Indeed, the story is of purāṇic times.

Sage Sanatkumāra narrates this story to sage Vyāsa. Rāvaṇa was killed by Viṣṇu in his incarnation as Rāma. Rāma then returned to Ayodhya and ascended the throne. Rāma once asked sage Agastya, 'Between Śiva and Vāyu who is superior?' Agastya answered, saying that both are equal. Hearing these words, Hanumat, the son of Vāyu, decided that he should possess and adore Śiva's phallus icon. He therefore went to Laṅkā. Hanumat reached Laṅkā and requested Bibhīṣaṇa to give him one 'Śiva-*liṅga*', and Bibhīṣaṇa showed him six. When Hanumat picked up the white one, Bibhīṣaṇa said. 'Kubera as a devotee of Rudra had worshipped this white '*liṅga*', but when Rāvaṇa snatched it away from him, Kubera lost all his grandeur and so you should take good care of this *liṅga* image'. Hanumat then straightway went to Avantīkapuri i.e. Ujjayini. He reached Ujjayini city in seven days and on Rudra-*sara*, he set up the *liṅga*. It became famous by the name Hanumatkeśvara. The story implies the importance of Ujjayini positioned in the zone of tropic of cancer or *karkavṛitta*.It signifies a geographical fact, to be discussed in the following pages.

Viṣṇumahātmya (*Skanda Purāṇa*) explains how Ujjayini became '*Saptakalpā*' (known by seven different names in seven different ages)[3]. One of the names of Ujjayini is Kuśasthalī. *Bhāgavata Purāṇa* (10.61-40), tells us that Kuśasthalī was the name of Dvāraka city also[4]. Śiva promised to protect Indra from Andhakasura (it may mean darkness?) and then Indra had established the position of the first sun. That *sthāna,* or *sthala* (position) is Kuśasthalī or Ujjayini, which is a great place for this reason it is said. It is to be noted that Ujjayini is considered to be a great place where the sun attains its highest position to the north of the equator and so must have been named Kuśasthalī, lying near the *karkavṛitta* or the line of the tropic of cancer ('*kusa*' means apex, highest point - '*Gīrvāṇalaghukośa*'). This myth indicates the importance of the city of Ujjayini from astronomical point of view. In addition, the Hanumatkeśvar story is also important from geographical point of view, in the context of location of two Laṅkās: 1) Astronomical, and 2) Rāmāyaṇic Laṅkā. Ujjayini had an ancient observatory and a centre for astronomical studies. In India the status of Ujjayini was similar to that of Greenwich and it was presumed by the early Indian astronomers that the middle line of the land, meaning of course the main longitude line, passed through Ujjayini[5]. According to Indian astronomers of ancient times, the city of Ujjayini was positioned on zero degree longitude.

Ujjayini and the astronomical Laṅkā

According to our early astronomers, the astronomical Laṅkā is said to be on the same meridian as Ujjayini (*'Siddhāntaśiromaṇī'* of Bhāskāracārya II) i.e. on the line passing through the north and south poles, Ujjayini, Kurukṣetra and other places to Mt. Meru (at the north pole). It has been denominated the **'madhyarekhā'** (the midline). This could be the first meridian for Indian astronomers. (*'Siddhāntaśiromaṇī'-Goladhyāya*-24). It was at Ujjayini, at 75° 46' east of Greenwich. The verse is-

yallaṅkojjayinī puropari kurukṣetrādi deśan spṛśan |
sūtram merugatam budhairnigaḍitā sā madhyarekhā bhuvaḥ ||[6]

The need for establishing astronomical Laṅkā was as follows: Late D.B. Svami Kannu Pillai says in his *'Indian Chronology'* as follows (quoted from G. Ramdas): 'Indian astronomers got over the difficulty (of calculating time at a particular place) by calculating time in the first place according to the central latitude and longitude and then by applying the necessary corrections in order to deduce the time at any place[7].'

The zero or central longitude is that of Ujjayini and the zero or central latitude is the equator. [For equator various names were used. **'kumadhya'** (centre of the earth) **'nirakṣadeśa'** (the zone of zero latitude) **'nirakṣareṣā'** (the line of 0 latitude) **'śūnya akṣaṃśa'** (0 latitude,' **'kuvṛtta'**, **'viśuvadvṛtta'**, **'bhūparighivṛtta'** (the equator) etc.]. These words are used by early astronomers like Aryabhata, Varāhamihira, Bhāskāracārya first and second etc. e.g. Aryabhata (fifth century) also calls astronomical Laṅkā at **'kumadhya'** as **'sthalajalamadhyallaṅkā'** (on the borderline of land and water) or as, '**tena sthalajalasandhau laṅkāvatiṣṭhate**' **|** (Laṅkā is situated at a point where land and water meet)[8].

To combine the central latitude and the central longitude at the intersection they proposed a hypothetical point ('Laṅkā-*puri*') situated on '**kumadhya**' (or on equator at 0^0 latitude also of the present times) and having the same longitude as Ujjayini. This was Laṅkā only for Indian astronomers. It was of course not Ceylon. It was neither Sumatra, nor Maldives or Malayadvīpā. It was only a hypothetical reference point (see fig. 1).

This point falls in deep Arabian sea to the south-south-west of Kerala. Being so far away from the mainland of *Bhāratavarṣa,* it cannot be Rāvaṇa's Laṅkā. It had only an imaginary existance, and so, this truth about the astronomical Laṅkā was very clear to Bhāskārācārya (II) and also other astronomers even of earlier period. This state of affairs must be realised in the context of the search for Rāvaṇa's Laṅkā.

In the opinion of D.B. Sahasrabuddhe[9], Bhāskārācārya's calculations of latitudes must be wrong or else Laṅkā at '**nirakṣadeśa**', which Bhāskārācārya thought is on zero latitude was actually 7^0-8^0 to the south of modern Ceylon - Sri Laṅkā, which in later times must have submerged in the sea, according to Sahasrabuddhe. His firm belief is that Laṅkā of Rāvaṇa was in Ceylon. Ceylon - Sri Laṅkā is at 7^0-8^0 N latitude.

N.S. Adhikari[10] held a view that the search for Rāvaṇa's Laṅkā should be conducted on Sumatra islands. For identifying Rāvaṇa's Laṅkā with Sumatra, he also relies on distances between Rāmāyaṇic sites and phonetic identity of some present sites in Sumatra, i.e. Samalaṅga or Sonilaṅkā and Laṅkāisāgar etc. with Rāmāyaṇic place - names. In his words, 'Sumatra is what has remained of that Laṅkā of by-gone fame and that this inference is furnished by the astronomical datum furnished by Bhāskārācārya'. Bhāskārācārya calls Laṅkā '**nirakṣadeśa**' because it was according to him situated at 0^0 latitude and therefore while describing Ujjayini, (Avantī) Bhāskārācārya says, '**nirakṣadeśāt kṣitiṣoḍaśaṁse bhavet avantī ganitena yasmat**'[11], is what N.S.Adhikari states.

Wilkinson gives the translation of this line from the verse as: 'As it is ascertained by calculation that the city of Ujjayini is situated at a distance from the equator equal to one sixteenth part of the whole circumference'. (This distance therefore multiplied by sixteen will be the measure of the earth's longitudinal circumference.) N.S. Adhikari further says 'Now, modern geographers locate the present Laṅkā or Ceylon at 7^0 or 8^0 above the equator. It is therefore obvious that Laṅkā of Bhāskārācarya was to the south of present Ceylon, at the 0^0 of the modern geographers and that Laṅkā must have been submerged under water (near 0^0 or the present Sumatra)'.

It must be noted here that Adhikari's statements are not tenable for the simple reason that Bhāskārācarya is talking about astronomical Laṅkā and not Rāvaṇa's Laṅkā. Also inference drawn by Adhikari from *Vāyu Purāṇa*[12] that Laṅkā was distinct from Jambūdvīpā and *Bhāratavarṣa*, is not acceptable, the reason for this is discussed in relevant context.

Vāyu Purāṇa says that there are six other *dvīpās* apart from Jambūdvīpā to its south, one of these six *dvīpās* being Malayadvīpā[15]. N.S. Adhikari quoting from *Vāyu Purāṇa* says that 'In Malayadvīpā on the top of Mt. Trikūṭa was Laṅkā situated[16]. To the east of this island lies a great Śiva temple in a holy place called Gokarṇa'....etc.

Does *Vāyu Purāṇa* say that Malayadvīpā lying to the south of the equator, beyond the salt-sea, apart from Jambūdvīpā and in the southern hemisphere of the globe, Rāvaṇa's Laṅkā was situated? It is most likely that *Purāṇās* like the *Vāyu Purāṇa* are really talking about Mt. Trikūṭa on that Malayadvīpā, which in fact was a subdivision of land or *'upadvīpā'* within the boundaries of Jambūdvīpā and *Bhāratavarṣa* (in Dravidian languages 'malai' means a hill).

V.H. Vader[13] holds the notion that Rāvaṇa's Laṅkā was on the equator, and that it was not Ceylon-Sri Laṅkā of present day. He further says that Malayadvīpā, as described in *Vāyu Purāṇa,* is today's Maldives island and that it was Rāvaṇa's Laṅkā. He too believes his theory is supported by great mathematician and astronomer Bhāskārācarya of the twelfth century, thus -

laṅkā kumadhye yamakoṭirasyāḥ |
prākpaścime romakapaṭṭaṇam ca ||
adhastataḥ siddhapuram sumerūḥ |
saumyetha yāmye vaḍavānalaśca ||[14]

Translated as: 'Laṅkā is situated in the middle of the earth. Yamakoti is situated to the east of Laṅkā and Romakapattana to its west. The city of Siddhapura lies underneath Laṅkā. Sumeru is situated to the north (under the north pole) and Vaḍavānala to the south of Laṅkā (under the south pole)'.

However, it must be realised that here also Bhāskāracārya is referring to astronomical Laṅkā and three other imaginary 'cities' (actually these are only hypothetical points for astronomical calculations referred to as '**puracatuṣṭayam**').

Rai Krisnadas[17] supported M.V. Kibe's more convincing theory that Vālmīki had visualised Rāvaṇa's Laṅkāpurī on a high-land and hill top, surrounded by watery area and it was at Amarkanṭak (situated within the boundaries of Jambūdvīpā and Bhāratvarśa). However, to clarify and justfy this he states that '*Bhāgavata Purāṇa*' mentions[18] eight *upadvīpās* (secondary units) of Jambūdvīpā, ('*Bhāgavata Purāṇa*': *skandha* 5: *adhyāya* 19) and there, Laṅkā and Siṃhala are mentioned separately. Rāvaṇa's Laṅkā cannot be outside the boundaries of *Bhāratavarṣa* (or India), and this is so because the nine sub-units of 'Bhārata' separated from each other by 'seas' which are assumed, do not count Laṅkā *as a dvīpā* (here he probably means nine varṣās of Jambūdvīpā, which in some *Purāṇās* being synonymous with *Bhāratavarṣa*, creates confusion). If Laṅkā were outside the boundaries of Bhārata, then the name of Laṅkā-*dvīpā* would have appeared in that list of nine sub-units. So, Laṅkā must be within the boundaries of Bhārata, Rai Krisnadas opines.

Mārkaṇḍeya Purāṇa mentions Laṅkā and Siṃhala as two separate *upadvīpās*. Thus -

laṅkākālājināścaiva śailikā nikaṭāstathā |[19]
ṛṣabhāḥ siṃhalāścaiva tathā kāñcīnivāsināḥ |[20]

Meaning: In the south are Laṅkā, Kālājina (Kālanjar) Sailika, Nikaṭa, Ṛṣabha, Siṃhala and Kañcī. Also, according to '*Bṛhatsaṃhita*' of Varāhamihira -

laṅkā kālājina saurikarṇatālikaṭaḥ |
marucīpaṭṭaṇaceryāyaka siṃhalā ṛṣabhāḥ ||[21]

Meaning: In the south are Laṅkā, the Kālājinās, Sauris, Kirṇas, Talikaṭa, Marucipaṭṭaṇa, Ceryā, Siṃhalas and Ṛṣabhās.

Scholars studying *Rāmāyaṇa* have interpreted **'laṅkā kumadhye'** of Indian astronomers in various ways. Hiralal[22], whose support to Kibe's theory of Laṅkā being on Amarkanṭak is not unreasonable. However, he takes '**kumadhye**' to mean 'at the centre of land' because he feels that it does not mean 'at the centre of water/ocean' (perhaps because he opposes the theory that island Ceylon in ocean was Rāvaṇa's Laṅkā). But his assumption regarding the meaning of '**laṅkā kumadhye**' is incorrect as '**kumadhye**' necessarily means on equator, whether it be on land or in water, as '**kumadhye**' is a word used here by astronomers.

Jacobi, Kibe, N. V. Rao, T.P. Iyer, V. D. Jha and a few other scholars are aware, that Indian astronomers of the past had assumed a hypothetical point on the equator and called it Laṅkā, where the equator is cut by the first meridian, zero longitude ('**madhyarekha**') passing through the poles, Ujjayini, Kurukṣetra and Mt. Meru (see fig. 1).

Both Kibe and T.P. Iyer were aware that there is another Laṅkā known to Indian astronomers. According to Iyer it was the 'Lingga' island in Sumatra. Iyer writes: 'The Hindūs of south India colonised Sumatra before Java, and long before Varāhamihira's time. (i.e. sixth century). The equator cuts it right at the top. This was Laṅkā outside the Rāmāyaṇa', he maintains[23]. Iyer locates Rāvaṇa's Laṅkā in Jabalpur district of M.P. M.V. Kibe writes, 'The Indian astronomer Bhāskārācārya (II) locates Rāvaṇa's Laṅkā (?) the destination of Rāma, on the equator in the ocean'. Kibe[24] identifies Rāvaṇa's Laṅkā on Amarkanṭak hill of Mt. Vindhya in eastern M.P. Some scholars identify it with an island near Sumatra or Java. A few would locate it in the Arabian sea or at the west-coast.

Scholars, who theorised that Rāvaṇa's Laṅkā should be looked for in M.P. were on the right track, but some of them seem to hold the notion that Indian astronomers were referring to Rāvaṇa's Laṅkā. In fact, this was not the case, as will be seen in the following discussion.

It should be realised that early Indian astronomers described their hypothetical Laṅkāpurī only from an astronomical point of view, as they had imagined it only for doing time and distance calculations for any point on earth. Thus, their Laṅkā, though only imaginary and hypothetical, had practical astronomical function and purpose. Poet of the epic *Rāmāyaṇa* on the other hand has described Laṅkā in great detail like any other place habitable by humans.

The astronomers did not bother whether their hypothetical point Laṅkā lay on land or in the deep sea, near or far away or whether it was habitable or even accessible. There would have been no problem if the Indian astronomers had called it by any other name (say 'Kalānpurī' instead of 'Laṇkāpurī'!). However, why the Indian astronomers named that point 'Laṅkā' may not be without reason.

Problem arises when scholars of *Rāmāyaṇa* assertively claim the identity of Rāvaṇa's Laṅkā with astronomer's Laṅkā and even go to the extent of saying that Rāvaṇa's Laṅkā might have got submerged into the sea, although *Rāmāyaṇa* at no place mentions that Rāvaṇa's Laṅkā was at '**kumadhya**' (the equator) or at the centre of the earth. Thus, we must distinguish between both these distinct Laṅkā's. Can it be proved that Indian astronomers did not really mean Rāvaṇa's Laṅkā and that for them Rāvaṇa's Laṅkā had a distinct geographical identity? It should also be examined whether the *purāṇakārās* were aware of the astronomical imaginary Laṅkā. Did they know the geographical location of Vālmīki's (and hence Rāvaṇa's) Laṅkā?

Another problem also crops up when 'tradition' is accepted uncritically, by scholars. Mark Collins[25] explains how 'traditional element can become a disturbing element even in scientific enquiry'. He writes about names and says: 'The geographical fancies of an early age are similarly propagated from generation to generation and sometimes find their way centuries later into the sober pages of technical literature. The nine fold division of *Bhāratavarṣa* (India) for instance given in the third book of *Viṣṇu Purāṇa* is repeated as late as the twelfth century by the astronomer Bhāskārācārya (II) in his '*Siddhāntaśiromaṇī*' and in the geographical section of Varāhamihira's '*Bṛhatsaṃhitā*' (Book XIV, sixth century A.D.)'.

If we try to examine and analyse the basic geographical concepts (up to the thirteenth century) of the *purāṇakārās* and also of the astronomers regarding the division of the globe, we find, for example, that Bhāskārācārya in his '*Siddhāntaśiromaṇī*' writes-

'Most learned astronomers have stated that, Jambūdvīpā embraces the whole northern hemisphere lying to the north of the salt sea (**'kṣara samudra'** or **'lavaṇa samudra'**) and that all the other six *dvīpās* and all the seven seas (including the salt sea) and that of milk, honey, clarified butter, sugarcane juice, wine and sweet water are all situated in the southern hemisphere'[26].

Thus, for all the Indian astronomers of those times, at the joining line of the land of Jambūdvīpā and salt water sea lay their **'kumadhya'**, **'nirakṣadeśa'** or equator, (also of the present times). To the south of equator lies the salt sea and to its south the sea of milk and the other oceans in succession, (see fig. 1) the last one being that of sweet water which surrounded Vaḍavānala. There were further divisions of land in *'varṣās'* formed by seas and mountains and also *khaṇḍās (dvīpās).* There were seven *varṣās* (one such is *Bhāratavarṣa*). In the middle of Illavṛttvarṣa stood Mt. Meru at the north-pole according to the geographical concepts of *purāṇakārās* and also of the ancient astronomers. *Bhāratavarṣa* lay to the south of Mt. Meru.

The point to be made here is that, although the astronomical measurements and calculations of the early Indian astronomers were remarkably correct, in that they are close to even those of the present values to a great extent, their ideas about the division of the land-mass and oceans on the surface of the globe were traditional and fanciful as they were simply borrowed down uncritically from the *Purāṇās.* The purāṇic notions of the world map had evolved out in course of time from the epics as has been pointed out earlier. Astronomers like Aryabhata {(B.476A.D.) (*'Aryabhaṭiyā'*)[27] } to Bhaskara (II), all shared the same geographical concepts. As a result, their astronomical Laṅkā chosen to be on the intersecting point of the equator (**'kumadhya rekha'**) and the Ujjayini meridian, falls on the (south) frontier or borderline of Jambūdvīpā land-mass and the northern water-front of the salt sea or *kṣara samudra.* In other words, the Jambūdvīpā border touched the salt sea front at **'kumadhya-rekha'**, the equator! (see fig. 1). Once accepted these traditions became conventions for Indian astronomers.

We will now see how a paradoxical situation arises from the geographical assumptions of these astronomers, in the context of location of Rāvaṇa's Laṅkā. Their astronomical Laṅkā lies on '**kumadhya-rekha**' i.e. on the joining line of land and salt water sea. Now this means that if this were Rāvaṇa's Laṅkā (Rāma's destination) there was no necessity of constructing a bridge to reach there, since it would then be situated on the Jambūdvīpā land itself, or at the most at the southern end of that land mass which touched the north water front of the salt sea of the south hemisphere. Their touching line was '**kumadhyarekhā**' ('**viṣuvadvṛtta**' or equator)

According to *Rāmāyaṇa* however, the construction of a bridge was a necessity. Therefore, Rāvaṇa's Laṅkā must be situated on such an inaccessible land which was moated with water and to reach there it was essential to construct a bridge over the waters of the sea or '*Dakṣiṇa Sāgara*' of Vālmīki! Laṅkā of Rāvaṇa also cannot be far away from Mt. Mahendra, Kiṣkindha and Pañcavaṭī. We can therefore safely infer that, astronomical Laṅkā on the equator or at '**kumadhya**' was not Rāvaṇa's Laṅkā, and this nebulous city as visualised by Vālmīki must be somewhere else. The present study of the epics and other ancient and modern records has led us to pinpoint a target area with the most convincing claim to identify it with rāmāyaṇic Laṅkā, which is not on '**kumadhya**' but near about *karkavṛtta* in north-eastern M.P. This has already been discussed in Chapters 5 and 6 of this book.

It will now be interesting to see what Marīci, the commentator of Bhāskārācārya (II) has to say about this paradox[28] in 'Marīci's commentary'[29]. Marīci explains the purāṇic version of the 'division of the globe', which he himself accepts! i.e. Jambūdvīpā occupies the northern half of the earth's sphere and joins the salt sea in/at the zone of '**nirakṣadeśa**' or **equator**. The lines are as follows -

'**atra bhūgolasyārdhamuttaram jambūdvīpām |**
tasya kṣārābdheśca sandhirnirakṣadeśaḥ' |

(and the geographical situation of seven *dvīpās* and seven seas in between them). Marīci says that 'the land of Jambūdvīpā and the waters of Lavaṇa samudra (salt-sea) meet at **kumadhya**, (the equator) and hence it follows that it is the zone of astronomer's Laṅkā. But, Laṅkā at **kumadhya** cannot be Rāvaṇa's Laṅkā as to reach there the existence of a bridge would be consequential in that geographical situation. The argument is given in following words -

'nanu lavaṇasamudrajambūdvīpāsandhipradeśasya bhūmadhyatvasiddheḥ praguktalaṅkākumadhyatvanupapattiḥ uktabhū golārdhasandhibhūparighivṛtte tasyā abhāvāt | anyathā setubandhānupapatteḥ' |

Marīci has further rightly pointed out that, we can imagine and accept the existence of quite a different Lavaṇa samudra, and that, that entire Lavaṇa samudra to be a part of Jambūdvīpā land-mass (of the northern hemisphere) within the boundaries of Bhāratvarśa. Marīci states that there existed such a Lavaṇa samudra, to the north of Laṅkā famed by *'Bhāgavata Purāṇa'* which imagines eight *upadvīpās* (sub-units) of Jambūdvīpā. King Sagara's sons were searching for their lost sacrificial horse and in their search as they exhumed the earth, the end result of their act was the Lavaṇa samudra filling the area which was embodied within Jambūdvīpā and therefore by corollary, to reach beyond this Lavaṇa samudra (*Dakṣiṇa Sāgara*) and Rāvaṇa's Laṅkā the famous *'setubandha'* (a bridge) was necessary. Thus, with reference to Lavaṇa samudra, Laṅkā (of Rāvaṇa) is an *'upadvīpā'* is what is indicated. Marīci says thus -

'na ca kṣārasindhorityanena sampūrṇasamudro jambūdvīpāntargataḥ iti kṣārasamudradakṣiṇataṭaparighau jambūdvīpārambhe laṅkāyāḥ satattvātkumadhyatvopapattiḥ setubandhopapattiśceti vācyam |
Sagaraputrairaśvānveṣaṇe mahīm khanadbhirjambūdvīpāsyāṣṭ āvupadvīpāḥ kalpitāḥ |
iti bhāgavate prasiddhatvāllaṅkāyā uttarabhage khananena lav aṇasamudrapravāhasyāgatatvāttasya jambūdvīpāntargatatvena prasiddheḥ setubandhopapatteḥ |
ata evābhitaḥ samudrasambandhāllaṅkāyā upadvīpatvam vyaktam' |

Thus, we can distinguish astronomical Laṅkā from Rāvaṇa's Laṅkā and arrive at a convincing and comprehensive picture of the distinct geographical positions of both (see fig. 1).

Marīci does not pin-point the exact geographical position of *Dakṣiṇa Sāgara* or Rāvaṇa's Laṅkā here, it is true. Marīci still proves his point, which supplies supporting evidence and strengthens the hypothesis put forward in this book. It is evident from the above that Marīci, the commentator of Bhāskārācārya of the twelfth century, was well aware that Rāvaṇa's Laṅkā and the '**sāgara**' which surrounded it were both within the boundaries of Jambūdvīpā and Bhāratavarṣa and that *Dakṣiṇa Sāgara* was a man-made *'samudra'* (sea). This truth was known to the purankaras and through the Purāṇās to the common people as well. However due to the emergence of a notion of astronomical Laṅkā it might have become necessary for someone like Marīci to bring forward the truth of two distinct Laṅkās.

A question that remains to be answered is, 'Why Indian astronomers had chosen the name 'Laṅkā' (and even 'Laṅkāpurī') for the hypothetical and imaginary point of their astronomical Laṅkā'. The *Purāṇās* had already been composed and got established and appeared in written versions in a settled form by the sixth century. It can be said that even before this time, the famed 'Laṅkā of Rāvaṇa' was known even to those early astronomers of India through local tales and traditions, literary or otherwise. Marīci's commentary itself provides a good proof for this. He talks about Rāvaṇa's Laṅkā being *Bhagvata-prasiddha* (well known to *'Bhāgavata Purāṇa'*). The Hanumatkeśvara story of the *purāṇakārās* reveals a geographical fact that must have been known to people at large, (the *purāṇakārās* and the astronomers as well) both by oral and literary traditions.

Kuśasthalī Ujjayini was the western limit of Mt. Vindhya, while Rāvaṇa's Laṅkā was in Kaimur ranges of Mt. Vindhya (almost nearly at the eastern limit) and was situated in the north-eastern peaks of Mt. Vindhya which spread, east-west, near about the line of the tropic of cancer (*karkavṛtta)*. Thus, the fact was known that in this way Mt. Vindhya formed a real 'Hunter' for the sun, with Ujjayini and Rāvaṇa's Laṅkā situated at its two ends. This could be the reason why these two place-names were woven, into the Hanumatkeśvara legend. The legend about Mt. Vindhya competing with Mt. Meru and Mt. Vindhya not allowing the sun to move further to the north beyond the *karkavṛtta* (at 23^0 30'N) also obviously has its origin in the geographical fact. The ancient astronomers were indeed aware of these facts and also of the fiction based on it.

It is tempting to put forward a conjecture that, there is a strong possibility that astronomers thus quite naturally chose the place-name Laṅkā for the imaginary astronomical Laṅkā point. These astronomers must be aware that Vālmīki's Laṅkā was around the same north latitude as that of Ujjayini (as indicated by Hanumatkeśvara legend.) In essence, like the *purāṇakārās* early Indian astronomers were aware of the fact that, Rāvaṇa's Laṅkā and Ujjayini lay nearly on the same latitude (as that of the tropic of cancer), they chose the same name Laṅkā for a spot or point-astronomical Laṅkā-which lay on the same longitude as Ujjayini as that line was the main longitude ('**madhyarekhā**') or the main meridian line for India of early ages. At the same time that point also lay on the '**Kumadhya**' or the main/zero lattitude or the equator. Perhaps this could explain why Bhāskāracārya's astronomical hypothetical point at the intersection of '**kumadhya**' (0^0 latitude) and '**madhyarekha**' (0^0 longitude) was given the name Laṅkā.

References: Latitude And Longitude Of Laṅkā

1. *'Bhāratiya Sanskṛti Kośa'*, vol. 9, (1976), p. 123
2. *'Skanda Purāṇa', Avantī Khaṇḍā* 5, Adhyāya 21: 8 , 9; 287:pp. 706, 707, Geeta Press Gorakhpur
3. Ibid. *'Viṣṇu Mahatmya'* Adhyāya:31:17, 18; 36:4, 5
4. *'Bhāgavata Purāṇa',* 10 Part 4:61:40, (ed. by S.L. Shastri; tr. and annotated by G.V. Tagare) (1983) p.1562, MLBD pbl. Delhi,
5. *'Bhāratiya Sanskṛti Kośa'*, vol.1, *(Tithicintamaṇī)*, p.600
6. Bhāskāracārya (II): *'Siddhāntaśiromaṇī'*-(tr. By Wilkinson) *Goladdhyaya-Bhuvanakośa*-24
7. D.B. Svami Kannu Pillai: *'Indian Chronology',* (quoted by G. Ramdas *'Rāvaṇa's Laṅkā* I.H.Q. (1928) p.340
8. Aryabhata: *'Aryabhaṭiyā', Goladdhyaya*-14, (with the commentary of Suryadeva, p.139 Yajvan*)* (Indian National Science Academy, New Delhi)
9. D.B. Sahasrabuddhe: *'Bhārata Sthalādarśa'*-Marathi-(1889), p.138
10. N.S. Adhikari:' Laṅkā of Rāvaṇa' (1922) p.498-503, [JBBRAS vol.XXV no.71-73]
11. Bhāskāracārya (II): *'Siddhāntaśiromaṇī'- Bhuvanakośa, Goladdhyaya,* 15
12. *'Vāyu Purāṇa'* 48:13
13. *'Vāyu Purāṇa'* Chapter 48, Bhuvanavinyasa:13
14. Ibid. 48: 20-31
15. V.H. Vader: *'Situation of Rāvaṇa's Laṅkā on the equator'* I. H.Q., vol .2, pp.345-351; QJMS, XVII pp.17-22

16. Bhāskārācārya (II) *'Siddhāntaśiromaṇī'-Bhuvanakośa, Goladhyāya,* 17
17. Rai Krisnadas: Nagarī Pracharini Patrika, 54:1, 2, 3
18. *'Bhāgavata Purāṇa', skandha* 5 *Adhyāya* 16, 19, p.711.736
19. *'Mārkaṇḍeya Purāṇa'* 191:55:20
20. Ibid.191:55:27
21. Varāhamihira: *'Bṛhatsaṃhitā'* (ed.by Kern) 14:11
22. Hiralal: 'The situation of Rāvaṇa's Laṅkā' Jha.comm.vol. (1937) Pune, pp.151-163
23. T. P. Iyer *'Rāmāyaṇa and Laṅkā',* (1940) (Bangalore) p.12,
24. M. V. Kibe *'Location of Laṅkā,'* (1927), Manohar Granthamala, Pune p.21
25. Mark Collins: *'The Geographical data of the Raghuvaṃśa and Daśakumāracarita',* (Leipzig), 1907, p.8
26. Bhāskārācārya (II): *'Siddhāntaśiromaṇī',* III, *'Division of the Globe',* 19 (tr. by Wilkinson) p.21-25, Bib India,Calcutta (1861)
27. Aryabhata:op[.cit. *'Aryabhaṭiyā'*
28. Bhāskārācārya (II): *'Siddhāntaśiromaṇī', Goladdhyaya,* pp.21-25 (With commentary by Marīci.)
29. Marīci, Ibid. p.59.

8

CEYLON - SRI LAṄKĀ AND RĀVAṆA'S LAṄKĀ

We have till now critically analysed and tried to elucidate the importance of objects, popular beliefs and researchers' concepts, the main characters of Rāmāyaṇa story, proper nouns and sites or places with place names, etc. from different Kāṇḍās of Rāmāyaṇa. There are many convincing reasons to uphold the position, that the location of Rāvaṇa's Laṅkā could not have been Ceylon, as it is popularly believed even today. Vālmīki Rāmāyaṇa does not supply any evidence in favour of the location of Laṅkā anywhere outside India, in Ceylon or to the south of river Narmada and Mt. Vindhya.

Ceylon is an island near the south-eastern tip of India. The distance between Talaimanar in Ceylon to Dhanushyakodi in India is 22 km (both being on the sea shore). Between Ceylon and India, where the sea is shallow, there are sunken rocky and sandy belts/ ridges, a nature's creation, which is in existence there from times immemorable. However, the sandy belt of 22 km length has been imagined to be the remains of a causeway (constructed by Nala vānara) to reach Ceylonese shore that is supposed to be none other than Laṅkā of Rāvaṇa.

If one wishes to uphold the traditional view some questions pertaining to the geography of the region will have to be answered. If Ceylon were Laṅkā, one expects to see near the seashore a mountain, with a table-land on its top. One should also then believe that Daṇḍakāraṇya, Pañcavaṭī, Kiṣkindha and Mt. Vindhya too should be shifted to south India and after Ceylon was linked with Rāvaṇa's Laṅkā, this has been done most suitably. Pargiter[1] has even gone to the extent of saying that, there is another Mt. Vindhya in India to the far south!

Sankalia observed that scholars believing in Ceylon-Laṅkā theory give either traditional or general arguments or of literary kind. V.V. Mirashi[2] argues that in the times of Kālidāsa (fourth century A.D.) Laṅkā was equalled to Ceylon. Sankalia[3] comments that, Kālidāsa and others only portrayed or narrated the then current view, whereas Varāhamihira (sixth century) or well- known Chinese travellers did not locate Laṅkā in the Indian ocean.

Rāmāyaṇa first became popular in U.P. and M.P. and then spread to south India and from there it was disseminated even out of India. It has logically been argued by Sankalia, that 'together with the interpolating of episodes, came the extension of the geographical dimensions'. Variations of the Vālmīki Rāmāyaṇa included local areas and location of Laṅkā gradually shifted southwards from Central India'.

U.P. Shah, T.P. Iyer, D.R. Mankad, Sankalia, Hiralal, Rai Krisnadas, G. Ramdas and others have discussed the problem of itinerary of Rāma's exile and journey to Laṅkā fairly exhaustively and the conclusions from their study and noncontroversial evidence gathered so far asserts that upto about the sixth century A.D. Mt. Citrakūṭa, Paṃpā, Kiṣkindha and of course the 'south-sea' and Laṅkā were all thought to be closely associated, and all were placed in north or central India. Sankalia in his book 'Rāmāyaṇa in Historical Perspective' has given reasons to dispose of Ceylon or Sri Laṅkā's claim to Rāvaṇa's Laṅkā. Two well-known Ceylonese scholars namely Anand Guruge[4] and Godakumbura[5], unhesitatingly say that Rāmāyaṇa story is not very popular in Ceylon. Godakumbura points out that in 'Bālarāmāyaṇa' of Rājaśekhara, (9th century) Rāvaṇa is addressed as Laṅkeśvara and nowhere called Siṃhaleśvara. P.V. Bapat[6] pointed out that 'early Pāli sources' confirm that there is no reference to the story of Rāma or Rāvaṇa, in the early canonical literature of Ceylon.

Rāmāyaṇa states that the 'city' of Laṅkā was situated on hill-top and was surrounded by 'Sāgara' or wetlands. It was really a land sub-division or upadvīpā, an 'island' only in that sense. Still, the whole island of Ceylon was called Sri Laṅkā, the city of rakṣasās, simply because it is an island in an ocean. This new identity given to the island, till then known as 'Siṃhala', was very easily and conveniently accepted. Even today this identity is so deeply rooted in the minds of people that it is never thought that Rāvaṇa's Laṅkā could be somewhere else. This notion is fixed in the minds of common people and the researchers alike. Here, it must be noted that classical Sanskrit writers never regarded Siṃhala *deśa* (or Siṃhala island) to be Laṅkā. Siṃhala is not mentioned in Vālmīki Rāmāyaṇa at any place. Laṅkā was the capital and Siṃhala was the janapada for them. These poets did not have much knowledge of island Siṃhala. Writers from Siṃhala might have imagined both to be the same, but classical Indian writers did not think so[7]. Ceylonese proper nouns like Sītā Eliya or Udu Rāvaṇa connected with Rāmāyaṇa came into existence because of Tamil influence. Murāri and Rājaśekhara distinguished Siṃhala from Laṅkā. Godakumbura[8], the Ceylonese scholar says that this confusion was not there in classical literature, but appeared in later period. He further says that 'Mahāvaṃśa' does not even mention the story of Rāma'. How Rāma-katha (story of Rāma) originated and got developed through the ages and in a variety of literature has been discussed by Camil Bulke. He has reviewed Sanskrit fiction, Sanskrit religious literature, as well as Buddhist and Jain literature[9].

According to *Mārkaṇḍeya Purāṇa*, Siṃhala (*deśa*) lies in the outer foot of southern part of the belly of 'kūrma' ('Dakṣiṇakukṣi' and 'bahya pada'). Siṃhala is associated with Ṛṣabhās and Kāñchī-nivāsis. Mārkaṇḍeya thus has mentioned Laṅkā and Siṃhala separately.

laṅkākālājināścaiva śailikā nikaṭāstathā |[10]
ṛṣabhāḥ siṃhalāścaiva tathā kāñcinivāsināḥ |[11]

D.C. Sarkar[12] on the contrary has said that 'Vālmīki quite clearly locates Rāvaṇa's abode far to the south of river Godavari, beyond the Sahya, Malaya and Mahendra ranges in the waters of the ocean, the location being supported by all 'early' Indian writers like Kālidāsa, Pravarasena, Kumāradāsa, Bhartṛhari and Bhavabhūti.' We have noted before the counter arguments by H.D. Sankalia, and others. Today the problem of location of Rāvaṇa's Laṅkā seems to have got caught up in such kind of mixed-up wild and clashing propositions.

H.D. Sankalia has pointed out that there are comparatively few references to Laṅkā and Siṃhala in Indian inscriptions, but these are very significant, as they definitely indicate that Ceylon came to be called Laṅkā and associated with rakṣasās, only after the fourth century, thus providing evidence that Rāvaṇa's (original) Laṅkā was not Siṃhala or Ceylon[13]. Who were the rakṣasās is another question which needs to be answered in this context. That they were aborigines, ādivāsis (tribals) of central India has now been proved beyond doubt and accepted by scholars. Romila Thapar has rightly pointed out that 'If historical survivals are to be sought then perhaps the one with the greatest potential for the Rāmāyaṇa would be a detailed examination of the central Indian Gonds and their neighbours to the east[14]'. G. Ramdas[15] after studying the language and the ways of life has identified the vānarās with the Śavaras and the rakṣasās with the Kui Gonds who have been living in central India (M.P.), a notion shared by some other scholars.

The Gond ādivāsis (aborigines) of Gondvana, that comprises of eastern Madhya Pradesh, claim their heritage from Rāvaṇa (*'Rāvaṇa-vaṃśīs'*). The Gonds in folk songs show in what high esteem Rāvaṇa and Meghanāda are still regarded by them[16]. This practice is not existent in Ceylon. Laṅkā therefore must be originally situated in the land of the Gonds[17]. As we know the Sāla tree (*Shorea robusta*) does not grow at all in Ceylon[18]. Sāla, which has its natural home in Madhya Pradesh is the tree of importance in Rāmāyaṇa.

'Nuvara Elia' is a mountain in Ceylon. The aborigines living in the forests in the neighbouring areas are 'Veddās'. The canonical writing of Ceylon, 'Mahāvaṃśa' does refer to Pulindās and Śavaras besides yakṣās and Nāgās as some of the original inhabitants of Ceylon. This thin thread however, is not sufficient to regard Ceylon as Rāvaṇa's Laṅkā. For a belief to get rooted and propagated there are reasons. For the last 1000 years or more Ceylon is thought to be Rāvaṇa's Laṅkā for some historical reasons. It has been 'an unfounded popular belief passed off as tradition'. We have seen before, that Rāvaṇa's Laṅkā had a long history even before Rāvaṇa was born, as per Uttarakāṇḍa, i.e. Brahmā's role in effecting its creation by Viśvakarma, antagonism between rakṣasās and gods, intervention by Viṣṇu and other gods, Kubera's hold over Laṅkā, Sumālī rakṣasa and his inciting Rāvaṇa for snatching away Laṅkā from Kubera etc.[19] No trace of this background mythology is given by Ceylonese stock of mythical stories. On the other hand, Narmada belt and to north of Mt. Vindhya is a fertile land of Rāmāyaṇa stories, place names, sites, etc. In Ceylon no such place names are found, and those showing similarity do not show any cultural relatedness.

The inner connection between Kubera (yakṣa), Rāvaṇa and their family deity Nikuṃbhilā has already been suggested by the present studies (see appendix C and D). In relation to this, in Ceylon there is no indication of any commonality of this kind. Also the present writer has brought to the notice of the readers the place of (river) Narmada in Rāvaṇa's ancestral tree and the fact that for this reason, very curious adjectives and names have been used for Narmada in our ancient literature (see Appendix C).

All such marks are from ancient Indian culture in general and they are exclusively related to the geography of that particular region, in this case a region to north of Mt. Vindhya. Although it is clearly indicated that Ceylon cannot be Rāvaṇa's Laṅkā (references cited before) many others believe that Ceylon was Laṅkā of Rāmāyaṇa and that Rāma had gone up to Ceylon. In central and north India and on the banks of Narmada are many places of pilgrimage, villages and many such sites with names related to Rāmāyaṇa story. e.g. Rāvaṇeśvara, Laṅkeśvara, Rāvaṇavādi, Rāvaṇagrām etc. and also Kuṃbhakarṇa tīrtha, Meghanāda tīrtha, Sugrīveśvara, Kubereśvara, Hanumatkeśvara, Kharaud, and many others. If Ceylon were related to Rāmāyaṇa story such culturally related things would be found there. However that is not the reality. Characters from Rāma's story like Kubera, sage Viśvāmitra or sage Agastya or even Sītā are of no significance in Ceylon. However, a word of caution here is that to consider only similarity of any names anywhere could be totally misleading.

Ceylon was originally known by the name 'Taṃbapannī' or 'Tāmraparṇī', and was known to Emperor Aśoka by the same name. Ptolemy's name for this island was 'Tāprobane'[20]. For Greeks the name of this island was Tāprobane. Before this period its name was 'Simoundou' which got changed to 'Salainke' and gradually the island came to be known as Ceylon. Another theory about this name is that it has its origin in the name of a Siṃhalī king Vijaya, 'Siṃhala' in Pāli became 'Celonā' and then Ceylon.

It is known that originally Laṅkā was not the name of this island and gradually the old names of persons, places and even rivers and mountains vanished and were replaced by new ones. Shobhana Gokhale[21] has used ancient inscriptions in India to study the times when such changes might have occurred in Ceylon. She says that Ceylon has taken Buddhism and Pāli language and Brahmi script from India and because of the cultural bond that has been there since long between the two countries, they remained connected. She has discussed various names Ceylon is known by, and primarily the times when the changes in names might have taken place. The oldest reference to Sri Laṅkā is found by the name 'Taṃbapannī' and is found in Aśoka's inscription[22] she notices.

According to the Ceylonese chronicles 'Dipavaṃśa' (fifth century A.D.) and 'Mahāvaṃśa' (sixth century A.D.), the name, 'Taṃbapannī', was given to a particular region where king Vijaya and his 700 aides landed on the sea-shore of Sri Laṅkā. The soil of that sea-shore was red coloured and reddened their hands, hence the name. There is no reference to the name Laṅkā in 'Dipavaṃśa', she observes and says that this legend is rather unconvincing.'

Mahāvaṃśa[23] records this name. She further states that 'It is surprising to note that the name 'Laṅkā' does not appear in (Indian) inscriptions before sixth century A.D. Gokhale, observed that on the contrary, Taṃbapannī was the name for the whole island. It was 'Tāprobane' for Greeks. Megasthenes has mentioned that Tāprobane was a land separated by the river Tāṃpraparṇī. The same name has been recorded by Periplus. It seems that the names Laṅkā and Siṃhala occur simultaneously in an Ikṣvāku record at Nāgārjunakoṇḍa. (Ikṣvāku period, south India, 300 A.D.)[24]. Island

Tāprobane was also known by the name 'Salaike' and the occupants were called 'Salai' according to Ptolemy.

Shobhana Gokhale says 'By about third century A.D. the name 'Tāprobane' disappeared from Indian inscriptions'. She also suggests a possibility that occupants of Sri Laṅkā established themselves in south Konkan too. The name Laṅkā was taken from Rāmāyaṇa, but it might have been taken from the Lithuanian word 'Laṅkā' reminiscent of an Indo-European word still in Lithuanian language, (meaning valley, strait, swampy, marshy land) or it could be a local name current even before the arrival of Indo-European speaking people.

In an inscription of sixth century A.D., the 'island' was not known by the name Laṅkā. Later Varāhamihira[25] has regarded Laṅkā and Siṃhala to be two distinct dvīpās. Periplus called it 'Pāre- Samudra' (Palae simaundu). Thus, the name of this island has changed from Taṃbapannī to Ceylon and today it is Sri Laṅkā and what is now known as Adam's bridge is believed to be Nalasetū. At present, questions are raised whether there really was a bridge? Was it man-made or a nature's creation? These questions are posed effecting in debate, discussions, research and politics too.

B.C. Law[26] has taken a review of known history of Ceylon. In the third century B.C. Aryans from the eastern and western coasts of India had already reached Ceylon under their leader, king Vijaya (a Siṃhalī). They reached Ceylon around 600 B.C. They subdued the locals and established a developed civilisation in Ceylon.

Around 247 B.C. Buddhism was officially introduced by Mahindra, the son of Aśoka, (third century B.C.). From third to second century B.C., Tamils arrived in Ceylon. This second era was of a constant pressure. Tamils, Paṇḍyās and Colās all came and tried to establish themselves. Siṃhalīs hardly ever gained victory over them. Siṃhalīs later accepted Buddhism. Their folk literature was not really influenced by Rāmāyaṇa. From A.D. 1111 to A.D. 1153 Parākramabāhu and his son Vijayabāhu ruled over the land. Vijayabāhu assisted by Paṇḍyās won victory over Colās. Tamil invasions and internal conflicts were going on. The capitals kept changing and the Tamils ultimately succeeded in occupying and settling in north Ceylon. After this, from A.D. 1505 to A.D. 1796,

Portuguese, Dutch and later British came to rule in the island. North Ceylon remained under Tamil domination. The central and south Ceylon came under the sway of Siṃhalīs, who spoke an Indo-European language and later had accepted Buddhism.

However, the studies presented in the previous chapters of this book supported by literary and geographical justification lead one to infer that Vālmīki's and Rāvaṇa's Laṅkā must have been in eastern M.P., (and not in Ceylon) as a hill-top settlement surrounded by watery, marshy, low-land area. It was a land sub-division, or upadvīpā, an island only in that sense. The cultural tradition and history of Ceylon does not make a thinking mind believe in the popular notion of Ceylon to be Laṅkā of Rāvaṇa. Rāvaṇa was indeed a part of Indian cultural tradition. The evidences discussed in this book point at the target area of Vālmīki's and Rāvaṇa's Laṅkā. The exact site is discussed in chapter 6 of this book.

References: Ceylon, Sri Laṅkā and Rāvaṇa's Laṅkā

1. F.E. Pargiter: 'The geography of Rāma's exile' in JRAS (1894),
2. V.V. Mirashi: 'Location of Rāvaṇa's Laṅkā', Journal of the Oriental Institute of Baroda. vol.XXIV. (1974-75), pp.356-368
3. H.D. Sankalia: *'Rāmāyaṇa in Historical Perspective',* (1973) p.141
4. Anand Guruge: *'The Society of the Rāmāyaṇa'*, (1960) Mahārāgāmā Sāman Press, Ceylon
5. Godakumbura: 'Laṅkā of the Classical Indian Writers', ALOCP 27, (1976), pp. 293-301
6. P.V. Bapat: (*Presidential address, All India Oriental Conference:* 27: Kurukṣetra, (1974)
7. C.E. Godakumbura: (1976): (Murāri and Rājaśekhara quoted by), op. cit.p.298
8. Ibid. p.301
9. Camil Bulke: *'Rāmakathā Utpatti aur Vikās'* (1962), Hindi Bhasha Parishad, University of Allahabad, U.P.
10. *'Mārkaṇḍeya Purāṇa',* 191:55:20
11. Ibid. 191:55:27
12. D.C. Sarkar *'Problems of the Rāmāyaṇa',* (1979), Andhra Pradesh. pbl. Hydarabad, p.16
13. H.D. Sankalia: *'Rāmāyaṇa in Historical Perspective',* Macmillan India Ltd. Bombay (1973), p.150

14. Romila Thapar: *'Exile and the Kingdom'* (1978), The Mythic Society, Bangalore, p.37
15. G. Ramdas: IHQ vol. IV (1928), pp339-46; vol. V (1929) pp.281ff
16. Durga Bhagavat: 'Folk songs from the Satpura valleys' Journal, University of Bombay, vol.III pt.4, Jan. (1960); 'Tribal Gods and Festivals in Central India', Asian Folklore Studies, vol. XXVII,-2(1968)
17. Hiralal: 'The situation of Rāvaṇa's Laṅkā' Jha comm. vol. (1937), p.155 (as recorded by Grierson.)
18. Ceylon Gazetteer,(1834), (ed. Chitty Mudliar)
19. 7:11
20. Ptolemy, [R.C. Majumdar, Classical accounts of India, (1960), Calcutta, p.361]
21. Shobhana Gokhale: 'Sri-Laṅkā in Early Indian Inscriptions' Annals BORI, LXXXV, (2004) *('Dipavaṃśa' and 'Mahāvaṃśa' quoted by),* pp.135-139
22. E. Hultzsch: CII, vol.I Oxford (1925), p.2, 66 (quoted by Shobhana Gokhale, Annals BORI, LXXXV, (2004))
23. W. Geiger: *'Mahāvaṃśa'*, 31 vol.61, tr.english (1908),
24. Epigraphia Indica volXX, (1929-30), p.23
25. Varāhamihira: *'Bṛhatsaṃhitā':* 14:11
26. B.C. Law: *'Chronicles of Ceylon',* RASB Monograph Series, (1947), vol. III

§§§

9

SUMMARY AND CONCLUSIONS

Rāmāyaṇa contains many riddles. The toughest one of these riddles being the geographical understanding of Rāma's exile, his journey from Ayodhya to Laṅkā and mainly the location of Laṅkā. Many researchers have rightly pointed out that Vālmīki's Laṅkā was not 1000 (or more) km away from the foot of Mt. Vindhya. It seemed to them doubtful whether the Laṅkā of Vālmīki indicated Ceylon. The place-names in *Rāmāyaṇa* may not all be mythical and many of these can be identified with actual sites in existence today. To get a coherent and believable picture of Vālmīki's *Rāmāyaṇa,* it was necessary to locate Laṅkā.

It can be said that if Sugrīva's *vānara* army after arduous journey could find Rāvaṇa's Laṅkā, we too may find it if we follow their steps with precision. Researchers in the last hundred or so years have tried to identify Laṅkā, with various sites.

The initiation, thinking and studies of Sardar M.V. Kibe, T.P. Iyer, U.P. Shah, D.R. Mankad, V.D. Jha, N.V. Rao, T. Amrithalingam, Sankalia, Romila Thapar, Hiralal, Rai Krisnadas, D.P. Mishra and many others have provided reasonable and decisive grounds to conclude that Rāmāyaṇic Laṅkā of Vālmīki must have been situated, necessarily to north of Mt. Vindhya. Few scholars believe that it should be located in eastern Madhya Pradesh.

The findings presented by other researchers while studying along these lines have been taken into consideration. Many aspects of the problem unattended by scholars so far, have been studied and many new evidences literary, geographical or otherwise are brought to light here in the present studies. The important Rāmāyaṇic sites identified are discussed in this book, providing literary and geographical justifications, based on topographical studies. The conclusions drawn from these studies are put down, briefly as follows. The important ones are -

(1) **Where was Daṇḍakāraṇya?** Public opinion, also shared by some scholars is that the Deccan plateau and Maharashtra is Daṇḍakāraṇya. The result of the present study suggests that it lay to the north of Mt. Vindhya, spread over southern regions of modern Uttar Pradesh, central and eastern regions of Madhya Pradesh touching northern Vidarbha. This conclusion is based on the story of king Daṇḍaka (given in the epic itself) who was cursed and got his empire ruined by dust-storm. This became Daṇḍakāraṇya. Later, when favourable conditions prevailed, it was again populated by *ṛṣīs*, sages, hermits, etc. and the area of their new settlement was called Janasthāna. The most probable location of Janasthāna is indicated by present studies. The story of king Śveta of Vidarbha, being one of the supporting evidences indicates the southern boundary of Daṇḍakāraṇya.

(2) **Pañcavaṭī:** Pañcavaṭī therefore cannot be at Nashik since the famous *'parṇakuṭī'* of Rāma was a part of Janasthāna and Daṇḍakāraṇya. There is no mention of Nasikya (or Nashik) in *Rāmāyaṇa*. Pañcavaṭī with a huge Banyan tree called 'Subhadra-*vaṭa'* as a landmark on its way must be situated near Mt. Citrakūṭa in Bundelkhand. The table-land or plateau in Reva district is identified with Pañcavaṭī of *Rāmāyaṇa*.

(3) **River Godavari:** Godavari of *Rāmāyaṇa* was not river Godavari flowing near Nashik in Maharashtra, but was *gupta*-Godavari with its rise in or near Mt. Citrakūṭa, or river Gadwā to its east with her origin most probably in the 'Godā *pahārā*'.

(4) **Kiṣkindhā:** Kiṣkindhā, the domain of *vānara*-kingdom is not situated at Anegundi (Karnataka state, South India) but it should

be searched for in U.P. where Ganga has her southern-most point touching the Kaimur ranges of Mt. Vindhya. Kiṣkindha must be located in the southern hilly region of Mirzapur district of U.P. abounding in rock shelters and caves. The evidence for this claim is gathered both from ancient literature as well as records from imperial gazetteers.

(5) ***Ṛkṣabila***: To the east of Madhya Pradesh lies Chhattisgarh state, to the north-east corner of which is Surguja district. Near the northern border of Surguja is Ramgarh hill. The singular large tunnel passing through this hill must be the *Ṛkṣabila* of *Rāmāyaṇa*. For identification of Laṅkā, the districts of Sidhi and Reva (lying to north of Surguja) of Madhya Pradesh are of special importance. The geographical positioning of Ramgarh hill, identified with *Ṛkṣabila,* actually points to the direction of Vālmīki's and Rāvaṇa's Laṅkā.

(6) ***Dakṣiṇa Sāgara:*** The birth story of *Dakṣiṇa Sāgara* given in Vālmīki *Rāmāyaṇa* had not drawn the attention of researchers till this date. The birth story of *Dakṣiṇa Sāgara* and loose threads from other sources, have been combined here. A conjectural theory was put forward by a few researchers that *Dakṣiṇa Sāgara* must be only a water reservoir of vast expanse. The present study provides most convincing internal evidence (from the epic itself) to that theory. The most probable location of *Dakṣiṇa Sāgara* must have been in south Ganga plain. The present study brings to light this fact.

(7) **Situation of Laṅkā:** Laṅkā, the Munda word, means a high land, a raised plateau, or a table-land on hill top as it also means an island that is surrounded by water on all sides. Vālmīki *Rāmāyaṇa* describes Laṅkā in this way. The place that fits very well with the description in *Rāmāyaṇa* has been searched, identified and located. A tentative theory is put forward that in Sidhi district of M.P. are a group of caves 'Rāvaṇa Mara' and other 'Mara caves'. These caves are situated on a south-eastern spur of a network of hills, with hill top settlements like Betdaha, Bansi, Nangva and others. This group of hills is situated in Singrauli basin to the west of backwaters of Rihand dam. It is hypothesised that hill ranges occupying this area can help in identifying Rāvaṇa's Laṅkā.

(8) **Latitude and longitude of Laṅkā**: The great Indian mathematician and astronomer Bhāskāracārya had mentioned Laṅkā in his '*Siddhāntaśiromaṇī*'. Its correct interpretation with the help of a legend of Hanumatkeśvara, a pilgrimage spot, proved the key for relocating the general area of Rāvaṇa's Laṅkā. Marīci's commentary on astronomer's Laṅkā provides a strong support for the argument presented in this book regarding the probable target area for which an internal evidence and geographical justification form the basis. The interpretation provided a strong supporting evidence for the inference drawn in this book regarding the probable location of Vālmīki's and Rāvaṇa's Laṅkā.

The present studies have also dealt with some other important aspects of Vālmīki *Rāmāyaṇa* like: The relationship between Rāvaṇa and his half-brother Kubera, the local deity of Laṅkā (Nikuṃbhilā), associations like Narmada, Sāla tree associated with Rāmāyaṇic sites, crocodiles often mentioned in *Rāmāyaṇa*, Puṣpak *Vimāna* as a flying vehicle etc.

All these conclusions can help in finding out where the most probable actual geographical locations of places as described in *Rāmāyaṇa* could be. The tentative sites of Pañcavaṭī, Kiṣkindhā, *Ṛkṣabila,* 'south-sea' and Laṅkā have thus come within the reach of our understanding, and these tentative conclusions are placed before the world of scholars. True, the geographical aspects with the support of literary evidences only have been studied here. However this is not the ultimate conclusion regarding the exact geographical location of Rāvaṇa's Laṅkā, as described by Vālmīki in his *ādi-kāvyā Rāmāyaṇa.*

The phase after this would be to explore the areas and various sites proposed by the present studies and carry out further multidisciplinary research. However, the present work definitely suggests that we are safely on the right track to trace the most believable locations of the original sites of many landmarks as described in Vālmīki *Rāmāyaṇa.*

The journeys undertaken by characters from Vālmīki *Rāmāyaṇa* on different occasions can be summarised as follows (H – Hermitage) (also see map 2):

Rāma and Lakṣmaṇa with sage Viśvāmitra: Ayodhya to Mithilā (Bālakāṇḍa)
Ayodhya → South bank of Śarayu (Ghāghra) → Ganga-Ghagra confluence → crossing Ganga → Ganga-Son doab (northern)-Malada-Karuṣa *deśa* or Tāṭakāvana → southern part of doab-Siddhāśrama near Kālakāvana → North bank of river Son → Towards north to Buxar → crossing Ganga → Ahalyāsrama → Viśāla nagarī → Mithilā nagarī.

Rāma, Lakṣmaṇa and Sītā: Ayodhya to Pañcavaṭī (Ayodhyākāṇḍa, Araṇyakāṇḍa)
River Tamasā/Kosālā *deśa,* river Gomatī → Śṛṅgaverapura (Guhā *sthāna)* → Ganga → Vatsa *deśa* → Ganga Yamuna Confluence → Bhāradvāja H. → crossing Yamuna → Śyāma-*vaṭa* → Citrakūṭā → Vālmīki H. → Atrī H. → Daṇḍakāraṇya → Virādha *sthāna* → Śarabhaṅga H. → Sutīkṣṇa H. → Pañcāpsara → Aśrama/ *maṇḍalās* (a stay of 10 years) → Sutīkṣṇa H. → Agastya's brother's H. (Pippalī vana) → *Agastya* H. → Jaṭāyu's abode → Pañcavaṭī

Abduction of Sītā by Rāvaṇa: Pañcavaṭī to Laṅkā (Araṇyakāṇḍa)
Daṇḍakāraṇya → Janasthāna and Pañcavaṭī → Rāma's *parṇakuṭī* → Kiṣkindha and Ṛṣyamūka → Paṃpā → Mahendra pass → Laṅkā

After abduction, Rāma and Lakṣmaṇa (Araṇyakāṇḍa, Kiṣkindhākaṇḍa)
From Janasthāna → Krauñcāraṇya → Kabandha *sthāna* → Mataṅga *sthāna* → Ayomukhī → opp. Mt. Ṛṣyamūka → Paṃpā → Mataṅgasara → West bank of Paṃpā → Śabarī H. → Kiṣkindha → Mt. Prasravaṇa or Mālyavān (stay of four months)

Hanumat group in search of Sītā: up to Ṛkṣabila and back to Kiṣkindha (Kiṣkindhākaṇḍa, Sundarakāṇḍa)
Ṛṣyamūka and Kiṣkindha → Kaṇḍu Muni's arid province → Vindhyan ranges → Mt. Rajata → Lodhra *vana* → Saptaparṇī *vana* → into *Ṛkṣabila* → Out of *Ṛkṣabila* → Vindhya + Mt. Prasravaṇa + *Sāgara* at the foothills of *Ṛkṣabila* → Towards north → Mt. Mahendra → Leap Over Mt. Maināka → Mt. Trikūṭa - mountains Laṃba and Ariṣṭa - Laṅkā → back to Mt. Mahendra → Madhuvana → Kiṣkindhā.

Onset of War - Rāma + Sugrīva's vānara army - Kiṣkindha to Laṅkā (Yuddhakāṇḍa)
Crossing Mt. Sahya + Malaya → ascending and descending Mt. Mahendra → north shore of *Dakṣiṇa Sāgara* → Nalasetū → south shore of *Dakṣiṇa Sāgara* → Mt. Suvela → Laṅkā

Hanumat - Hero of victory: Laṅkā to Ayodhya: (Yuddhakāṇḍa) Ganga-Yamuna confluence crossing → Śṛṅgaverapura → Bhāradvāja H. → Paraśurāma *tīrtha* → River Varūthi → River Gomatī → *Sāla* forest → Naṅdigrāma → Hanumat meets Bharata

Rāma's Puṣpak journey: Laṅkā to Ayodhya (Yuddhakāṇḍa)

Mt. Trikūṭa - Laṅkā battle ground → *Lavaṇa samudra* and Nalasetū → Mt. Maināka submerged in *Dakṣiṇa Sāgara* → *vānara* army camp point on north sea shore → Śiva *tīrtha* → Kiṣkindha (short stop) → Mt. Ṛṣyamūka → Paṃpā + Mataṅga *vana* → Kabandha *sthāna* → Subhadra *vaṭa* in Janasthāna → Pañcavaṭī + Jaṭāyu's death spot → *parṇakuṭī* → Godavari → Agastya H. → Śarabhaṅga H. → Virādha *sthāna* → Mt. Citrakūṭa → Atrī H. → River Yamuna → Ganga-Yamuna confluence + Bhāradvāja H. → River Ganga → Śṛṅgaverapura → Ayodhya.

Table 1

DISTANCES BETWEEN SOME IMPORTANT SITES FROM VĀLMĪKI RĀMĀYAṆA (As indicated by present study) (H. – Hermitage)

Ujjayini to Betdaha	Ujjayini to Laṅkā	750 km
Ayodhya to Prayag	Ayodhya to Bhāradvāja H.	150 km
Prayag to Rajapur Rajapur to Citrakūṭa	(Bhāradvāja H. to Citrakūṭa) Bhāradvāja H. to Rajapur Rajapur to Citrakūṭa	65 km 30 km
Citrakūṭa to Satna	Citrakūṭa to Sutīkṣṇa H.	64 km
Jaitwara (dist. Satna) to Sarang (dist. Satna)	Sutīkṣṇa H. to Agastya H.	35 km
Sarang (dist. Satna) to Reva Plateau	Agastya H. to Pañcavaṭī	<20 km
Devtālāb to Betdaha (as the crow flies)	Pañcavaṭī to Laṅkā	<100 km
Devtālāb to Mirzapur (as the crow flies)	Pañcavaṭī to Kiṣkindhā	<100 km
Mirzapur to Ramgarh Hill (Surguja) (as the crow flies)	Kiṣkindha to Ṛkṣabila	<250 km
Mirzapur to Ahraura		<50 km
Ramgarh hill to Betdaha (as the crow flies)	Ṛkṣabila to Laṅkā	100-125 km
Mirzapur to Betdaha (as the crow flies)	Kiṣkindha to Laṅkā	<125 km

Table 2

LATITUDE, LONGITUDE AND ELEVATIONS OF SOME LANDMARK PLACES FROM VĀLMĪKI RĀMĀYAṆA

(As indicated by present studies)

Place	Survey Sheet No.	Latitude	Longitude	Altitude
Ayodhya	63-J	26^0 48′	82^0 12′	91 m
Śṛṅgaverapura	63-G/10	25^0 34′	81^0 39′	86 m
Prayag (Allahabad)	63- G/15	25^0 27′	81^0 48′	92 m
Citrakūṭa Hill	63- C/16	25^0 10′	80^0 51′	173 m
Anasūyā Hill and Atrī Hermitage	63-C/16	25^0 4′	80^0 52′	242 m
Virādha Kuṇḍa	63-C/16	25^0 2′	80^0 52′	283 m
Śarabhaṅga Hermitage	63-D	24^0 58′	80^0 51′	-
Sutīkṣṇa Hermitage (Satna)	63 D/14	23^0 58′	80^0 21′	314 m
Agastya Hermitage (Sarang Dist. Satna)	63 H/7	24^0 18′	81^0 29′	244 m
Goda Pahar Reserved Forest	63-H/5	24^0 45′	81^0 15′	282 m
Reva	63-H/2+6 & 63 H/10+14	24^0 32′	81^0 18′	306 m
Devtālāb (Reva Dist.)	63 L/1+5	24^0 40′	81^0 43′	350 m
Mirzapur	63 K/4+8 & 63 K/12+16	25^0 08′	82^0 33′	83 m
Ramgarh Hill (Surguja Dist.)	64-J/9 +13	22^0 53′	82^0 54′	968 m
G. V. P. Sagar Dam, Renukut	63-L/15 & 64 I/9+13	24^0 11′	82^0 39′–83″	264 m
Betdaha Sidhi Dist.	64 I/1+5 & 64 I/9+13	23^0 57′	82^0 23′	608 m
Mara (Sidhi Dist.)	64 I/9+13	23^0 55^0	82^0 31^0	480 m
Ujjayini	46 M/12+16	23^0 10′	75^0 46′	535 m

§§§

APPENDIX

(A) *MAKARĀS* OF *RĀMĀYAṆA*

Rāma, with his followers sat worrying on the shores of *Dakṣiṇa Sāgara*. Without crossing the sea they could not reach Laṅkā. Rāma then requested Sāgara to suggest a way out, and asked, "*dānavās* (Crocodiles?) have infested your waters; (*Mahādānavasaṅkula*) [*Caṇḍanakragrāhaghoram*, 6:4:112][1] (*Makrairnāgabhogaiśca*, 6:4:116)[2] and therefore, how do we cross your expanse?" Sāgara explained saying, 'Out of lust, want, fear or love (or because of all these), I cannot deprive my waters abounding in crocodiles of their perpetual motion'.

na kāmānna ca lobhādvā na..bhayātpārthivātmaja |
grāhanakrākulajalam stambhayeyam kathañcana ||[3]

Sāgara then suggests that if a bridge is constructed over the waters, he would make a firm land base for it and hold it. Rāma was still nervous as *Dakṣiṇa Sāgara* was crowded by frightful and ferocious aquatic animals, mainly crocodiles.

ayam hi vipulo vīro sāgaro makarālayaḥ |[4]

Ultimately Sāgara assured Rāma, that the crocodiles would not come out and attack the *vānarās*, till the *vānara*-army had crossed the bridge that was to be constructed by Nala *vānara* over the waters. The verse is--

grāhā na prahariṣyanti yāvatsenā tariṣyati |[5]
harīṇām taraṇe rāma kariṣyāmi yathāsthalam ||[6]

That *Dakṣiṇa Sāgara* was an abode of crocodiles has been stated often in *Rāmāyaṇa*[7, 8]. Rāma and Lakṣmaṇa had used shields made from the skin of crocodiles in Laṅkā war.

Sugrīva had alarmed the *vānarās* about a ferocious aquatic creature named Aṅgārakā or Saiṃhikā, capable of catching the victim by its shadow. It is said that the aquatic demon was there to guard *Dakṣiṇa Sāgara*. Hanumat had then succeeded in killing the creature and had entered Laṅkā. The description indicates a water predator. *Ānanda Rāmāyaṇa* gives a story that Hanumat's sweat drops were swallowed by a crocodile and it gave birth to his son named Makaradhvaja, whom Hanumat met at the gates of Laṅkā.

Constructing a bridge over the vast waters was the only solution, which Sāgara had suggested, because the main obstacle was the presence of crocodiles in its waters. Rāma says that navigation is not possible there. This indicates that the 'sea' was muddy, marshy, with rocks standing in between and it was not a very deep water reservoir, which otherwise would have made it possible for Rāma's men to cross it with the help of boats and rafts. When Rāma had crossed river Ganga of enormous expanse, Guhā had helped Rāma with his 500 boatmen and there is no mention of crocodiles in that description. We meet cursed *apsarās* (celestial damsels) transformed into crocodiles many a times in ancient mythology. Khara *rakṣasa's* son is named 'Makarakṣa', *Rāmāyaṇa* informs.

In the context of these *makarās*, river Narmada (and other rivers in that region) is distinctive and its characteristics should be taken note of. Narmada has her rise in Madhya Pradesh at Amarkanṭak hills in Vindhyan ranges. The river descends towards the west, forming falls and water pools. After flowing for a distance of 500 km it meets the Arabian sea. Madhya Pradesh, especially the Kaimur ranges, has large areas covered with forests even today. Narmada is described as a river, which never becomes thin or dry and has formed innumerable marshy lands. Thick tropical forests on the river banks are naturally crowded by animals of all kinds. The predators depending upon herbivorous animals are found in great numbers in such forests. *Makarās* or crocodiles of Narmada belt are one of the important predators often mentioned in epics and other ancient literature. It is therefore not surprising that river Narmada also has a name 'Makaragāminī'. Some of the names Narmada is known by are extremely interesting. A collection of thousand names for Narmada, listed in '*Narmada Sahasṛanamavali*'[9] include the following names: *Nakṛeśi* (*nakra-makara* - crocodile), *Siṃhikā, Siṃhī, Siṃhapālinī, Gṛahinī, Gṛahaṇa, Gehā, Gṛaheśā, Gṛahavallabhā, Godhā, Godhāminī* (*gṛāhā, godhā* means Crocodile and *godhā* means monitor lizard also). As a river goddess Narmada is presented in paintings and popular mass art prints as sitting on lotus flower held and supported by a crocodile as a *vāhana* (vehicle).

Three species of crocodiles are found in India[10].

(1) *Ghariyal*: (*Gavialis gavialis* or *Gavialis gangeticus*) the species has characteristically thin and long jaws and are found only in India.

They are strictly only fish eaters, having their long, narrow snoots as a perfect weapon for catching fish. They are found only in large rivers of north India like Ganga, Sindhu, Brahmaputra and Mahanadi. They prefer to remain in deep waters and are the most aquatic of the crocodiles. Being only fish eaters they do not cause concern amongst humans or other animals, since they do not walk overland as do *maggaras* and they do not attack. They are never found in marshy lands or large ponds. Thus, while crossing great rivers like Ganga and Yamuna, crocodiles were not the main hurdle, as there was in the shallow, marshy water currents or reservoirs.

(2) The second type, *Crocodylus porosus,* is found in salty waters, coastal areas and swamps. They are the largest of all types measuring more than two to three metres in length.

(3) The third type is the *'maggara.'* They are very swift in movement. Their prey catching efficiency is enormous. They have the broadest jaws, but their length does not exceed two metres. They are found all over India. In a river like Narmada, surrounded by thick forests and in marshy, shallow, waterlogged areas they live happily. They often come overland. Narmada is a home for *maggaras (Crocrodylus palustris)* [Dr. Varadagiri (of Bombay Natural History Society) personal communication].

Rāmāyaṇa describes a variety of monkeys and deer. The easiest prey for *maggaras* are the deer. Thus *maggaras* are the most important crocodile type, of M.P., Chhattisgarh etc. The word *'timi'* is used for a large fish. It can be imagined that the word *'timiṅgala'* might have been used in the epics and other ancient literature to mean *maggara, susara* or *ghariyal. Rāmāyaṇa* describes *Dakṣiṇa Sāgara* around Laṅkā to be *lavaṇārṇava* or *lavaṇāṃbhās* or *lavaṇa samudra* (salt water sea) whether the word *'lavaṇa'* means 'salty' or the word *'lavaṇa'* is of non-Aryan origin and means 'a low level land-mass' as Rai Krisnadas[11] has suggested will have to be examined. The crocodile species, which was having its habitat in the target area can throw more light on this matter.

Baburnama[12] describes *maggara* as 'water-tiger' (Persian *'Sir-abi'*) or *makara*. Babar had noticed all three types of crocodiles of India.

The valleys of rivers Narmada, Son etc. in shallow, marshy water-logged areas are crowded with *maggaras* and this is expressed in cultural, religious and other practices of people of Madhya Pradesh, southern U.P., Chota Nagpur, western Bihar etc. It is interesting to note that from the word *'makara'* there are maximum number of place names found only in M.P., and some examples are noteworthy. A village called 'Makarapataka' is near Bhedaghat (dist. Jabalpur). An inscription found in the area says that it is situated on the right bank of river Narmada[13]. V.V. Mirashi opines that four miles to the west of Bhedaghat, at the toe of a hill, is a village named 'Magarmuha'. He has identified it with 'Makarpataka' since 'Magarmuha' is also on the right bank of river Narmada[14]. Similarly in eastern part of M.P., there are villages with names like Makarohar (significance mentioned in chapter 6), Makrouri, Makardha, Magror, Makari, Magarvadha and alike. The number of such names is larger in M.P. as *maggaras* are abundant in Narmada belt. Interestingly, information of this kind helps us in solving some riddles of mythology, history, geography, etc. Based on such information one can do archaeological studies, carry out excavations etc. in the target area. Large rivers like Ganga had dolphins and whales in ancient times. (There is a *ślokā* in *Rāmāyaṇa* describing whale fish.) Such records and archaeological research can throw light on the geographical characteristics of a particular place. For instance, in the context of crocodiles the following information and an inference drawn from it are interesting.

Ghariyal is found in large rivers like Sindhu, Ganga, Brahmaputra and their larger tributaries. *Ghariyal* is also found in Mahanadi of Orissa and Kaldan of Arkan. *Ghariyal* never comes on land. Also it never enters the sea waters. Therefore, the existence of *ghariyal* in

Mahanadi of Orissa and Kaldan indicates that in remote times these two rivers must be joining Ganga. *Ghariyal* is an animal of .great antiquity and its remains are also found in the Sivalik ranges of Himalayas[15]. However, the *makarās* of *Rāmāyaṇa* are the *maggaras*, abundantly found in Narmada belt and the region around.

References: Makarās of Rāmāyaṇa

1. 6:4:112
2. 6:4:116
3. 6:15:6
4. 6:15: Entry no. 314
5. 6: 15:7
6. 6:15: Entry no. 262
7. 6:2:5
8. 6:3:14
9. *'Narmada Sahasṛanamavali'* in *'Narmada Parikṛamā'* (ed. and Compiled by Omkaranandagiri, 2002)
10. M.C. Downes: *'A Bibliography of the Recent Crocodilians'* (1970)
11. Rai Krisnadas: *'Rām vanavās ka bhūgol'* Nagarī Pracharini Patrika, 54:1-3 p. 117
12. 'The *Baburnama',* vol. 2, (Tr. by Beveridge*)* (1970) p.501*,*
13. P.K. Bhattacarya: 'Epigraphia Indica' vol.II pp.7 ff (cited from*'Historical Geography of M.P. From Early Records'* (1977) p.234
14. V.V. Mirashi: CII, no. 60 p.314 [cited from P.K. Bhattacharya (1977), p.234, 235]
15. *'Imperial Gazetteer of India',* Indian Empire, vol. 1, (1909)

(B) THE GREAT LEAP OF HANUMAT

Hanumat was the chief aide of Sugrīva, the king of *vānarās.* Rāma and Lakṣmaṇa get acquainted with Hanumat in *Kiṣkindhākaṇḍa*. We meet him later in *Sundarakāṇḍa* and *Yuddhakāṇḍa*.

Unless Hanumat jumps across *Dakṣiṇa Sāgara, Rāmāyaṇa* story cannot progress. The birth story of Hanumat is curious[1]. Hanumat, like *pāṇḍava* Bhīma is wind-god Vāyu's own son Marutī, (the son of Marut), while *vānarī* Añjanā's husband, Kesarī *vānara* is his *kṣetraja (*adoptive) father. Añjanā is a rebirth of an *apsarā* Puñjikasthalā[2] (this name represents a particular constellation). Vāyu's promise to Añjanā was that she will get a strong bodied, brilliant and radiant son from him, who will be especially skilled in taking leaps like Vāyu himself. Thus-

mahāsattvo mahātejā mahābalaparākramaḥ |
laṅghane plavane caiva bhaviṣyati mayā samaḥ ||[3]

Jāṃbavan praises Hanumat by calling him *'plavatāmuttamo'*[4] meaning the best skilled jumper, and says, 'O the mightiest of *vānarās*! Arise and cross this vast ocean'.

uttiṣṭha hariśārdūla laṅghayasva mahārṇavam |[5]

Marutī, being Vāyu's son, says that as far as jumping skill is concerned, he is the master of that skill and there is no one else like him. Thus-

marutasyaurasaḥ putraḥ plavane nāsti me samaḥ |[6]

Scholars agree that *rakṣasās* and *vānarās* were human beings, the aborigines, living in forests. It can be imagined that only they could move through thick forests, finding their way without getting exhausted. Moving amidst high hills and thick forests was something only forest dwellers could do. Kabandhā's advice to Rāma to make an alliance with Sugrīva was therefore a well thought out strategy. Sugrīva's *vānara* army with heroes like Hanumat, Jāṃbavan, Añgada and others proved to be the best assistance, Rāma could get to put up a fight with Rāvaṇa. These forest dwellers might have 'monkey' as their totem. Words like *'vānara', 'harī', 'kapi', 'plavaga', 'plavaṅgama', 'śākhāmṛga', 'golāṅgula',* and *'ṛkṣa'* all mean *vānara,* a monkey (*ṛkṣa* also means a bear).

Chota Nagpur is occupied by tribal people (the natives) of communities like Munda, Oraon, etc. They have clan names like Tigga, Hilman, Bajaranga, Gadi, which mean *'vānara'*. Bhuiya people of Singbhum consider themselves to be the descendants of Hanumat. Researchers have pointed out that aborigines from some communities proudly tie-up a dangling tail on their body[7].

Hanumat, the jumping expert - Hanumat's feat of crossing over the sea should be examined here. We must remember that

Rāmāyaṇa is essentially poetry and hence there is bound to be much exaggeration. What exactly is the meaning and context of the picture painted by Vālmīki can still be studied. How did Hanumat cross the sea when there was no bridge over the sea waters? Did he swim through the waters or flew through the sky? Did he jump? Or simply waded through the muddy waters? We will now examine this point without taking it literally. *Sundarakāṇḍa* explains –

sa tu vīryavatām śreṣṭhaḥ plavatāmapi cottamaḥ |[8]

Hanumat was the mightiest of the *vānarās* and the best jumper. He goes through the sky but by taking a leap over the waters. He does not fly through the sky like a winged bird. Even in mass art, popular paintings, etc. Marutī is never shown to have wings, although he is shown in the skies with Mt. Dronagiri on the palm of his hand. Thus he never flies. He inflates his own strong body to resemble Mt. Meru and then by jumping or by taking long and high jumps and leaps, Hanumat crosses over *Dakṣiṇa Sāgara*. His enlarged body allows him to take a great leap. If Hanumat had flown or swam, he need not expand his body to an enormous size. What he would need in such a case is speed and a body of light weight and small size. *Rāmāyaṇa* doesn't say that he swam through the waters. The inference therefore is that Hanumat took a long jump, (or by touching Mt. Maināka immersed in the sea waters, Hanumat took two or more jumps).

'mahāmerupratīkāśam mām drakṣyadhvam plavaṅgamāḥ' |[9]

The accepted meaning of '*plava*' or '*plavaṅgama*' is 'to jump' and 'to swim' both. *Rāmāyaṇa* however does not describe Hanumat as expert swimmer. The scenery around, the aquatic animals (excepting Saiṃhikā and Surasā who are killed by him and he again jumps) springing up from the waters, etc. are also not described. He jumps into and through the sky. Also it is clear that swimming through *Dakṣiṇa Sāgara* was out of question because it was marshy and heavily infested with crocodiles. U.P. Shah[10] has argued that the sense of swimming in words '*puplave*' or '*plavamāna*' cannot be overlooked. However, this notion is not acceptable for obvious reasons as follows:

1. Hanumat's prowess[11] as an expert jumper is often described and compared with that of Vāyu, his father, and also with Garuḍa,

the king of birds, (*Kiṣkindhākaṇḍa)* and at that very instance, of crossing over the sea, the fact of his being the son of Vāyu is brought forth by the epic poet[11].

2. After viewing the sea, the *vānarās* discuss among themselves each one's capacity to take leaps or jumps and then it is pronounced that Hanumat is the best of all.
3. Jāṃbavan finally reminds Hanumat that, Hanumat as an infant had taken a great leap towards the rising sun, thinking it to be a radiant fruit. Hanumat therefore is described by Vālmīki as an expert jumper, and not a swimmer or a flyer, is very clear from the descriptions in the epic.

The significance of this inference is that Hanumat being a *vānara*, this was his specially acquired skill to take long and high jumps through the trees and mountains as expertly practiced not only by monkeys but also by forest dwellers, and that is exaggerated to the level of a fantasy by Vālmīki.

References: The Great Leap of Hanumat

1. 4:65:8-18
2. 4:65:8, 9
3. 4:65: entry no.1353
4. 4:65:34
5. Ibid.
6. 4:66:7
7. V.D. Jha: *'Investigations into the Archaeology of Surguja'* (1973)
8. 5:2:5
9. 4:66:18
10. U.P. Shah: *'Introduction to Uttarakāṇḍa'* of *'Vālmīki Rāmāyaṇa'* c.e. (1975) p. 47 (refers to 1: 57; 5: 35.5.)
11. 4:65:18, 19

(C) *RIVER NARMADA*

The story of *Rāmāyaṇa* describes many rivers, e.g. the great Ganga, Yamuna, Śarayu, Son (Sumāgadhī), Gupta Godavari of the north, Gomatī, upper Tamasā and Tamasā (Tons), Paṃpā, Vaitaraṇī, Mandākinī, Alakanaṅda and Narmada. Which one of these rivers was of supreme importance providing flesh and blood to the story of the epic? The answer is not simple. Outwardly none of the rivers has received any special importance.

In *Bālakāṇḍa,* Śarayu or Ghāghra is mentioned, as it is near Ayodhya. Ganga, and Yamuna have to be crossed over like Ghaghra. Ganga descending from the Himalayan heights is again the story mainly of Bhagīratha and Sagara, Rāma's ancestors. *Araṇyakāṇḍa* refers to a number of rivers and the Ganga-Yamuna confluence. When Rāma settles in Pañcavaṭī, the beautiful Godavari with her surroundings draws reader's attention. *Kiṣkindhākaṇḍa, Sundarakāṇḍa, Yuddhakāṇḍa* and *Uttarakāṇḍa* do not specially describe any one river. Even today no river can claim to be the mother nurturer river of Rāma-*katha.* Ganga and Yamuna are important but Rāma does not come across these rivers again. Sītā and Rāma worship these rivers so that they reach the far bank safely.

Narmada is a river, which does not overtly receive any significance in the story. It remains in the background like a backstage worker for the drama. However, it is river Narmada that plays an important role in the story. According to P.V. Kane[1] an express reference to river Narmada has not so far been traced in the Vedic literature. Various *Purāṇās* and epics mention Narmada. Ptolemy refers to Narmada as 'Nammados'[2]. It is one of the seven holy rivers of India. *Skanda Purāṇa* has one full section, the *'Reva Khaṇḍā'* devoted to Narmada. Reva is another name of Narmada. The name Narmada means the one that heightens beauty. Literally numerous legends and tales, place-names and *tīrthās* have come to exist in Narmada belt. Many of these names, stories, spots and sites revolve around Śiva, Rāvaṇa, Kubera, Sahasrārjuna and Hanumat. In the present times Narmada is adored by devout people piously and devotees undertake *'parikramā',* a circuit route around the river. A verse from *'Narmadāmahātmya'* says **'narmadā sadṛśī loke na gaṅgāpi varānane'**[3] meaning 'no other river (of India) including river Ganga enjoys the reverence of this kind'

Narmada has her origin in Amarkanṭak hill of the Maikal range of Mt. Vindhya. Therefore her explanatory names are *mekalasuta* and *mekalakanyaka*. In *Rāmāyaṇa* story, Narmada is never crossed over by any character, as a result the river is not considered important by readers. Narmada may not be of significance for Rāma, but it is still a very important river, for the aborigines dwelling amidst the Vindhyan ranges and forests, valleys and plains of Narmada belt. River Narmada is also adored by rāmāyaṇic characters like Sahasrārjuna Kārtavīrya, Rāvaṇa, Kubera, *vānarās, Nāgās, yakṣās, gandharvās, rakṣasās,* etc.

Narmada was conferred with a boon of immortality by Śiva. The hill was therefore, named Amarkanṭaka. The name may also have its origin in *'kaṅṭakā'* meaning bamboo groves which filled the area in remote times. The river flows in westward direction and still her connection with the region from where she issues out never breaks. A place name of a certain pilgrimage on the banks of Narmada indicates such correlation. Narmada has not just few but literally thousand names e.g. *Nāgābhagini, Makaragāminī, Nakṛeśi, Saiṃhikā, Nageśi, Dhanadeśvarī, Sahasradhārā*[4] etc. The river is also known as Mandākinī and Trikūṭa or Trikuṭī as a consequence of rāmāyaṇic influence. Some of these names explain her character and associations.

Haihayadhipati Sahasrārjuna Kārtavīrya had a confrontation with Rāvaṇa on the banks of river Narmada, (near Māhiṣmatī) which could not come in the sweep of any one of them. The story is indicated by the name *'Sahasradhārā'*. Mt. Vindhya and especially river Narmada have been described in great details by Vālmīki[5, 6]. Narmada belt is basically a region of aborigines and even their home is under the influence of the epic. Although Narmada is not directly connected to Rāma story, she is connected through the medium of numerous characters, indirectly, e.g. some of the names given in *Narmada Sahasṛanamavali*, (thousand naṃes of Narmada) are particularly strange and curious:

Bhrāmarī (from Mt. Bhramara) was the goddess of Janasthāna. Bhrāmarī was also the name of goddess Viṅdhyavāsini as given in *Śabdeśwari*[7].

Bibhīṣaṇavarapradā (the one favouring Bibhīṣaṇa)

Yakśinī, Yakṣapālikā, Yogamāyā, Rakṣikā, Rakṣasabhakṣyā,

Rāmakāryakarī, Rāma, Rāmarājyapratiṣṭhitā, Rāsabhī, Rāsabhaprītā (*rāsabha*-an ass, a hardy animal used by Rāvaṇa to pull his cart-chariot) are among the thousand names of Narmada.

Some names are even related to Laṅkā e.g. *Laṅkāpālī, Laṇkeśī, Lokalokā prapūjitā Lavaṇābdhitarī Laṅkā, Laṇkeśī, Laṅkāpālīkā* (*Lāṅk* = type of grain) or (Laṅk = name of an *asura*)[8].

These proper nouns clearly indicate the correlation Laṅkā has with Narmada, and with this it indicates the geographical location of Laṅkā in Narmada belt, one can easily conjecture. *Rāmāyaṇa* informs us[9] that, Rāvaṇa is from a *rakṣasa* lineage with Narmada *gandharvī* (river Narmada personified by the poet) playing an important role. The birth story of Rāvaṇa indicates (see Appendix D) that the most probable location of Rāvaṇa's ancestral home Laṅkā was in Narmada belt. Some more names of Narmada also draw our attention, as they remind us of the Rāma-*kath*ā e.g. *Siṃhī, Siṃhikā, Siṃhapālikā, Śabarī, Śabarātmikā, Hanumatprītimāpanna, Harī-rūpa, (harī-vānara) Harī-priyā*

Kārtavīrya - Vilāsā

Kārtavīrya Prabodhinī

Kālanjarnivāsinī (Kālanjar is a name of a small hill near Citrakūṭa, *Kālanjara is one more name of Śiva.* Narmada is believed to be the daughter of Lord Śiva so her name Kālinjarī.)

Khareśī (khara - an ass, or Khara *rakṣasa)*

Kharabhakśī

Kharadūṣaṇamardinī

Gṛahinī (*gṛaha* - crocodile)

Godhā, Godhāminī (*godhā* - crocodile or a reptile)

Dhaneśā, Dhanapālī (*Dhaneśā and Dhanadā*-Kubera), *Dhaneśapoṣiṇī, Dhanadeśvarī*

Naravāhanaśobhādhya (Naravāhana - Kubera)

Jaleśī, Jalaśayyā, Jalasāgaravāsini (The word *'sāgara'* may mean a sea, a lake, water logged area etc. Many such *sāgarās* or water bodies are formed by Narmada in the surrounding area.) *Ṭaṅkinī, Ṭaṅkarūpā Ṭaṅkātmā, Ṭaṅkāneśvarī* are some of the names of Narmada.

Śabdeśvarī has given names of *asura* pairs one of which is *asura* Laṅka and his aide *asura* Ṭaṅkaṭa (also a male *asura*). Names of *rākṣasīs* are Ṭaṅkaṭā, Laṅkaṭaṅkaṭā and Laṅkinī. However, *Śabdeśvarī* does not give the source of these names. *Ṭaṅka* or *Ṭaṅkikā* (Sanskrit) means hand-axe or a tool for breaking stones. It is possible that Laṅka and Ṭaṅkaṭa were from an expert stone breaker tribe. Laṅkā, the hill-top city was '**ṭaṅkacchinnā caturdiśī**', as if chiselled from all four sides[10]. River Narmada is also known to break rocks and stones by the force of her current. Thus, she might have been given names like *Ṭaṅkinī* etc. Another possibility is that if 'Laṅka' and 'Ṭaṅkaṭa' are the names of *rakṣasās* (or *rākṣasīs*) and their particular tribe, then Rāvaṇa, as their headman can be named *Laṅkanāyakā, Laṅkanātha, Laṅkāpatī,* etc. If this is the basis of their abode-name, (city of Laṅkā) from the Laṅkā tribe, then Rāvaṇa (or later Bibhīṣaṇa) can be named Laṅkā-*nātha,* Laṅkā-*dhipatī, Laṅkeśa, Laṅkeśvara,* etc, the names Rāvaṇa and Bibhīṣaṇa are known by. In the absence of any information about the source of these words all this is only a conjecture at the moment.

There are innumerable pilgrimages in Narmada basin connected with *Rāmāyaṇa*. Some names are Meghanāda *tīrtha,* Garjana *tīrtha,* Rāvaṇeśvara, Vaṭeśvara, Piṅgaleśvara, Kuberabhavana, Kuberbhaṅḍāri, Aṅgāreśvara, Marutālaya, Yamā *tīrtha,* Ahalyā *tīrtha* etc. At a place named 'Māhiṣmatī', is a temple of Rāvaṇeśvara. These names of *tīrthās* also suggest a very close relation Narmada has with characters from Rāma-*kath*ā. Similarly there are a number of pilgrimages of Śiva and legends connect them with Rāma story, e.g. Ahalyeśvara, Hanumatkeśvara, Vānareśvara, Gomateśvara, Kubereśvara and many more Śiva pilgrimages. To summarise, the evidences compels one to connect Rāma *katha* with river Narmada, as the most important river providing the flesh and blood to the story of Rāma.

References: River Narmada

1. P.V. Kane: 'History of Dharmaśastra', (1953) vol.IV, Adhyāya 15, BORI, Pune,pp.703-707
2. Ptolemy II, i: 31, 32, (R.C.Majumdar '*Classical accounts of India*' (1960), p.369

3. *Bhāratīya Sanskriti Kośa'* (1987):4:p.700, Bharatiya Sanskriti kosh Mandal, Pune
4. *'Narmada Pradakṣiṇā'* (ed. and compl. by Omkaranandagiri), (2002), p.181-196
5. 7:31:9-40
6. 7:32:40-42
7. *'Śabdeśvarī'* (ed. Aravindakumar and Kusumakumar) (1999) p.169
8. *'Gīrvāṇalaghukośa'* p.409
9. 7:5:27, 28, 29
10. 7:5:21

(D) *RĀVAṆA AND LAṄKĀ OF KUBERA*

The history of Laṅkā as given in *Rāmāyaṇa*[1] informs us that it was created by Viśvakarma originally for *daityās (rakṣasās)* like Māli, Sumālī and Mālyavān who were married to three daughters of a *gandharvī* named Narmada. When they started harassing gods, Viṣṇu killed Māli in a battle. Fearing Viṣṇu's might *rakṣasās* then fled to *pātāla*. After this, Laṅkā was ruled by Vaiśravaṇa (Kubera). He was gifted with Puṣpak *Vimāna* by Brahmā, who also made him *'Lokapāla'* (regent of the north), and *'Nidhīśa'* (the lord of all treasures). Rāvaṇa was then born. Sumālī filled with envy, instigated Rāvaṇa to restore Laṅkā to *rakṣasās*. Kubera was subdued and Rāvaṇa ascended the throne of Laṅkā vacated by Kubera.

Kubera's mother Ilvilā was the daughter of king Tṛṇabindu and Alaṃbuṣā (daughter of Alaṃbuṣa *rakṣasa*)[2] whose name was also Sālakaṭaṅkaṭaā[3]. Rāvaṇa too was in the lineage of Alaṃbuṣa *rakṣasa*[4]. Thus, Sālakaṭaṅkaṭā was a common stock of *yakṣarāja* Kubera and *rākṣasarāja* Rāvaṇa.

According to the scholars like U.P. Shah[5] and T.P. Iyer[6] Sālakaṭaṅkaṭas were a tribe. Thus one should start by following the word. The tribe name, *'Kaṭaṅkaṭa'*[7] means: (1) Fire (2) Gold (3) Gaṇeśa (4) Śiva (5) Plumbago (citrak plant). *'kaṭakin'* means a mountain. There is a queer word *Laṅkāṭaṅkaṭā* given in *'Śabdeśvarī',* denoting an *asura* woman. Laṅkanāyakā, Laṅkanātha, Laṅkāpatī are the names for Rāvaṇa[8].

There are *rākṣasīs,* (females) with names like Ṭaṅkaṭā, Laṅkaṭaṅkaṭā and Laṅkinī. This information is singular and curious. The meaning of the word *'Ṭaṅkaṭā'* is not given. *'Śabdeśvarī'* sadly, does not give the source of these very peculiar words.

Now what does the word 'Laṅkā' mean? In Sanskrit it means: adulteress, twig, Laṅkā (a type of grain) and *sprukkā. Sprukkā* also means a thorny plant, Dantī *vanaspatī, piṇḍakā* plant, (*piṇḍakāḥ* in Sanskrit means to have control over senses), *rakṣasa* or *Uda* (plant). The word 'Laṅkā' also means nude woman or prostitute[9]. *'Ṭaṅk'* means an axe, a spade or a tree named *'Kuṭha'.*

Uttarakāṇḍa[10] informs us that Iḍviḍā (Ilvilā), was the wife of Pulastya and mother of Viśravās, daughter of Tṛṇabindu *(Prācina Caritrakośa)* and Alaṃbuṣa.

Aiḍaviḍ was the son of Iḍviḍā (Ilvilā) and Viśrava. Thus, Kubera (Vaiśravaṇa, or Aiḍaviḍ) is the great great grandson of Sālakaṭaṅkaṭa or Alaṃbuṣa *rakṣasa.*

Sālakaṭaṅkaṭa-Alaṃbuṣa is also an initial forefather of Rāvaṇa. Sālakaṭaṅkaṭa is therefore the family name of Kubera, who like Rāvaṇa is in the lineage of Pulastya as well as Brahmā. Kubera thus was Rāvaṇa's half-brother. U.P. Shah[11] suggests that the word *'Kaṭaṅkaṭa'* seems to be of non-Aryan origin and Sālakaṭaṅkaṭa was one of the four *vināyakās* who create *vighna* (obstacles) and who are therefore malicious deities. This tradition of *vināyakās* is fairly old. Thus, the tradition of *Sālakaṭaṅkaṭas,* enemies of gods, who first lived in Laṅkā, as recorded in *Uttarakāṇḍa* is also very old. They could be Gonds. 'Gondavana' was called *'Gaḍh-Kaṭaṅgaḥ'* by Abul Fazl in his *Ain-I-Akbari* (one is reminded of a similar name 'Kāmakataṅkaṭā' of Kāmākhyā goddess) U.P. Shah notices.

P.V. Kane[12] mentions a place, 'Vaiśravaṇeśvara'. This *tīrtha* is in Śrī *parvata* (or Śrīśaila) in Amarkanṭaka hill is noteworthy. The significance of Kubera, sites for *yakṣās* and places where *yakṣa* images are found, are remarkably high in number in north India, M.P. and Maha Kosālā. Eminent scholar V.S. Agrawala in his book, *'Ancient Indian Folk Cults',* has brought to light, the antiquity, importance and greatness of *yakṣa* cult[13]. This fact is of prime importance for our studies, even if this link is a later addition in *Rāmāyaṇa*.

There are no evidences from ancient literature or from other sources suggesting that while ruling in Laṅkā or thereafter Kubera was ever known to have crossed over Mt. Vindhya to come to its south. After he was driven out of Laṅkā by Rāvaṇa, Kubera preferred to go towards the Himalayas as if to retire forever. His second abode was the famous Alakāpuri or 'Vasuokasārā' (or Vasvokasārā), where Himalayan river Mandākinī flows.

Kubera is indicated by several other names Soma, Seṭha, Bhaṇḍārī, Nikuṃbha and many others. In the context of our search for Laṅkā, one name in particular is of prime importance. That *yakṣa*-name is 'Nikuṃbha' (an ancient name also for Gaṇeśa).

Nikuṃbha *dānava* was the son of Pralhada[14] and had two sons, Sunda, husband of Tāṭakā, and Upasunda. The name Nikuṃbha is found at many other places in ancient literature. Rāvaṇa's brother Kuṃbhakarṇa and wife Vṛtrajvālā had a daughter named Nikuṃbhī[15] and two sons, Kuṃbha and Nikuṃbha. One of the sons of Bali *daitya* was Nikuṃbhanābha. Kuṃbhil was also a name for Nikuṃbha. *'Harivaṃśa'* includes a chapter *Ṣaṭpuravadha*[16]. Ṣatpura was the dwelling place of Nikuṃbha *daityās*, who practiced *māyā.*

There are some more curious relationships that show resemblance in names and except the family of Rāvaṇa are not found elsewhere. For instance the names of Sumālī's family members are found only here. Sumālī's daughter is Kuṃbhīnasī and his wife (Narmada *gandharvī's* daughter) is curiously named 'Vindhyāvalī'. Narmada *gandharvī* was the grandmother of Rāvaṇa. It can therefore be argued that all these names and relations are not only of ancestral nature but also have geographical significance. These names suggest that they were correlated to Nikuṃbhilā, who must have been the mother goddess of *yakṣās* and consequently related to the *yakṣa-rakṣasa* tradition, of both Kubera and Rāvaṇa. It is next to impossible to believe that such a correlation (this, of course according to the epic, being originally of Kubera'*s yakṣa* tradition) did not exist as the evidences gathered are numerous and of various nature. This also means that Nikuṃbhilā must be a *yakśinī* or a *mahāyakśinī.*

The *rākṣasīs* frighten and threaten Sītā captive in Aśokavana, saying:

surā cānīyatām kṣipram sarvaśokavināśinī |
mānuṣam maṁsamāsādya nṛityamotha nikuṃbhilām ||[17]

Meaning- 'Bring that intoxicating drink *'sura'* that ends all our agonies at the earliest and then we will relish this human flesh and dance in front of goddess Nikuṃbhilā'.

It appears from the description that Nikuṃbhilā was a deity and a mother goddess of the locals of Laṅkā. This name singularly has a restricted sphere of influence. According to the epic,

sa tu prekṣya hanūmantam vrajantam yatra rāghavaḥ |
nikuṃbhilamadhiṣṭḥāya pāvakam juhuvendrajit ||[18]

Further *ślokās*[19] indicate that Indrajit went to goddess Nikuṃbhilā's *sthāna* and at that *caitya* (fire-home) he lit the *'homa'*-fire as a procedure to worship Nikuṃbhilā, before going to the battle ground. *Yuddhakāṇḍa*[20] further clearly says that Indrajit then went to that *'yajña-bhūmī'* (fire-place). He performed a sacrifice killing a beast and by throwing blood in the fire, he then offered it (to the goddess) following the rules of the rites ceremoniously. It was only then that the *rakṣasās* prepared themselves for the war. In the same Nikuṃbhilā grove, stood a very large *vaṭavṛkṣa* (Banyan tree), blue like a cloud. Indrajit adored this tree.

Now here, we have to consider that Kubera also has a name 'Vaṭa'. 'Vaṭavāsin' is a name for *yakṣa* creed or sect, as it can also be deduced from some rites and practices. For example, one such practice popular amongst folks is known (region not given). It is believed, that *yakśinī* goddess named 'Vaṭavṛkṣavāsinī', is a folk deity who uses a Banyan tree for her abode. She is believed to be 'Mahāyakśinī' and fulfils all the desires of the worshipper. She wears red or black coloured clothes. This obviously indicates that she asks for a victim. Remarkably, the *'mantra'* (chant or formula) that is used to please her is supposed to be a creation/composition of a *ṛṣī* named 'Viśrava[21]'! Thus, the above information, suggests that the sequel of this is a belief that the *Mahāyakśinī* on a Banyan tree is to be worshipped by *ṛṣī* whose name should be 'Viśrava'. We may now very safely conclude that Nikuṃbhilā was a common family deity of Rāvaṇa and Kubera.

Here we should remember that at no time Kubera was ever connected with Sri Laṅkā (Ceylon). As we have seen, Kubera has always been a regent of the north, and therefore Laṅkā that was possessed by Kubera, was the Laṅkā of Rāvaṇa. It can never be Ceylon. There is a weak reference indicating an occurrence of *yakṣās* and *nāgās* in Ceylon but no marks of cultural association have been noticed in that land.

According to a tale given in *Ānanda Rāmāyaṇa*[22], Nikuṃbhilā was connected with Rāvaṇa's family. The tale is about two *rakṣasa* brothers Ahirāvaṇa and Mahirāvaṇa, the friends of Rāvaṇa.

M.V. Kibe[23] has mentioned that the Gond tribe worships forty one deities, which are located under a tree outside their habitation. These are, *'Bodaka devā'* (of Banyan tree), *'Ningī devā'* etc. *Ningī devā* especially is offered human sacrifice. These facts of their cultural life seem to be reflected in the epic myth. V. Raghavan[24] says that the sacrificial ceremony of Nikuṃbhilā which was known as 'Nikuṃbaniā' was performed on a hill named 'Ākāśagirī'.

References: Rāvaṇa and Laṅkā of Kubera

1. 7: 3:
2. *'Prācina Caritrakośa'* p.42
3. *'Mbh'. Droṇaparvan.*7:84: 24, 26, 29
4. *'Prācina Caritrakośa'*, p.1038
5. U.P. Shah: *'Introduction to the Uttarakāṇḍa of Vālmīki Rāmāyaṇa'* c.e. Baroda(1975)p.45
6. T.P. Iyer: op.cit. (1940), p.76
7. *'Gīrvāṇalaghukośa'* p.137
8. *'Śabdeśvarī',* p.191, 205
9. *'Gīrvāṇalaghukośa',* p.137
10. 7:2:1-34
11. U.P. Shah: op.cit. (1975), p.44 - 46
12. P.V. Kane: *'History of Dharmaśastra',* List of Tīrthās, p.817, BORI Poona
13. V.S. Agrawala: *'Ancient Indian Folk Cults'* (1970) pp.165-199, Prithvi Pbl. Vārāṇasi
14. *'Mbh'. Ādiparvan.*1:59:17-19
15. *'Śabdeśvarī':* p. 202
16. *'Harivaṃśa'*, 82:2:5-90, 29 B *Pariśiṣṭa* I, p.288, c.e.vol.II (1971) BORI, Poona

17. 5:22:41
18. 6:69:23
19. 6:69:23-26
20. 6:69:26-28
21. *'Bhāratiya Sanskṛti Kośa'* 8:p. 471
22. *Ānanda-Rāmāyaṇa' Sārakāṇḍa* 1,(tr.V.V.Bapat)pp.63-65)
23. M. V. Kibe: *'Location of Laṅkā'* Manohar Granthamala Pune; (1947), p.53
24. V. Raghavan: *'Rāmāyaṇa in Greater India'* (1975) p.79, South Gujrat Univercity

(E) *APPROACHES TO LAṄKĀ*

Rāvaṇa returns to Laṅkā on foot from Pañcavaṭī with Sītā, as his chariot is totally destroyed by Jaṭāyu. *('bhagnadhava','viratho', 'hatāśvo', 'hatasārathih')*[1]. Rāvaṇa comes across some hills, which must be near Kiṣkindha and Mt. Ṛṣyamūka and then river Paṃpā, (**sa ca pampāmatikramya laṅkāmabhimukha purīm**)[2] and 'turns' towards Laṅkā, indicating changing direction. After this he comes across Mahendra *dvāra.* As described in the epic, Mahendra *dvāra* that was blocked by Supārśva, was obviously an easy approach to Laṅkā before crossing over *Dakṣiṇa Sāgara.*

Araṇyakāṇḍa mentions that Akaṃpana, the *rakṣasa* who backed out from the war at Janasthāna, went running, to Laṅkā to deliver the news to Rāvaṇa, of the massacre Khara and other *rakṣasās* had to face at the hands of Rāma. This obviously means that Janasthāna and Laṅkā were not too far away from each other. There is no mention of any *sāgara* on his way. This verse is omitted from the critical edition of Baroda.

tvaramāṇastato gatvā janasthānādakaṃpanaḥ |
praviśya laṅkām vegena rāvaṇam vākyamabravīt ||[3]

Rāma killed 14,000 *rakṣasās* along with their generals Khara, Dūṣaṇa and Triśirā. Seeing this, mournful, purple with rage and defaced Śūrpaṇakha went to Rāvaṇa's court in Laṅkā and lamented with resentment in front of Rāvaṇa, who was sitting amongst his ministers. The verse is -

tataḥ śūrpaṇakhā dīnā rāvaṇam lokarāvaṇam |
amātyamadhye saṅkruddhā paruṣam vākyamabravīt ||[4]

Neither Akaṃpana nor Śūrpaṇakha had to cross *Dakṣiṇa Sāgara*. It appears from this, that there was another secret approach to Laṅkā which was known only to Rāvaṇa and his subjects. It was available to them to reach the world outside Laṅkā by land. Laṅkā was inaccessible and therefore crossing the dreaded and scary sea approachable by walking only from the north was the only approach known even to Sugrīva the wise king of *vānarās*.

Rāmāyaṇa describes Rāvaṇa's Laṅkā-Gokarṇa journey (This Gokarṇa is of north India) and also his victory march. None of these travel accounts mention or describe any of the places from south India. Rāvaṇa's wanderings were restricted to places located to the north of Mt. Vindhya.

References: Approaches to Laṅkā

1. 3:49:15 Bd
2. 3:52:5 Bd
3. 3:31:1 By
4. 3:31:1 Bd

(F) *THE PUṢPAK VIMĀNA*

Rāmāyaṇa informs us that Rāma's return journey to home city Ayodhya was by a vehicle which was a thing an enemy would be envious of. It was a creation of celestial artisan Viśvakarma, who had created it for Brahmā. It was handed over to Kubera, from whom Rāvaṇa had snatched it away by force. 'Puṣpak' would move at the will of the host it is described. Rāvaṇa used to mount on it and wander around.

When Hanumat entered Laṅkā and sneaked through Rāvaṇa's palace he got the glimpses of Puṣpak of which the description in *Sundarakāṇḍa*[1] is: 'That vehicle looked like a mountain wonderfully glittering with many metals. It resembled the sky, studded with stars and the moon. It was looking like clouds splashed beautifully with many colours, studded with gems, precious stones like corals and vaidurya and... decorated with artificial images of animals like deer and elephants holding lotus leaves. There was also an image of Lakṣmī sitting on a lotus flower floating in water'.

The description of an image of Gajalakṣmī on Puṣpak *Vimāna*, according to H.D. Sankalia could be a later addition[2]. When Rāma and Lakṣmaṇa viewed Puṣpak they were wonderstruck, since such a thing was not known in Ayodhya! Puṣpak is described in great detail in *Yuddhakāṇḍa* as well as in *Uttarakāṇḍa*. Some descriptions of it in *Rāmāyaṇa* itself suggest it to be a vehicle to be lifted by carriers of palanquin.

A description in *Uttarakāṇḍa* is especially noteworthy[3]. It says that Rāvaṇa went towards Kārtikeya's Śaravana (in Himalayan ranges) and there Puṣpak could not ascend the mountains! *Rāmāyaṇa* also informs us that thousands of *bhūtagaṇas* were the carriers of Puṣpak. Puṣpak had windows, doors and columns but nowhere is mentioned as having wings excepting one mention of it being an air-craft carried by swans. There are of course a few references of its movement in the sky. *Uttarakāṇḍa*[4] states the following- 'When Rāma gave a command; the aircraft approached to him and 'said humbly' that it was Rāma's attendant and had surrendered to Rāma. Hearing these soft words, uttered by the director deity of the vehicle-'... etc.

These directors must have been the carrier servants of Puṣpak *Vimāna*, and this can also be inferred, by some other evidences from ancient literature. Puṣpak needed carriers for its movement is clear from the following:

Vanaparvan[5] describes Śiva's journey towards Bhadra *vaṭa*: 'Like the sun ornamental with the flash of lightening, Śiva seemed radiant with Pārvati. Ahead of him *naravāhana bhagavān* Kubera was 'marching' with Guhyakas sitting in his beautiful Puṣpak *Vimāna*'. It also describes the people following Śiva, those walking by his two sides and those mounted on the chariots. An unambiguous inference may be drawn from this, that Kubera, mounted on Puṣpak *Vimāna,* was moving on land along with others. All these descriptions suggest that this famed vehicle was a large, heavily decorated palanquin and Puṣpak *Vimāna* was one such *vāhana* (a vehicle) to be carried by *'nara'* (men), [and hence can be called 'Nārayāna!']. For this very reason, undoubtedly, Kubera was also known by the name 'Naravāhana', it is clear[6]. According to *'Bhāgavata Purāṇa' 'nārayāna'* means a *śibikā* (or a palanquin)[7].

Sometimes a city is described as 'moving in the skies'. (E.g. king of Saubha city was Śalva, who's *'vimāna'* was called 'Saubha') This means that the city was situated on highland or hill top and *'vimāna saubha'* must also mean a chariot, the descriptions there indicate[8,9].

Rāvaṇa wandered around mounted on Puṣpak. It is only after he raped Raṃbhā, Nalakūbara's wife, that he was cursed and could not use Puṣpak anymore. Rāvaṇa used an ass-drawn chariot, as he went towards Pañcavaṭī and on battleground he used a horse-drawn chariot, *Rāmāyaṇa* states.

It may be added here that Hanumat and other *vānarās* also are said to move through the sky. These descriptions can only be taken to mean that *vānarās,* mountain-dwellers could move through high hills and mountains.

In Rāmāyaṇic period, on plains or on battleground horse-drawn chariots could be used only if rough roads were made for the purpose. We may also recall here, that Jaṭāyu noticed Rāvaṇa taking Sītā by *'ākaśa mārga'* (through the skies) but then he is said to have put up a fight with Rāvaṇa and broke down and destroyed his chariot and forced Rāvaṇa to abandon it. The exact word used here is *'viratha'*. This also supports our inference.

The word *'yāna'* is used for a vehicle, chariot, aircraft or even a cart in *Raghuvaṃśa*[10] and in *'Bhāgavata Purāṇa'*[11]. In *Mahābhārata* the word *'yāna'* means a journey, expedition, procession, *'dolī'* or *'dolā'* (a palanquin) etc. *Rāmāyaṇa* uses the word *'yāna'* or *'vimāna'* to denote a palace, house, palanquin[12]. In *'Harivaṃśa'* the word *'vimāna'* is used to denote a type of seat[13].

'Vimāna' (adj.) means insulted, measure, air-vehicle, chariot, a horse, palace, a seven-storied building, a boat, house by the side of a larger house'[14]. *Vimānavidyā* also means temple architecture and word *vimāna* is used for a temple or for an apex of a temple e.g. in south Indian temple architecture. A description from *'Bhāgavata Purāṇa'*[15] is an evidence to presume that Puṣpak *Vimāna was*

really a palanquin. 'All those ladies had decorated their necks with golden ornaments and their ears with bright dangling ornaments. They had wrapped themselves in rich clothes and they were sitting with their husbands in *vimānās*. They were all moving by the side of Satī's house...' seeing all that Satī thought ...etc.

We can safely deduce from this description, that those vehicles were passing close by Satī's house hence she could notice all the details. This again indicates that those vehicles must be slow moving palanquins, or *'dolīs'* since Satī and Śiva had their dwelling place high up in Himalayas. Thus the word *'vimāna yāna'* used here does not appear to mean an air-plane. An interesting version of *Rāmāyaṇa* supports this theory in a queer way. *Adbhuta Rāmāyaṇa* informs us that Puṣpak was an excellent chariot, (***'Puṣpako rathasattamaḥ'***) though it could move through the skies! It further says that warrior Sītā was leading her women's army as the battle was going on and then for the next events the verse is -

rathādavaskandya satī pāpata raṇamūrddhani |[16]

Means, She jumped from the chariot on the battle ground (and ultimately killed Rāvaṇa). This delineation clearly points to the fact that Puṣpak was a chariot moving on the battle ground.

A verse from *'Raghuvaṃśa'*[17] indicates that Puṣpak was a palanquin. It says that the great and revered Rāma was mounted on Puṣpak *Vimāna*, which was moving with a slow pace and in front of which Rāma's subjects were marching. After covering a distance of half a *krośa* they took a halt in that spacious and grand pleasure garden near Ayodhya, where Shatrughna had already made the preparations... etc.

All the above evidences and the description of Puṣpak given by *Rāmāyaṇa* collectively indicate that Puṣpak V*imāna* was actually a very skilfully constructed vehicle, large in size, richly decorated, beautiful palanquin or a chariot and it was not an air-plane. If we imagine the social conditions prevailing in the times of *Rāmāyaṇa*, we are forced to conclude that Puṣpak could not have been an air-plane as some people believe. For an air-plane to exist in those times, it would be necessary that many other simpler, less complicated things existed.

Of course in ancient India too, like elsewhere in the world, men had some vague ideas of fabricating some crude gadgets with the help of which they thought one could fly like birds. References from ancient literature point at such efforts[18]. 1) There were '*tripurās*' crafted by Mayāsura. 2) 'Mahāvihaṅga' described in king Bhoja's '*Samarāṅgaṇasūtra*' 3) '*Bṛhadvimānaśāstra*' of Bhāradvāja in his '*Anśubodhinī*'. Recently R.K. Shukla[19] has claimed to have done the geographical study of *Rāmāyaṇa* in all its aspects and for this he claims to have used a wider imagination and original method and an untraditional perspective. For instance, the things man could not achieve 200 years ago or cannot achieve even today could not exist three or four thousand years ago. However, Shukla says that the mention of Puṣpak *Vimāna* in *Rāmāyaṇa* (and its description) proves that it was an air-plane, 'air-transport' (p.135) of 'fast speed' existed then. He writes, 'probably, wireless was well known to the Aryans' (p.143). 'Mechanical instruments or 'cranes' were used for uprooting and transporting the unwanted trees and boulders to the seashore'[20, 21]. R.K. Shukla of course firmly believes Ceylon to be Rāvaṇa's Laṅkā.

In those times there were no air-planes, but there were *yānās* and *vimānās* (palanquins) which were carried and moved by men with great efficiency. There was neither wireless system nor mechanisms of any kind, but there was a system of *dūtās* (messengers) and there were no ships and bigger boats but there were ferries or rafts. There were no cranes, but men used ropes, bamboos, logs and 'machines' constructed out of these simple things for carrying heavy loads. This will be a logically viable and believable proposition.

References: The Puṣpak Vimāna

1. 5:8-17
2. H.D. Sankalia: '*Vālmīki Rāmāyaṇa in Historical Perspective' Macmillan India Ltd. Bombay* (1973) p.39, 40
3. 7: 16:7, 18
4. 7:73:14-16-By; 7:66:7,8 Bd
5. *'Mbh'. Vanaparvan. Āraṇyakaparvan.*3:221:1, 5
6. '*Raghuvaṃśa*' 9:11
7. '*Bhāgavata Purāṇa*'10:59:36

8. *'Bhāgavata Purāṇa'*.10:76: *Adhyāya* 15:20
9. *'Mbh'. Vanaparvan, Āraṇyakaparvan* 3, *Adhyāyās* 15:23
10. *'Raghuvaṃśa'*, 15:45, 7:51, 16:68, 10:46
11. *'Bhāgavata Purāṇa'* 4:3:6
12. 4:49:23
13. *'Harivaṃśa'* 12:299:25
14. *'Gīrvāṇalaghukośa'* p.443
15. *'Bhāgavata Purāṇa* 4:3, 6
16. *'Adbhuta Rāmāyaṇa'Uttarakāṇḍa, Sarga* 23:23-25;25:39 [tr. By B.V. Bapat (1910) Modavṛutta press
17. *'Raghuvaṃśa'* Adhyāya 13:79
18. *'Bhāratiya Sanskṛti Kośa'*: 8, p.711
19. R.K. Shukla: *'The Geography of the Rāmāyaṇa'* (2003), p.135, 143, Koshal Book Depot, Delhi
20. 6.22-60 (cited by R.K.Shukla)
21. 6:15: foot note: 293

(G) *MOUNT MAHENDRA*

Vālmīki *Rāmāyaṇa* mentions a few special features of Mt. Mahendra and that Mt. Mahendra was situated at a strategic point, set by sage Agastya on the north shore of *Dakṣiṇa Sāgara* with one of its spurs thrust into the sea. Mt. Mahendra had a *dvāra* towards *Dakṣiṇa Sāgara* (Mahendra-*dvāra,* or a pass). *Rāmāyaṇa* describes Agastya as the master or preceptor of all mountains[1]. *Kiṣkindhākaṇḍa* says that Mt. Mahendra is inhabited by Siddhās and Caranās and on every *'parvakāla'*, god Indra visits the mountain. It also clearly says that beyond Mt. Mahendra and the south sea is a wonderful island, i.e. Laṅkā, with an extent of 100 *yojanās;* **'dvīpastasyā pare pāre śatayojanamāyataḥ'** |[2] and is quite inaccessible. Rāvaṇa (on foot), carries off Sītā from Pañcavaṭī and enters Laṅkā area via Mahendra-*dvāra*, perhaps a very narrow pass in the mountain. Mt. Mahendra is first mentioned by Sugrīva and then by Saṃpātī, who meets Hanumat and his search party after they come out of *Ṛkṣabila*. Supārśva's account suggests that Mt. Mahendra was quite away, (half a day's distance) from *Ṛkṣabila* hill, from where Saṃpātī could actually see Laṅkā, 100 *yojanās* away, but not Mt. Mahendra.

If Laṅkā were 100 *yojanās* away from *Ṛkṣabila* and 100 *yojanās* away also from Mt. Mahendra (the length of Nalasetū from Mt. Mahendra to Mt. Suvela at Laṅkā) obviously Mt. Mahendra was not close to *Ṛkṣabila* and this matches well with Supārśva's account. It is naturally not within Svayaṃprabhā's view either. Having known the fact from Saṃpātī that Mahendra-*dvāra* was a shortcut to Laṅkā, *vānarās* taking this hint, go first in the south direction. Thus -

abhijidabhimukhā diśamyayurjanakasutāparimārgaṇonmukhāḥ |[3]

and then go to the north shore of the 'south sea'. (However, there is no mention of Hanumat using Mahendra-*dvāra*).

'dakṣiṇasya samudrasya samāsādyottaram diśam'[4]

They all then ascend Mt. Mahendra, from where Hanumat takes his first leap in south direction towards Laṅkā, 100 *yojanās* away. Later, Rāma with *vānara* army also did not use the Mahendra pass possibly because it being very narrow, would not have allowed the entire army to pass through it in a short time.That Mt. Mahendra was at the north shore of the sea can easily be inferred from the descriptions in the epic itself.

(1) Rāma and the *vānara* army after descending Mt. Mahendra are still on the north shore of *Dakṣiṇa Sāgara.* (2) Saramā consoles Sītā by informing that Rāma having crossed the sea has now reached the south shore at the gates of Laṅkā.

uttīrya sāgaram rāmaḥ sahavānarasenayā |
sanniviṣṭaḥ samudrasya tīramāsādya dakṣiṇam ||[5]

Ancient literature gives us some interesting pieces of information about Mt. Mahendra. 'Kirāta' community lived in Vindhyan ranges[6]. *Mahābhārata* states that Bhīma had conquered seven Kirāta kings, inhabitants of Mt. Mahendra in Videha (Bihar)[7]. Kirātās have also been referred to in *Bhīṣmaparvan* of *Mahābhārata*[8,9]. All this information about Mt. Mahendra, or Ptolemy's Meandros, raises a question as to whether Mt. Mahendra of Agastya (and Vālmīki) can be identified with Mahendragiri of eastern ghats in Orissa as Pargiter and some other researchers believe? The description of Mt. Mahendra given in

Purāṇās mentions it to be one of the seven *kulācalās.* According to *'Prācina Sthalakośa',* Mt. Mahendra is also sometimes called Śrīśaila *parvata* in purāṇic literature. Curiously, Mahendra was a place adored by Bhārgava Rāma (Paraśurāma Jāmadajña). It was a place where Brahmā had performed sacrifice. It is said to be a spot where Bhāgīrathī Ganga sank herself in Maṇikarṇika *sarovara* (a lake). Here Ganga is called Brahmaśāla. *Maharṣi* Mataṅga had his hermitage here (Mataṅgakedāra). Devavana, Kuṇḍoda *parvata,* and rivers Bahudā and Nandā are said to be in the vicinity of Mt. Mahendra. All this information seems mixed up indeed; since as a matter of fact, Maṇikarṇika is in Vārāṇasi area whereas one river Bahudā flows in Orissa. The important question is, which one was Mt. Mahendra of Vālmīki?

It is stated elsewhere that Mt. Mahendra is associated with Paraśurāma Bhārgava[10-15], who lived in times much earlier than Rāma *daśarathī.* While giving the explanatory tale of why Bhārgava Rāma created Śūrpāraka *deśa* (in the western ghats!), *Brāhmāṇḍa Purāṇa* says that when king Sagara's sons started digging up the earth in the bed of river Ganga in the south Ganga plain, a disaster of Gokarṇa getting drowned into those waters would befall on *śuṣka brāhmaṇās* and therefore on their request Paraśurāma created Śūrpāraka *deśa.* There is one Gokarṇa in north India, the place Śiva adored, the second one in south India and the third one in Orissa (as Gokarṇeśvara on Mahendragiri) near Jajpur (Cuttack district) on the banks of river Brahmanī. It appears that the story of Paraśurāma is popular and seems to have got mixed up with *'Gaṅgāvatarana'* legend.

Mt. Mahendragiri, as it is known (highest peak 2700 Metres), is situated 106 km north-east of Araku valley in eastern ghats of Orissa, in district Gajapati, which is situated to the immediate south of Ganjam, and to the north of Parlakimedi. This Mahendragiri has sites like Kunti or Gokarṇa *mandira* and also temples of *Pāṇḍavās,* Bhīma and Yudhiṣṭhira. This Mt. Mahendra might have one long spur. However, it is nearly 50 km from the shores of eastern sea and also far away from south Ganga plain. The Mahendragiri of eastern-ghats therefore cannot be Mt. Mahendra (of sage Agastya) with one of its spurs intruded into

Dakṣiṇa Sāgara, dug up by king Sagara's sons. There seems to be a mix-up of two different legends here. Then, the question is

(1) Was sage Agastya's Mt. Mahendra set in *Dakṣiṇa Sāgara* exhumed by king Sagara's sons different from Mt. Mahendra of eastern-ghats associated with sage Paraśurāma Bhārgava? (as the present studies have suggested) or,

(2) Did Vālmīki (or the later hands) fantasize the then well known great Mahendragiri (of eastern ghats) to be situated on the north shore of the exhumed *Dakṣiṇa Sāgara?* How could Vālmīki simply use the name and fame of Bhārgava Paraśurāma abode Mahendragiri of eastern-ghats for quite a distinct hill range in the vicinity of that dug up *Dakṣiṇa Sāgara* of the south Ganga plain? Interestingly, Rāma's return journey from Laṅkā to Ayodhya by Puṣpak V*imāna* does mention golden mountain Maināka that had created a resting place for Hanumat and was immersed in the waters of *Dakṣiṇa Sāgara,* but, surprisingly does not mention Mt. Mahendra at all.

hiraṇyanābham śailendram kāñcanam paśya maithilī |
viśramārtham hanūmato bhitvā sāgaramutthitam ||[16]

A word of caution is necessary here regarding the identification (and/or) existence of Mt. Maināka in the locale of *Rāmāyaṇa*. It is true that the geographical data of epic text should not be taken too litrally and topographical details could be more dependable in establishing the probable location of any site in question, in the present day maps. Bhagavansingh Suryavanshi[17], who investigated the source of *Mahābhārata* geography lead him to conclude that Maināka was known to the Aryans for long and was a part of Himalayan range. It was adjacent to Bindusarovara-spot where river Ganga appeared for the first time and got divided into (three main or) seven channels. Based on his inference it can be said that initially Mt. Maināka (with its legendary wings) might have been given a place in Rāma story by the epic poet/s and then in later times Mt. Mahendra of Paraśurāma might have crept in the story under Bhārgava/ Brāhminical influence. Mt. Maināka certainly has a greater role to play in the Rāma story. *Mahābhārata* states that Bhāgīrathī Ganga sank herself in Maṇikarṇika *sarovara* on Mt. Mahendra, creating a confusion since this indirectly means that some limited, compact area (in south Ganga plain) was also associated with a hill (range?) named 'Mahendra', or else, *Mahābhārata* also has simply used the name of 'Mahendragiri' of Orissa, for the site of *Gaṅgāvatarana*. It is often mentioned in ancient literature that Maṇikarṇika lake, or *tīrtha*, was in Vārāṇasi area[18] or in south Ganga plain. In the end, the only probable conjecture one can make here would be that, Rāmāyaṇa describes Agastya's Mt. Mahendra with a narrow pass towards the sea. It was said to be on the north shore of *Dakṣiṇa Sāgara*. Mt. Mahendra had one of its spurs intruded into those waters, so that both Hanumat and Nala *vānara* found a convenient and suitable starting point on the firm ground from where to leap or construct a bridge to cross over the expanse of water called *Dakṣiṇa Sāgara*. With all this, a suggestion that Mt. Mahendra of Agastya and Vālmīki could not be Mahendragiri of Orissa can remove the anomaly mentioned above.

At this very juncture it will have to be examined if Bhārgava Paraśurāma and (his) Mahendragiri are later additions in *Rāmāyaṇa* and if the same presumption slowly got established as part of local tradition. This question remains unanswered.

As far as the target site for Laṅkā suggested by present studies is concerned, it is believed by the locals of the area of Sidhi district, that father of Paraśurāma, sage Jamadagnī, had his hermitage at Deogarh on the banks of river Reṇū or Reṇukā (Rihand) that has been named so after his wife Reṇukā, who was of Ikṣvāku lineage[19]. It is to be noted that there is a small hill/village named 'Renukut' close to Obra dam and to the north-east of G.V.P. Sagar. A Śiva *sthāna*, called 'Reṇukeśvara' also exists near by, its antiquity being unknown. Could this be Paraśurāma's favourite abode Mt. Mahendra? It is curious that one of the caves of the Mara group, the locals believe, contains the *'farsā'* (*parśū*), the famous weapon of the legendary Paraśurāma Bhārgava.

References: Mt. Mahendra

1. 3:10:77-83; entry no. 185,186
2. 4: 40:24
3. 4:62:15:

4. 4: 63:4
5. 6: 24:14
6. *'Prācina Sthalakośa'* pp.490-92
7. *'Mbh'. Āraṇyakaparvan*. 48:20
8. *'Mbh'. Bhīṣmaparvan.*6:10:49, 55
9. *'Mbh'. Sabhāparvan.*2:27:13
10. *'Brāhmāṇḍa Purāṇa'* Part III, section 3: chapter 44:36, 37
11. Ibid. 3:47
12. *'Mbh'. Shantiparvan.*49,
13. *'Mbh'. Anuśasanaparvan.*137.12
14. *'Mbh'. Vanaparvan.*117.14
15. *'Mbh'. Sabhā. Tīrthā.* Adhyāya: 85, 87, 99
16. 6:111:12
17. Suryavanshi Bhagavansingh: *'Geography of the Mahābhārata'* (1986), Ramananda Vidyabhavan, New Delhi, p.113
18. P.V. Kane: *'History of Dharmashastra'*, vol.IV, List of Tīrthās, p.634, 635
19. V.D. Jha: *'Investigations into the Archaeology of Surguja'* (1973) p.70

§§§

ŚLOKĀS IN DEVANĀGARĪ

Chapter 1: Introduction and Review of Literature

1) स गिरेश्चित्रकूटस्य सालमासाद्य पुष्पितम् । (2:92:13)

Chapter 2: Daṇḍakāraṇya, Janasthāna and Pañcavaṭī

1) सरय्वाश्चोत्तरे तीरे यज्ञभूमिर्विधीयताम् । (1:11:15)

2) अथ संवत्सरे पूर्णे तस्मिन्प्राप्ते तुरंगमे ।
सरय्वाश्चोत्तरे तीरे राज्ञो यज्ञोभ्यवर्तत ॥ (1:13:1)

3) एष ज्ञातिसहस्रेण स्थपतिः परिवारितः ।
कुशलो दंडकारण्ये वृद्धो भ्रातुश्च ते सखा ॥ (2:78:11)

4) सुरम्यमासाद्य तु चित्रकूटम् ।
नदीम् च ताम् माल्यवतीम् सुतीर्थाम् ॥ (2: 50:22)

5) निवर्तय रथम् शीघ्रम् दंडकान्नय मामपि । (2: 54:3)

6) पम्पानदी निवासानामनुमन्दाकिनीमपि ।
चित्रकूटालयानाम् च क्रियते कदनम् महत् ॥ (3:5:16)

7) इतो द्वियोजने तात बहुमूलफलोदकः ।
देशो बहुमृगः श्रीमान्पञ्चवट्यभिविश्रुतः ॥ (3: 12:13)

8) स देशः श्लाघनीयश्च नातिदूरे च राघव ।
गोदावर्याः समीपे च मैथिली तत्र रंस्यते ॥ (3: 12: 18)

9) ततः स्थलमुपारुह्य पर्वतस्य विदूरतः ।
ख्यातः पंचवटीत्येव नित्यपुष्पितकाननः ॥ (3: 12: 22)

10) दक्षिणाम् दिशामाक्रामत्ततो राजर्षिनंदनः ।
शैवलस्योत्तरे पार्श्वे ददर्श सुमहत्सरः ॥ (7:66:12)

11) इल्वलो नाम दैतेय आसीत्कौरवनन्दन ।
मणिमत्याम् पुरि पुरा वातापिस्तस्यचानुजः ॥ (Mbh.Vana.Ara.3:94:4)

12) पुरस्तादिह वातापिः परिभूय तपस्विनः ।
उदरस्थो द्विजान्हन्ति स्वगर्भोऽश्वतरीमिव ॥ (3:41:39)

13) अनूपं सिंधुराजस्य ददर्श त्रिदिवोपमम् ।
तत्रापश्यत्स मेघाभम् न्यग्रोधमृषिभिवृतम् ॥ (3:33:27)

14) नाम्ना सुभद्रम् न्यग्रोधम् ददर्श धनदानुजः ।
तम् तु गत्वा परं पारम् समुद्रस्य नदीपतेः ॥ (3:33:27, 35, 36)

15) निषादविषयम् हत्वा शाखया पतगोत्तमः । (3:33:32)

16) दृश्यतेऽसौ जनस्थाने सीते श्रीमान् वनस्पतिः । (6:123:42)

17) इतो द्वियोजने तात बहुमूलफलोदकः ।
देशो बहुमृगः श्रीमान्पञ्चवव्यभिविश्रुतः ॥ (3:12:13)

18) एतदालक्ष्यते वीर मधूकानाम् महद्वनम् ।
उत्तरेणास्य गन्तव्यम् न्यग्रोधमभिगच्छता ॥ (3:12:21)

19) ततः स्थलमुपारुह्य पर्वतस्य विदूरतः ।
ख्यातः पञ्चवटीत्येव नित्यपुष्पितकाननः ॥ (3:12: 22)

20) गंगायमुनयोः संधिमादाय मनुजर्षभ ।
कालिन्दीमनुगच्छन्ती नदीम् पश्चान्मुखाश्रिताम् ॥ (2:55:4: By)

21) यत्र भागीरथी गंगा यमुनामभिवर्तते । (2:48:2)

22) ततः परम् जनस्थानात्त्रिक्रोशम् गम्य राघवौ ।
क्रौञ्चारण्यम् विविशतुर्गहनम् तौ महौजसौ ॥ (3:65:5)

Chapter 3: Kiṣkindhākaṇḍa of Rāmāyaṇa

1) अभिषिक्ते तु सुग्रीवे प्रविष्टे वानरे गुहाम् ।
आजगाम सह भ्रात्रा रामः प्रस्रवणम् गिरिम् ॥ (4: 26:1)

2) अप्सरासु च मुख्यासु गन्धर्वीणां तनूषु च ।
यक्षपन्नगकन्यासु ऋक्षविद्याधरीषु च ॥ (1:16:5)

3) जाह्नवी सर्वतः पुण्या ब्रह्महत्यानिवारिणी ।
तत्रापित्रविशेषेण यत्र विन्ध्येनसंगता ॥ (*'Tīrthayātrāprabaṅdha'*)

Chapter 4: Ṛkṣabila and Dakṣiṇa Sāgara

1) एष विन्ध्यो गिरिः श्रीमान्नानाद्रुमलतायुतः ।
एष प्रस्रवणः शैलः सागरोऽयं महोदधिः ॥ (4:52:12)

2) ततस्तस्मिन्बिले दुर्गे नानापादपसंकुले (4:49:16)

3) मलयोयं गिरिवरो भयं नेहास्ति वालिनः । (4: 2:14By)

4) इदं हि मायाविहितं सुदुर्गमम् प्रभूतवृक्षोदकभोज्यपेयम् । (4: 52:32)

5) येनेदं काञ्चनं दिव्यं निर्मितं भवनोत्तमम् । (4:50:11)

6) पप्रच्छ का त्वम् भवनं बिलं । (4: 49:32)

7) शाश्वतः कामभोगश्च गृहं चेदं हिरण्मयम् । (4: 50: 15)

8) प्रविवेश गुहां घोरां किष्किन्धां रामशासनात् । (4:32:1)

9) मयेन दानवेन्द्रेण त्वद्भयात्सख्यमिच्छता । (*'Purvardha'*)
दुहिता तव भार्यार्थे दत्ता राक्षसपुंगव ॥ (*'Yuddha'* 6:7:6) By

10) दक्षिणस्योदधेस्तीरे विन्ध्योऽयमिति निश्चितः । (4: 59:7)

11) ह्रियमाणा मया दृष्टा रावणेन दुरात्मना । (4:57:15)

12) उत्तीर्य सागरं रामः सह वानरसेनया ।
संनिविष्टः समुद्रस्य तीरमासाद्य दक्षिणम् ॥ (6:24:14)

13) दक्षिणस्य समुद्रस्य समासाद्योत्तरां दिशं । (4:63:4)

14) शतयोजनविस्तीर्णः सागरो मकरालयः । (5:34:7)

15) दूरादयश्चक्रनिभस्य तन्वी तमालतालीवनराजिनीला ।
आभाति वेला लवणाम्बुराशेर्धारार्निबद्धेव कलंकरेखा ॥

(*'Raghuvaṃśa'* 13:15)

16) साहाय्यं वानरेन्द्रस्य यदि नाहं हनूमतः ।
करिष्यामि भविष्यामि सर्ववाच्यो विवक्षताम् ॥ (5:1:76)

17) ततः स लंबस्य गिरेः समृद्धेः ।
विचित्र कूटे निपपात कूटे ॥ (5: 1:189)

18) स लम्ब शिखरे लम्बे लम्बतोयदसंनिधे । (5: 3:1)

19) स नगाग्रे च ताम् लंकाम् । (5:2:8)

20) गिरिर्मूर्घ्नि स्थिताम् लंकाम् । (5:2:18)

21) स्थिता पारे समुद्रस्य दूरपारस्य राघव ।
नौपथश्चापि नास्त्यत्र निरादेशश्च सर्वतः ॥ (6:3:20)

22) उत्तरं तीरमासाद्य खस्थ एव व्यतिष्ठत । (6:11:8)

23) एवमुक्तस्तु धर्मज्ञः प्रत्युवाच बिभीषणः ।
समुद्रं राघवो राजा शरणं गन्तुमर्हति ॥ (6:13:13)

24) खानितः सगरेणायमप्रमेयो महोदधिः ।
कर्तुमर्हति रामस्य ज्ञातेः कार्यं महोदधिः ॥ (6:13:14)

25) गुरोर्यियक्षोः कपिलेन मेध्ये रसातलं संक्रमिते तुरंगे ।
तदर्थमुर्वीमवदारयद्भिः पूर्वः किलायं परिवर्धितो नः ॥

(*'Raghuvaṃśa'* 13:3)

26) अहमिक्ष्वाकुनाथेन सगरेण विवर्धितः ।
इक्ष्वाकुसचिवश्चायं ना वसीदितुमर्हति ॥ (5:1: 77)

27) गोदावरीं जनस्थानामिमां प्रस्रवण गिरिम् । (3:60:14, By)

28) बहुदृश्यदरीकुञ्जे तस्मिन् प्रस्रवणे गिरौ । (4:26:5; 4:6:10)

Chapter 5: The Birth Story of Dakṣiṇa Sāgara

1) मा शुचः पुरुषव्याघ्र वधोऽयम् लोकसम्मतः । (1:40:17)

2) कपिलेनाप्रमेयेण दग्धा हीमे महाबल ।
सलिलं नार्हसि प्राज्ञ दातुमेषाम् हि लौकिकम् ॥ (1:40:18,19)

3) येषां स सगरो नाम सागरो येन खानितः ।
षष्टिः पुत्रसहस्राणि यं यान्तं पर्यवारयम् ॥ (1:5:2)

5) स राजा सगरो नाम यः समुद्रमखानयत्
इष्ट्वा पर्वणि वेगेन त्रासयन्तमिमाः प्रजाः ॥ (2:102:19)

6) तदर्थमुर्वीमवदारयद्भिः पूर्वः किलायं परिवर्धितो नः ।
(*'Raghuvaṃśa'* 3:13:3,)

7) स तं देशं तदा पुत्रैः खनयामास पार्थिवः ।
आसेदुस्ते ततस्तत्र खन्यमाने महार्णवे ॥
(*'Harivaṃśa Sagarotpattī'*, 14:23-26)

8) कालकेयाः इति ख्याताः सहस्राणि चतुर्दशाः । (7: 23 entry no. 442)

9) अयोद्ध्यामायतो ह्येषः पन्थः परमदुर्गमः । (6:109:7)

10) तस्मात्तद्बाणपातेन अपः कुक्षिष्वशोषयत् ।
विख्यातं त्रिषुलोकेषु मरुकान्तारमेवच ॥ (6:22:37, By)

11) अत्त पूर्वम् महादेवः प्रसादमकरोद्विभुः ।
एतत्तु दृश्यते तीर्थं सागरस्य महात्मनः ॥ (6:111: entry 3395)

Chapter 6: Identification of Rāvaṇa's Laṅkā

1) कर्मनाशाज्जलस्पर्शात् पुनः संस्कारमर्हति । (*'Tirthasār'*)

2) नदीं वैतरणीं घोरां रुधिरौघनिवाहिनीम् ।
खड्गपत्रवनंचैव भीमां पश्यसि रावण ॥ (3:51:18)

Chapter 7: Latitude and Longitude of Laṅkā

1) यल्लंकोज्जयिनीपुरोपरि कुरुक्षेत्रादिदेशान् स्पृशन् ।
सूत्रं मेरुगतं बुधैर्निगडिता सा मध्यरेखा भुवः ॥
(*Siddhāntaśiromaṇī: Goladhyāya:* 24)

2) तेन स्थलजलसंनिधौ लंकावतिष्ठते । (*Aryabhaṭiyā:Golapada:*14)

3) निरक्षदेशात् क्षितिषोडशांशे भवेदवंती गणितेन यस्मात् ।

(*Siddhāntaśiromaṇī:Goladhyāya:*15)

4) लंका कुमध्ये यमकोटिरस्या : । प्राक्पश्चिमे रोमकपट्टणं च ॥
अधस्ततः सिद्धपुरं सुमेरूः । सौम्येऽथ याम्ये वडवानलश्च ॥

(*'Siddhāntaśiromaṇī'* of Bhāskaracārya:*Bhuvanakośa:Goladhyāya* 17)

5) लंका कालाजिनाश्चैव शैलिका निकटास्तथा ।

(*'Mārkaṇḍeya Purāṇa'* 191:55:20)

ऋषभाः सिंहलाश्चैव तथा काञ्चीनिवासिनाः ॥

(*'Mārkaṇḍeya Purāṇa'* 191:55:27)

6) लंका कालाजिनसौरिकर्णतालिकटः ।
मरुचीपट्टणचेर्यायक सिंहला ऋषभाः ॥

(Varahamhira, *Bṛhatsaṃhitā* 14:11)

8) अत्र भूगोलस्यार्धमुत्तरम् जम्बुद्वीपम् । तस्य क्षाराब्धेश्च
संधिर्निरक्षदेशः ।

9) ननु लवणसमुद्र जम्बुद्वीपसंधिप्रदेशस्य भूमध्यत्वसिद्धेः
प्रागुक्तलंकाकुमध्यत्वानुपपत्तिः
उक्तभूगोलार्धसंधिभूपरिघिवृत्ते तस्या अभावात् ।
अन्यथा सेतुबन्धानुपपत्तेः ।

(Marīci's commentary on *'Siddhāntaśiromaṇī Goladhyāya'* 21:25)

10) न च क्षारसिंधोरित्यनेन संपूर्णसमुद्रो जम्बुद्वीपान्तर्गत इति
क्षारसमुद्रदक्षिणतटपरिघौ जम्बुद्वीपारंभे
लंकायाःसतत्त्वात्कुमध्यत्वोपपत्तिः सेतुबन्धोपपत्तिश्चेति वाच्यम् ।
सगरपुत्रैरश्वान्वेषणे महीं खनद्भिर्जम्बुद्वीपस्याष्टावुपद्वीपाः कल्पिताः ।
इति भागवते प्रसिद्धत्वाल्लंकाया उत्तरभागे खननेन
लवणसमुद्रप्रवा(ह)स्याऽऽगतत्वात्तस्य जंबुद्वीपान्तर्गतत्वेन प्रसिद्धेः
सेतुबन्धोपपत्तेः ।
अत एवाभितः समुद्रसम्बन्धाल्लंकाया उपद्वीपत्वम् व्यक्तम् ।

(Marīci's commentary on *'Siddhāntaśiromaṇī Goladhyāya'* 21:25)

Chapter 8: Ceylon - Sri Laṅkā and Rāvaṇa's Laṅkā

1) लंका कालाजिनाश्चैव शैलिका निकटास्तथा ।

(*'Mārkaṇḍeya Purāṇa'*:191:55:20)

ऋषभाः सिंहलाश्चैव तथा काञ्चीनिवासिनाः ॥

(*'Mārkaṇḍeya Purāṇa'* 191:55:27)

Appendix

(A) Makarās of Rāmāyaṇa

1) न कामान्न च लोभाद्वा न भयात्पार्थिवात्मज ।
   ग्राहनक्राकुलजलं स्तम्भयेयं कथंचन ॥ (6: 15:6)

2) अयं हि विपुलो वीरो सागरो मकरालयः । (6:15 entry 314)

3) ग्राहा न प्रहरिष्यन्ति यावत्सेना तरिष्यति । (6:15:7)

4) हरीणां तरणे राम करिष्यामि यथास्थलम् । (6:15 entry no.262)

(B) The Great Leap of Hanumat

1) महासत्वो महातेजा महाबलपराक्रमः ।
   लङ्घने प्लवने चैव भविष्यति मया समः ॥ (4:65:entry no. 1353)

2) उत्तिष्ठ हरिशार्दूल लङ्घयस्व महार्णवम् । (4: 65:34)

3) मरुतस्यौरसः पुत्रः प्लवने नास्ति मे समः । (4: 66: 7)

4) स तु वीर्यवतां श्रेष्ठः प्लवतामपि चोत्तमः । (5:2:5)

5) महामेरुप्रतीकाशं मां द्रक्ष्यध्वं प्लवंगमाः । (4:66:18)

(C) River Narmada

1) नर्मदा सदृशी लोके न गङ्गापि वरानने ।
   [*'Bhāratiya Sanskṛti Kośa'* (1987):4,p.700]

(D) Rāvaṇa and Laṅkā of Kubera

1) सुरा चानीयतां क्षिप्रं सर्वशोकविनाशिनी ।
   मानुषं मांसमासाद्य नृत्योमोऽथ निकुम्भिलाम् ॥ (5:22:41)

2) स तु प्रेक्ष्य हनूमंतं व्रजन्तं यत्र राघवः ।
   निकुम्भिलामधिष्ठाय पावकं जुहुवेन्द्रजित् ॥ (6:69:23)

(E) Approaches to Laṅkā

1) स च पम्पामतिक्रम्य लञ्कामभिमुख पुरीम् । (3:52:5)

2) त्वरमाणस्ततो गत्वा जनस्थानादकम्पनः ।
   प्रविश्य लंकां वेगेन रावणं वाक्यमब्रवीत् ॥ (3: 31:1.By)

3) ततः शूर्पणखा दीना रावणं लोकरावणम् ।
अमात्यमध्ये संक्रुद्धा परुषंवाक्यमब्रवीत् ॥ (3:31:1)

(F) **The Puṣpak Vimāna**

1) रथादवस्कन्द्य सती पापत रणमूर्द्धनि । (*Adbhuta Rāmāyaṇa*)

(G) **Mount Mahendra**

1) द्वीप तस्यापरे पारे शतयोजनमायतः । (4: 40:24)

2) अभिजिदभिमुखा दिशंययुर्जनकसुतापरि मार्गणोन्मुखाः (4:62:15)

3) दक्षिणस्य समुद्रस्य समासाद्योत्तरं दिशम् । (4: 63:4)

4) उत्तीर्य सागरं रामः सहवानरसेनया ।
संनिविष्टः समुद्रस्य तीरमासाद्य दक्षिणम् ॥ (6: 24:14)

5) हिरण्यनाभं शैलेन्द्रं कांचनं पश्य मैथिलि ।
विश्रमार्थं हनूमतो भित्वा सागरमुत्थितं ॥ (6:111:12)

BIBLIOGRAPHY

BOOKS

Agrawala V.S., *'Ancient Indian Folk Cults'*, Prithvi Publ. Vārāṇasi, 1970

Agrawala V.S., *'India as Known to Pāṇinī'*, 1956

Agrawala V.S., *'India as known to Pāṇinī'*, Lucknow University, 1953

Al-beruni, *'Al-beruni's India* Vol. 2' (translated and annotations by Sachau E.C.), London, 1910

Ali S.M., *'The Geography of the Purāṇās'*, People's Publishing House, New Delhi, 1966

Amrithalingam T., *'Rāmāyaṇa Vimarśa'*, (quoted Rao N.V. op. cit.), Madras

Apte V.S., *'Sanskrit-English dictionary'*, Bombay, 1978

Aravindakumar and Kusumakumar (ed.), *'Śabdeśvarī'*, 1999

Aryabhata, *'Aryabhaṭiyā'*, *Goladhyāya*-14, (with the commentary by Suryadeva, Yajvan*)*, Indian National Science Academy, New Delhi

Awasthi A.B.L., *'Studies in Skanda Purāṇa'*, Parts 1 and 2, Kailash Prakashan, Lucknow, U.P., 1976

Awasthi A.B.L., *'Studies in Skanda Purāṇa'*, Kailash Prakashan Lucknow, 1976

Bajpai K.D., *'The Geographical Encyclopedia of Ancient and Medieval India'*, Indic Academy, Vārāṇasi, 1967

Bajpeyi K.D., *'Yugo Yugomen Uttarabhārat'*, Hindi, Vārāṇasi, 1955

Bapat B.V. (translated), *'Adbhuta Rāmāyaṇa' Uttarkaṇḍa, Sarga* 23:23-25; 25:39, Modavṛutta press, 1910

Bapat V.V. (translated pp.63-65), *'Ānanda-Rāmāyaṇa' Sārakāṇḍa* 1,

Bhāratiya Sanskṛti Kośa' Vol.1-10, Bharatiya Sanskriti Kosh Mandal, Pune, 1965/1987

Bhāskāracārya II, *'Siddhāntaśiromaṇī', Goladhyāya,* (with commentary by Marīci)

Bhāskāracārya II', *'Siddhāntaśiromaṇī* III', *'Goladhyāya' 'Bhuvanakośa'* (Division of the Globe), (translated Wilkinson), Bib. India, Calcutta,1861

Bhat S.C. (ed), *'Encyclopedia of District Gazetteers'*: Vol. V.

Bhatt G.H. (ed), *'Vālmīki Rāmāyaṇa',* Books I-VII; c.e., Oriental Institute, Baroda, 1959-75

Bhattacharya P.K., *'Historical Geography of M.P. from Early Records'* MLBD, Vārāṇasi, 1977

Bhavabhūti, *'Uttararāmacarita'* Act 1, Chaukhamba Press, Vārāṇasi, 1953

Bradley F.B., *'Chota Nagpore',* 1910

Buddha Prakash, *'Notices of Central Asiatic Geography in the Rāmāyaṇa',* Bharatiya Vidya Publication, Bombay, 1957

Bulke Camil, *'Rāmakathā Utpatti Aur Vikās',* Hindi Bhasha Parishad, University of Allahabad, U. P., 1962

Chaudhari S., *'Index to Place Names in the Varāha Purāṇa'*, 1993

Chitrav S., *'Prācina Caritrakośa'*, Bharatiya Charitra Kosh Mandal, Poona, 1964

Chitrav S., *'Prācina Sthalakośa'* I, Bharatiya Charitra Kosh Mandal, Pune, 1969

Chwang Yuan, *'On Yuan Chwang's Travels in India',* (ed. Watters Thomas, Rhys Davids T.W. and Bushell S.W., 2 Vols.), London, 1904

Cunningham A., *'The Ancient Geography of India',* ed. Majumdar Shastri, Calcutta, 1924)/Vārāṇasi, 1963

Cunningham A., ASIR, Vol. XXI, 1894

Das Navinchandra, *'Ancient Geography of Asia compiled from Vālmīki Rāmāyaṇa'*, Bharat Bharati Oriental Publ., Vārāṇasi, 1971

Devīkośa' (quoted *'Bhāratiya Sanskṛti Kośa',* Vol. 7)

Dey N. (quoted Prācina Sthalakośa), Patañjali (entry *'Kālakāvana'*) 1979

Dey Nundalal, *'Geographical Dictionary of Ancient and Medieval India,'* Cosmo Publication, 2nd ed., New Delhi, 1979 and Oriental Reprint, Delhi, 1927/1971

Downes M.C., *'A Bibliography of the Recent Crocodilians',* 1970

Fazal Abul, *'Ain-I-Akbari',* (translated Jarret), Calcutta, 1949

Fleet J.F., *'Indian Antiquary',* 1893, *'The topographical list of 'Bṛhatsaṃhitā'*

Gadgil Amrendra (ed.), *'Gaṇeśa kośa'*, 2nd ed., Shri Ganesh Kosh Mandal, Pune, 1981

Gazetteer of the Palamau District, Chapter 1

Geiger W. (translated English) *'Mahāvaṃśa'*, 31 Vol. 61, 1908

Godse D.G., *'Mātāval'*-Marathi, Popular Prakashan, Mumbai

Grant Charles (ed.), *'Gazetteer of the C.P. of India',* second ed. Delhi, 1870

Gupta Paramanand, *'Geography in Ancient Indian Inscriptions'*, D.K. Publication House, Delhi, 1973

Guruge Anand, *'The Society of the Rāmāyaṇa'*, Mahārāgāmā Sāman Press, Ceylon, 1960

Harivaṃśa', 'Sāgaracaritam' Vol. I and II, c.e., BORI, Poona, 1969/1971

Heu-en-Tsang, *'Ancient Geography of India'*, Vol. I and II (translated Beal S.) London, 1884

Hiralal R.B. and Russel R.V., *'Tribes and Castes of the C.P. of India'* in 4 Volumes, McMillan, London, 1916

Hiralal, *'Descriptive list of Inscriptions in Central Provinces and Berar'*, 1916, Govt. Press Nagpur, quotes from Bergees, Ind. Antiq. Vol. XXXIV, 1905

Hiralal, 'The situation of Rāvaṇa's Laṅkā', Jha comm. Vol. (1937), (as recorded by Grierson.)

Imperial Gazetteer of India', dist. Banda, U.P., India

Imperial Gazetteer of India', Districts Sidhi, 1994 and Reva Vol. IV, 1907

Imperial Gazetteer of India', Indian Empire, Vol. 1, 1909

Imperial Gazetteer of India', North-Western Provinces, Bundelkhand, Vol. 1, 1875

Imperial Gazetteer of India', Sidhi District, 1994

Imperial Gazetteer of India', Vol. XIII

Imperial Gazetteer of India', Vol.9

Imperial Gazetteer of Surguja' (1905), 'Chhattisgarh and Feudatory states,'

Imperial Gazetteer' of Mirzapur, U.P., Banaras Division,

Imperial Gazetteer', Vol. V

Iyer T. Paramasiva, *'Rāmāyaṇa and Laṅkā'*, Bangalore, 1940

Jacobi H (ed. and publ.), *'Paumacariyam', Vimalasuri*; Vora Shantilal (translated) *'Paumacariyam', Sandhi* V; B.R. Publ. Corp. Delhi

Jacobi Herman, *'Rāmāyaṇa'*, (quoted Kibe M.V. in *'Rāvaṇa's Laṅkā Discovered'* as app. a) Baroda, 1893-1960

Kane P.V., *'Dharmashastraka Itihas'*, (translated in Hindi, Chaube Arjun Kashyap), Hindi Samiti Suchana Vibhag, Lucknow, 1966

Kane P.V., *'The History of Dharmashastra'*, Govt. Oriental series, BORI Poona, 1963

Karandikar A.J., *'Mahābhāratachi Parśvabhūmī-Paschim Asia'*, 1980, (Marathi), Shubhada Sarasvat Publication, Pune

Kautilīya Arthashastra'-Encyclopaedia Asiatica

Keay F.E., *'Kabīr and his Followers',* Association Press, YMCA, Calcutta/ O.U.P., 1931/1995

Kern H. (ed.), Varāhamihira: *'Bṛhatsaṃhitā',* Calcutta, 1865

Kibe M.V., *'Location of Laṅkā'*, Manohar Granthamala, Pune, 1927/1947

Kielhorn (ed.), *'Vyākaraṇa Mahābhāṣya of Patañjali',* Bombay, 1892

Kielhorn, *'Epi. Indica'* 7:86

Kochar Rajesh, *'Vedic People: Their History and Geography',* Orient Longman, 2000

Kosambi D.D., *'An Introduction to the Study of Indian History',* Bombay 1956/75

Kosambi D.D., *'The Culture and Civilisation of Ancient India',* London 1965

Lal B.B. *'Excavations at Śṛṅgaverapura'*, Memoirs of ASI, Vol. I, no. 88, 1993

Law B. C., *'Historical Geography of Ancient India'*, Calcutta, 1954

Law B.C., *'Geographical Aspects of Kālidāsa's Works',* Indian Research Institute, Calcutta, 1954

Law B.C., *'Geographical Essays'* Vol. I, Luzac & Co. London, 1937

Law B.C., *'Mountains of India: A Historico-Geographical Study',* Publ. 5, Calcutta, (1944)

Law B.C., 'Tribes in Ancient India, no. 4, BORI, Poona, 1973

Law B.C.: *'Rivers of India: A Historico-Geographical Study'*, Calcutta, 1944

*Lele (*translated in Marathi*), 'Devī Bhāgavata'*

Lele Ganesh Shastri, *'Tīrthayātrāprabaṅdh'* Deshmukh and Co., Pune, 1885/1964, (based on Sardar Abasaheb Vinchurkar's All India Pilgrimage in 1770)

Lokmanya Tilak B.G., Ch.X 'Vedic Maths - The Matutinal Deities' from 'The Arctic Home in the Vedas' (1983 edition) Publ: messers Tilak Bros. Pune, pp.245-247.

Majjhima Nikaya': 1:378 (quoted by Chitrav S., *'Prācina Sthalakośa'*)

Majumdar R.C., *'Ancient India'* Book I, Motilal Banarasidas Publication, Delhi, 1960

Majumdar R.C., *'The Classical Accounts of India',* Firma K.L. Mukhopadhyay Publication, Calcutta, 1960

Mark Collins, *'The Geographical Data of the Raghuvaṃśa and Daśakumāracarita',* Leipzig, 1907

Matsya Purāṇa'

Mc Crindle J.W., *'Ancient India as Described in Classical Literature'*, Calcutta, 1906

Mirashi V.V. (quoted), *'Kautilīya Arthaśastra' 1.3,* (1958) *'Ramagiri of Meghadūta is Ramtek'* (Marathi), Vidarbha Samshodhan Mandal, 1958

Mirashi V.V., 'Location of Rāvaṇa's Laṅkā', Journal of the Oriental Institute of Baroda Vol. XXIV, 1974-75

Mirashi V.V., C II, no. 60 page 314 (cited from Bhattacharya P.K.), 1977

Mishra D.P, *'The Search for Laṅkā',* Agam Kala Prakashana, Delhi, 1985

Moniar Williams, 'Sanskrit English Dictionary', MLBD, Vārāṇasi, 1981

Mora Jatak' 2:36 (quoted by *'Bhāratiya Sanskṛti Kośa',* p.138 ed. by Mahadeoshastri Joshi, (1968) Bharatiya Sanskriti Kosh Mandal, Pune

Mudliar Chitty (ed.), Ceylon Gazetteer, 1834

Muzumdar B.C., *'Orissa in the Making'*, University of Calcutta, 1925

Nandargikar G.R. (ed. and translated), *'The Raghuvaṃśa of Kālidāsa'* with commentary by Mallinatha, MLBD, 1982

Oak J.V., (3rd ed.), *'Gīrvāṇalaghukośa'* (Sanskrit-Marathi), Jamshedpur, 1960

Omkaranandagiri (ed. and compiled), *'Narmada Sahasṛanamavali' in 'Narmada Parikṛamā'*, 2002

Padma Purāṇa' Ādiparvan

Paṇḍya S.N., *'A Geographical Horizon of the Mahābhārata'*, Bharat- Bharati Publication, Vārāṇasi-5, 1980

Panikkar K.M., *'Geographical Factors in Indian History'*, Bombay, 1955

Pargiter F.E. (ed.), *'Mārkaṇḍeya Purāṇa'*, The Asiatic Society of Bengal, Calcutta /Indological Book House, Delhi, 1904/1969

Pargiter F.E. (translated notes), *'Mārkaṇḍeya Purāṇa',* Asiatic Society of Bengal, Calcutta, 1904

Pargiter F.E., *'The Geography of Rama's exile',* 1894

Pathak Visuddhanand, 'History of Kosālā', MLBD Publication, Vārāṇasi, 1963

Periplus, (translated Schoff W.H. of *'Periplus of the Erythraean Sea'*), 1912

Pillai Svami Kannu D.B., *'Indian Chronology',* (quoted by G. Ramdas *'Rāvaṇa's Laṅkā* I.H.Q., 1928)

Pliny, *'Natural History'* (Mc Crindle, *'Ancient India as Described in Classical Literature'*), Edinburg, 1901

Ptolemy, (ed. Mc Crindle J.W., 1881-1888 also ed. Shastri Majumdar, 1927), *'Ancient India'* Calcutta

Ptolemy, Vol. II (Majumdar R.C., Classical Accounts of India, Calcutta, 1960)

Raghavan M.D., *'India in Ceylonese History and Culture'*, chapter II - Ceylon and Her Immigrants, published by Indian Council for Cultural Relations, 1964

Raghavan V. (ed.), *'Rāmāyaṇa Tradition in India'*, Sahitya Academy Publ. Delhi, 1980

Raghavan V., *'The Rāmāyaṇa in Greater India'*, South Gujarat University, 1975

Rai Ramkumar, *'Mahābhāratakośa'* Chaukhamba Sanskrit series no. 98, Vārāṇasi, 1966

Rai Ramkumar, *'Vālmīki Rāmāyaṇa Kośa'*, Chaukhamba Sanskrit Series no. 168, Vārāṇasi, 1965

Ramakrishnan R.K., *'Rāvaṇa and Laṅkā'*, Global Vision Publication, New Delhi, 2003

Roy Sarat Chandra, *'The Oraons of Chota Nagpur'*, Brahmo Mission Press, Calcutta, 1915

Roychaudhari H., *'Studies in Indian Antiquities'*, Calcutta, 1958

Sahasrabuddhe D.B., *'Bhārata Sthalādarśa'* Marathi, Pune, 1889

Sankalia H.D. (ed.), *'Pre-history and Proto-history of India and Pakistan'*, Deccan College, Poona, 1962/1974

Sankalia H.D., *'Historical Geography of Madhya Pradesh'*

Sankalia H.D., *'Rāmāyaṇa: Myth or Reality'* (1973) New Delhi and *'Rāmāyaṇa in Historical Perspective'* (1973), Macmillan India Ltd., Bombay

Sarkar D.C., *'Cosmology and Geography in Early Indian Literature'*, *'Indian Studies: Past and Present'* Calcutta, 1967

Sarkar D.C., *'Problems of the Rāmāyaṇa'*, Andhra Pradesh, publ. Hyderabad, 1979

Sarkar D.C., *'Studies in the Geography of Ancient and Medieval India'* Delhi, 1960 and MLBD, Vārāṇasi, 1971

Sarkar D.C., Select Inscriptions Vol. I, Calcutta, 1942

Satavalekar S.D. (translated and edited with notes), *'Vālmīki Rāmāyaṇa'*, Books I-VII, Marathi edition, Publ. Swādhyāya Mandal, Pardi, Balsad, Gujarat, 1967

Shastri J.L. (ed), Tagare G.V. (translated and annotated), All *Purāṇās*, MLBD, Publ., Delhi 1983

Shastri Shakuntala R., *'Kaumudī mahotsava'*, Bombay, 1952

Shukla H.L., *'Archaeology of the Indian Cave Theatre: A Study of Ramgarh Hill of Chhattisgarh'*, B.R. Publishing Corp., Delhi, 2002

Shukla R.K., *'The Geography of the Rāmāyaṇa'*, Koshal Book Depot publ., Delhi, 2003

Singh M.R., *'A Critical Study of the Geographical Data in the Early Purāṇās'*, Punthipuṣpak Publication, Calcutta, 1972

Singh Suryavanshi Bhagavan, *'Geography of the Mahābhārata'*, Ramanand Vidyā Bhavan, New Delhi, 1986 -Appendix V, Location of Laṅkā

Skanda Purāṇa', Maheśvara-Kumārikā *Khaṇḍā*, Geeta Press, Gorakhpur

Skanda Purāṇa', Avantī Khaṇḍā 5, Geeta Press, Gorakhpur

Smith Daniel: *'Select Bibliography of Rāmāyaṇa Related Studies', Anantacharya Indological series, no. 21, Bombay, 1989*

Sukhtankar V.S. and Belvalkar S.V. (ed), *'Mahābhārata'*, Volumes I to XII, c.e. BORI, Pune, 1933-1956

Thakkar A.V., *'Tribes of India'* parts I and II, Bharatiya Adim Jati Sevak Sangh, Kingsway Publication, Delhi, 1950 and1951

Thapar Romila, *'Exile and the Kingdom: Some Thoughts on the Rāmāyaṇa'*, The Mythic Society, Bangalore, 1978

The Baburnama', (English), Vol. II (translated Beveridge A.), Lusac and Co., London/Bombay, 1922

Vaidya C.V., *'The Riddle of the Rāmāyaṇa'* revised edition, New Delhi, 1971

Vaman Purāṇa'

Varāhamihira, (ed Kern H.), *'Bṛhatsaṃhitā'*, Calcutta, 1865

Varāhamihira', *'Bṛhatsaṃhitā'*, *'Bhavabhūti'*, *'Uttararāmacarita'*, *'Murāri'*, *'Rājaśekhara'*, *'Bālarāmāyaṇa'* (all quoted by Rao N.V. in Introduction to his play *'Sītā Josyam'*, 1990)

Vasu S.C (translated), *'Aṣṭadhyāyi of Pāṇinī'*, 3 Vols., Allahabad, 1891-97

Vora Asha (translated), *Banavari*, *'Pañcavaṭī, Indian Approach to Environment'*, 1992

Yule, (quoted *'Prācina Sthalakośa'*)

ARTICLES

Adhikari N.S.,'Laṅkā of Rāvaṇa', 1922, JBBRAS, Vol. XXV, no. 71-73, 1922

Agashe S., *'Nashikche Nāmarahasya'* (Marathi), Mumbai Loksatta, 10th Dec. 2006

Agrawala V.S., 'Ancient Indian Geography', IHQ, XXVIII, no.3, 1952

Arian, Indica-4, Mc Crindle, Cunningham ASIR 1.1

Asian Researches 14.402

ASIR, Vol. II,

Bajpeyi K.D., '*Geographical Encyclopedia of Ancient and Medieval India*', Vol.1, India Academy, Vārāṇasi, 1967

Ball V., '*Indian Antiquary*', 2,1873

Bapat P.V., *Presidential Address, All India Oriental Conference*, 27, Kurukṣetra, 1974

Beglar and Cunningham, ASIR, XIII, 1882

Beglar, JRAS, 1894

Begler and Cunningham, ASIR Vol. XIII, 1882, (*Report of Tours in the South-Eastern Provinces, 1874-75, 1875-76*)

Bhagavat Durga, '*Folk Songs from the Satpura Valleys*' Journal, University of Bombay, Vol. III, pt. 4, Jan. 1960. '*Tribal Gods and Festivals in Central India*', Asian Folklore Studies, Vol. XXVII, 2, 1968

Bhandarkar D.R., '*Daṇḍakāraṇya*', fn.1, Jha Comm. vol., Poona, 1937

Bloch T., '*Ramgarh Hill Caves and Inscriptions*', ASIR, 1903-04

Burgess, '*The Ramagarh Hills in Surguja*', Ind. Anti., Vol. XXXIV, 1905

Cockburn, JRAI XVII, 1988

Corp. Inscr. 1:4:2:385 (quoted by *Pracina Sthalakośa*)

Cunningham A., ASIR (Reva, Bundelkhand, Malva and Gwalior), Vol. XXI, 1883-84

Cunningham A., ASIR 1974-75, 75-76, Vol. XIII, 1904

Cunningham A., ASIR, Vol. XIII

Cunningham, ASIR, Vol. 8, 1874-76

Cunningham, ASIR, Vol. XXI, 1883-1884

Dalton, JASB, Vol. XXXIV, pt. 1 and pt.2, 1865

Diskalkar D.B., '*Ceylon and Laṅkā are Different*' (Correspondence, QJMS XVIII, 1927-28)

District Gazetteer of India', Mirzapur issue, Vol. XXVII, 1911

District Gazetteer of Mirzapur', Vol. XXVII, 1909

Epigraphia Indica, Vol. XX, 1929-30

Epigraphia Indica', Vol. II (pp 7 ff) cited from Bhattacarya P.K., '*Historical Geography of M.P. from Early Records*', MLBD Publ., Vārāṇasi, 1977

Excavations at Śṛṅgaverapura'; Memoirs of ASI, no.88, 1993

Ghosh J.C., '*Rāvaṇa's Laṅkā located in Central India*', Annals, BORI, Vol. XIV, 1938-1939, I.H.Q. Vol. V

Ghosh J.C., '*Siṃhala in Central India*' New India Antiquary, Vol. I, 1938

Ghosh Manoranjan, *'Rock Paintings and other Antiquities of Pre-historic and later Times'*, Memoirs of ASI, no.24, Chapter no. 1 and 4, 1998

Godakumbura C.E., *'Laṅkā of the Classical Indian Writers'*, All India Oriental Conference Proceedings, 27th session, 1976

Gokhale Shobhana, *'Sri Laṅkā in Early Indian Inscriptions'* Annals, BORI, LXXXV, 2004. (*'Dipavaṃśa' and 'Mahāvaṃśa'* quoted by ....)

Hiralal *'The Situation of Rāvaṇa's Laṅkā'* Jha Comm. Vol., Poona, 1937

Hiralal, (quotes from Bergess, *'Ind. Antiq'*. Vol. XXXIV, in *'Descriptive list of inscriptions in the C. P. and Berar'*), Govt Press, Nagpur, 1916

Hultzsch E., CII, Vol. I, Oxford, 1925 (quoted by Gokhale Shobhana)

Hunter W.W., *'Statistical Account of Bengal'*, Vol. XVII, London, 1877

Imperial Gazetteer of India', 1911, special issue of Mirzapur, XXVII

Imperial Gazetteer of India', Vol. XVII, Oxford, 1908

Imperial Gazetteer of Reva State', Vol. IV, 1907

Jha V.D., *'Investigations into the Archaeology of Surguja'*, 1973

Kane P.V., JBBRAS, 27:38

Kibe M.V., *'Location of Laṅkā in Amarkanṭaka in Modern Literature' 'New Indian Antiquary'*, no. I, April-June, 1946

Kulkarni V.M., *'Origin and development of the Rāma story in Jain Literature'*, J.O.I. Baroda, IX, no. 2, 1960-62

Kumāradāsa, *'Jānakīharaṇa'*, canto. (quoted by Godakumbura *'Laṅkā of the Classical Indian Writers'* in All India oriental conference proceedings 27), 1976

Law B.C., *'Chronicles of Ceylon'*, RASB Monograph Series, Vol. III, 1947

Law B.C., *'Geographical Essays'*, Vol. 1, Luzac and Co., London, 1937

List of Ancient Monuments in the Chota Nagpur Division'

Mankad D.R., *'Introduction to the Kiṣkindhākaṇḍa of Vālmīki Rāmāyaṇa'* c. e. Baroda, 1965

Mirashi V.V. *'Corp. Inscr.'*, Vol. IV, Part 1

Mishra D.P, *'Mahakosal Historical Society Papers'*, Vol. I, Bilaspur, 1932

Mishra D.P., 'The Location of *'Kiṣkindhā'* in *'The Search for Laṅkā'*, Agam Kala Prakashan, Delhi, 1985

Muzumdar B.C., *'Sonepur Plates of Kumāra Someśvaradevā'*, Epi. Indica, Vol. XII, no. 29, 1925

Ouseley J.R., *'On the antiquities of Surguja and its Neighborhood'* JASB, Vol. XVII, pt. 1, 1848

Rai Krisnadas, *'Rām Vanavās ka Bhūgol', 'Ṛṣyamūka - Kiṣkindha ki Bhaugolic Awasthiti'*, Nagarī Pracharini Patrika, 52:4

Rai Krisnadas, '*Rām Vanavās ka Bhūgol*', Nagarī Pracharini Patrika, no. 54:1-3

Ramakumar Rai, '*Vālmīki Rāmakośa*', Chaukhamba Sanskrit Series, Vārāṇasi, 1965

Ramdas G., '*Aboriginal Names in the Rāmāyaṇa*', JBBORS, Vol. XI, 1925, '*Aboriginal Tribes in the Rāmāyaṇa*', I.H.Q. Vol. IV, 1928, '*Man in India*', Vol. V, '*Rāvaṇa and His Tribes*', Vol. VI

Ramdas G., '*Rāvaṇa and His Tribes*', Vol. V and VI, 1929

Ramdas G., '*Rāvaṇa's Laṅkā*', I.H.Q. Vol. I and IV, 1928

Ramsay Cobden L.E.B., '*Statistical account of Bengal*', Vol. XVII, 1905

Rao Narla Venkateshvar, Introduction to his play - '*Sītā Josyam*', 1990, (Marathi translation by Sadhle Nalinī, Marathi Sahitya Parishad, Hyderabad)

Roychaudhari H.C., 'The Study of Ancient Indian Geography', IHQ, June 1928

Sankalia H.D., '*Times of India*', Bombay, February 23, 1976, (quoted by N.V. Rao N.V., op. cit.)

Shah U.P., '*Introduction to the Uttarakāṇḍa of Vālmīki Rāmāyaṇa*', c.e. Baroda (1975)

Shah U.P., '*Rāmāyaṇa in Jain Tradition*', (1961), International Rāmāyaṇa Seminar Proceedings

Shende, '*Routes between Āryāvarta and Dakṣiṇapatha*', PIHC, 1943

Shukla H.L., '*Kosalānaṅda Mahākāvyam*', (based on palm-leaf manuscripts of 1664), BORI, Pune, VII A, 2000

Thapar Romila, '*The Rāmāyaṇa: Theme and Variation*', 1982, in S.N. Mukerjee (ed.) '*India: History and Thought*', Calcutta. Also see '*Cultural Pasts*' in Collected Works, 2000

The Wealth of India' 1972; Vol. IV, ('*A Dictionary of Indian Raw Materials and Industrial Products*', Publication and Information Directorate, CSIR, New Delhi)

Vader V.H., '*Situation of Rāvaṇa's Laṅkā on the Equator*', I.H.Q., Vol.2, QJMS, XVII

Yardi M.R., '*The Rāmāyaṇa: Its Origin and Growth*', a statistical study, BORI, Poona, 1994

ABOUT THE AUTHOR
Sukanya Agashe

Born in Pune in 1944 Sukanya chose Microbiology as her field and obtained M.Sc. and Ph.D. from the University of Mumbai. However, she left the field of scientific research and plunged into social activities from 1978 onwards, joined People's Science Movement and worked as socio-cultural activist till 1992.

She, at the same time, ventured into fiction as well as non-fiction writing, which was published in various Marathi periodicals and magazines. These articles were of literary criticism or covered various relevant socio-cultural issues. She started writing short stories and poems for children. The subjects and their treatment both were quite unconventional. Her collection of poems 'Napasanchi shala' ('A school of failures') and a biography 'Dr Kotnis' were well received. Both fetched her Maharashtra State Awards.

Two of her short story collections drew the attention of connoisseur readers and she received awards for these including a Maharashtra State Award. Her translation from Hindi of the biography of renowned Hindi writer late Shri Hajariprasad Dwivedi was published by the 'Sahitya Academy', Delhi.

Having keen interest in Indian Mythology, Sukanya has written stories and plays based on myths, which were published in various magazines. A collection of her articles 'Magova Mithakancha' will soon be published.

For more than a decade, she did independent research on 'The Search For Rāvaṇa's Laṅkā' and was guided later by Dr Romila Thapar. The present book is the outcome of this research. She lives in Mumbai since 1970.